PROBLEMS
IN
CRIMINAL PROCEDURE

Fourth Edition

By

The Late Joseph D. Grano
Distinguished Professor of Law
Wayne State University

Leslie W. Abramson
Professor of Law
University of Louisville
Louis D. Brandeis School of Law

AMERICAN CASEBOOK SERIES®

Mat # 40180417

American Casebook Series and West Group are trademarks registered in the U.S. Patent and Trademark Office.

COPYRIGHT © 1974, 1981 WEST PUBLISHING CO.
COPYRIGHT © 1997 By WEST GROUP
© 2004 West, a Thomson business
     610 Opperman Drive
     P.O. Box 64526
     St. Paul, MN 55164–0526
     1–800–328–9352

ISBN 0–314–15003–X

Preface to the Fourth Edition

This is the fourth edition of this book of classroom problems in Criminal Procedure. The problem method is the best way to teach the Criminal Procedure course. Unlike classroom hypotheticals, problems require careful and somewhat sophisticated advance preparation. Students must organize the facts and identify the relevant issue(s), decide which cases from the readings are applicable, analyze and synthesize the applicable cases, and defend an outcome that usually is contestable. Rigorous case analysis is still required, because a good problem often presents an issue of the case law's uncertain reach. The problem method requires students to read, understand, and apply cases and their rationales, just like real lawyers and judges.

Class begins with a student identifying the issue(s) that the problem presents and discussing the solution that the reading material suggests. Other students then offer their views. Sometimes students role play as defense lawyers and prosecutors and argue the problem as a trial motion or an appeal. When a problem issue is a close call, the discussion may end with a vote about the way a court would probably decide, rather than according to the students' preferences.

Criminal Procedure issues sometimes do not lend themselves to problem analysis. Some topics like the exclusionary rule or the use of prophylactic rules like *Miranda* may indicate putting the problem method aside temporarily and discussing the issue at hand. No method of instruction requires 100% commitment.

The citations to the cases from which the problems are taken are in the back of this book. The problems were chosen because the facts presented good issues, not because of the court's analysis. Sometimes the facts have been changed to improve the problem. Comparing the student's analysis with that of the case does no harm as long as it *follows* the student's analysis.

This Fourth Edition builds on the solid foundation Professor Joseph D. Grano provided for law teachers and law students as a Professor of Law for three decades until his death in 2001.

LESLIE W. ABRAMSON
LOUISVILLE, KY.

February, 2004

*

iii

Table of Contents

PROBLEMS
IN
CRIMINAL PROCEDURE
Fourth Edition

*

Chapter 1

SEARCH AND SEIZURE

A. FOURTH AMENDMENT ACTIVITY: DEFINING A "SEARCH" AND "SEIZURE" FOR FOURTH AMENDMENT PURPOSES

Whether Fourth Amendment activity has occurred is sometimes a threshold issue in search and seizure cases. Absent such activity, the Fourth Amendment's probable cause, warrant, and reasonableness requirements simply do not apply. A finding of Fourth Amendment activity, however, does not tell us whether that activity complies with Fourth Amendment requirements.

The problems in Subsection 1 examine the state action requirement. Although often treated as an exclusionary rule issue, the question of state action has more to do with the presence or absence of Fourth Amendment activity. Without state action, Fourth Amendment activity cannot occur; without Fourth Amendment activity, the Fourth Amendment exclusionary rule cannot apply. Whether a state wants to enforce state trespass and state breaking and entering laws with an exclusionary rule aimed at private conduct is not a matter of Fourth Amendment concern.

The problems in Subsection 2 explore whether state activity that uncovers evidence or intrudes in some way on the person is a search. The problems allow both for application of the current doctrine and critical evaluation of that doctrine. If the old "trespass" approach was inadequate, and if *Katz*[a] leaves a lot to be desired, what "test" could be used that would be adequate and yet not do violence to the Fourth Amendment's text and purpose? Because the *Katz* issue is both fundamental to a free society and rather confounding, an ample selection of problems is provided.

The "seizure" issue, considered in Subsection 3, is often considered when stop and frisk is studied, and this is perfectly appropriate. Nevertheless, this issue is conceptually related to the "search" issue. Despite the emphasis on the reasonable person's perceptions, the seizure issue, more than the search issue, seems to focus on what the police actually did. Do you agree that the emphasis is somewhat different? Should it be? Problem 13, though somewhat long factually, covers the major issues.

a. Katz v. United States, 389 U.S. 347, 88 S.Ct. 507, 19 L.Ed.2d 576 (1967).

1

In all the problems in this chapter, students may want to consider whether the "good faith" exception to the exclusionary rule has (should have) any bearing on the outcome.

1. THE STATE ACTION REQUIREMENT

(1) Officer Cooper asked Shawn Anderson, an employee of a private mail drop company in Anchorage, Alaska, to notify him of shipments made by "foreign persons who were dressed in flashy clothes, appeared to be carrying large amounts of cash or wearing expensive jewelry, and appeared to be Jamaican." Later that day, Patrick Thompson, a Jamaican who was wearing an open shirt and a necklace with a gold medallion, brought Anderson a package for shipping. Thompson filled out the Federal Express airbill and paid the $45.00 charge with a $50.00 bill that he pulled from a three inch wad of bills.

After Anderson notified Cooper of her suspicions, Cooper came to the premises, shook the package, and had a dog sniff it. The dog did not alert. Cooper also showed Anderson a group of pictures from which she identified Thompson. Cooper then left, telling Anderson to send the package if Federal Express arrived.

Anderson then got permission from Federal Express to open the package. (Federal Express airbills state that their agents may open and reject packages.) Officer Cooper also called and said that he had done some checking and believed that Anderson could open the package. With Cooper still on the phone, Anderson opened the package and found almost $20,000 in cash. Later, and after Anderson had resealed it, Cooper took the package from Anderson, opened it, seized the money, and determined that a number of bills corresponded to bills previously used in recorded drug purchases.

Charged with distributing cocaine, Thompson moved to suppress the money. The judge granted the motion, finding that Anderson's inspection did not implicate the Fourth Amendment but that Cooper's examination of the serial numbers on the bills did. What result on the prosecution's appeal? Did Fourth Amendment activity occur at any point? Would any part of your analysis be different if Anderson had not resealed the box? How significant is Cooper's phone call?

(2) Harold Cheesman, an airplane supply company employee, testified at the defendant's suppression hearing that a woman had informed him by phone of her suspicion that the defendant was storing stolen company inventory in a garage that the defendant rented from her. Although the woman offered to let Cheesman check the garage, Cheesman decided to go to the police. The police refused to act without a criminal complaint, and they advised Cheesman to check his inventory for missing items. Cheesman's testimony continued:

A.   At this point, I asked for somebody to go with me. They didn't feel they should send anybody with me until I had seen if there was anything in there. And after that, they said I should file a complaint.

Q.   So, then, one of the officers indicated that you could go there?

A. They never said either way. They just refused to give me any help.

Q. But you still didn't know whether you could go to the garage?

A. Not really. They told me that if I went there and did find something, then to report it back to them.

The police officers who spoke to Cheesman also testified that they had not authorized Cheesman to enter the garage. One officer did recall saying that if Cheesman found stolen items, the police would "follow up."

After leaving the police, Cheesman went to the garage. When the woman unlocked the door, Cheesman entered and found company items that had been stolen. Using this information, the police obtained a warrant, searched the garage, and seized the items.

What result? Should the police have done anything to restrain Cheesman? What? Were they in a position to give him legal advice—for example, as to whether an owner can give someone permission to enter a leased garage? Did the police stand idly by? If they did, is that enough to convert private behavior into a Fourth Amendment search? Did the police invite Cheesman to search the garage? (Given Cheesman's entry, did Fourth Amendment activity occur when the police subsequently entered the garage?)

(3) Deidri Mitchell, employed as a Security Officer (SO) by Woodward and Lothrop in Washington, D.C., followed defendant Alston from a fitting room past several cash registers to the store exit. Using her two-way radio, Mitchell then called her supervisor, Special Police Officer (SPO) Brenda Lee, also employed by the store, and reported that she had observed a pink and white garment in Alston's tote bag while investigating a complaint of possible shoplifting. Noticing Mitchell's radio, Alston started to run, but Mitchell caught up with her outside the store and brought her to the store's security office. There, in the presence of Lee and other SPO's, Mitchell searched the tote bag and recovered items of stolen clothing.

Pursuant to the D.C. Code, the mayor commissions SPO's to protect private property for corporations or individuals. Although SPO's are paid by the party whose property they protect, the Code gives them the same powers of arrest for crimes committed in their presence and within their jurisdiction that law enforcement officers have. SO's are licensed by the mayor to prevent crimes such as theft, but unlike SPO's, they have no greater power to make arrests than ordinary citizens, and they must carry identification cards to this effect. The Code requires both SPO's and SO's to wear different uniforms than the city police wear, but the Chief of Police is permitted to waive this requirement in the case of SPO's.

What result on Alston's motion to suppress?

2. ACTIVITY THAT CONSTITUTES A SEARCH

(4) Acting on reports of sexual activity in highway public rest rooms, police hid a video camera in an outside wall, thus enabling them to watch and film what was occurring in front of and in the two toilet stalls inside. The stalls had no doors, but the stall interiors could not be seen from the entrance to the rest room or from the urinals, which were partitioned from the toilets. The officer operating the camera knew when persons entered or left the rest room by the sound of the door, and the officer activated the camera whenever he thought illegal activity might occur.

Using the camera, a police officer observed defendant Casconi expose himself in a stall and begin to masturbate. The officer also observed Casconi cover himself whenever someone else entered the rest room. The officer did not see anyone look over, under or into Casconi's stall, and apparently no one else saw Casconi's activities. Later, the officer again used the camera to observe defendant Owczarzak masturbate in the common area directly in front of the stalls.

Convicted of public indecency, both defendants now appeal. What result? Did Fourth Amendment activity occur? Would it matter whether the police filmed all stall occupants or only those suspected of criminal conduct? Can a person have an expectation against a particular method of surveillance?

Would anything change if the stalls had doors and the camera was hidden in the ceiling? If a person must assume the risk that children, scavengers, and snoops will gain access to the person's trash, why would a person not have to assume the risk of such individuals looking over or under even a closed stall? Should privacy expectations against the public define privacy expectations against the government? Would a sign warning of surveillance have any bearing on your analysis? Should a search be deemed to occur whenever an officer intends to look for evidence? If not, can the *Katz* test be improved? How?

(5) The defendant lives in the lower, front apartment of a two-story four-unit building. A common path between his building and an adjacent two-unit building, owned by the same landlord, leads to a back yard surrounded by a chain link fence. The tenants of the six units have common use of the yard. The yard is not used by people who have business with the tenants.

Suspecting narcotics activity, Officer Valdes maintained surveillance from the street in front of the defendant's apartment while Officer Knapp kept vigil, with permission, from a neighbor's garage abutting the back yard. In one forty-five minute period, Valdes saw six individuals on separate occasions enter the defendant's apartment. The defendant on each occasion exited the apartment and walked to the back yard along the common path. Each time, Knapp saw the defendant retrieve something from a shaving kit in a rubbish pile under the tree and return to the apartment, after which the visitor departed. After conferring, the two officers walked the common path into the back yard, retrieved a closed shaving kit from the rubbish pile, opened the kit, and discovered narcotics.

What result on defendant's motion to suppress? When, if ever, did Fourth Amendment activity occur? What if the officers did not have to open the kit to see narcotics?

(6) Defendant's house sits on a half-acre lot enclosed by a ten-foot metal fence on the north side (the back), a six-foot metal fence on the east side, and a chain link fence on the west side. A garage is located in the northwest corner.

Suspecting that the defendant's home was being used as a drop house for drug traffickers, federal agents installed a video camera on top of a power pole behind the defendant's back fence. The camera permitted the officers to see drugs being taken from false automobile gas tanks in the defendant's back yard. Searches pursuant to warrants based on these observations produced evidence that the defendant now wants to suppress.

What result? Is it relevant (1) that power company employees working on the poles could see into the yard, (2) that a person of average height could peer over the east fence, or (3) that back yard activities could be observed by aerial surveillance? Does this problem involve the curtilage? Does it matter?

(7) The defendant's home is in the middle of his 155 acre farm, about a half mile from a dirt road. Because of dense trees, the home and farm buildings are not visible from the road. The farm is surrounded by a low fence with an access gate. Several "No Trespassing" signs are posted, including one adjacent to the access gate.

Police officers with a tip that did not establish probable cause went to the defendant's farm looking for bait money from a robbery. Acting upon the tip, they used a shovel to probe the ground next to a chicken coop adjacent to the home. The officers discovered the money after displacing a few inches of soil.

What result on defendant's motion to suppress? What if the chicken coop had been 200 feet from the house? What if the officers found the money by entering the chicken coop? What distinguishes the risks we must assume from those we need not? Compare this problem with the preceding two.

(8) Pennsylvania police received an anonymous tip, allegedly from a private pilot, that defendant had marijuana growing in his pole-barn. Three officers in a police helicopter then flew over the barn at an altitude of 500 feet and observed through the transparent, plastic roof a color identical to that of growing marijuana. Coming down to 50 feet, and hovering for 15 seconds, they observed the tops of plants pressed against the barn's roof. The plants clearly matched the distinctive color, size, and configuration of marijuana. The officers then obtained a warrant to search the pole-barn, which had completely opaque sides, was

18 feet high, and was located 446 feet from the road and 251 feet from the defendant's home.

Did Fourth Amendment activity occur? What if defendant testifies that he experienced noise and vibration during the surveillance? Does this have any bearing on whether a search occurred? What if the officers could not see the plants even at 50 feet without binoculars? (Federal regulations permit fixed-wing aircraft to fly at 500 feet in non-congested areas; the regulations permit helicopters to fly lower if this can be done "without hazard to persons or property on the surface.")

(9) Anthony Scherer invited two men to his farm to build duck blinds. Unknown to Scherer, one was a government informant and the other a federal agent posing as the informant's cousin, Jim. Scherer's wife gave the two men broad permission to look around the grounds and in the barn for wood to build the blinds. On one trip to the barn, the agent, who was investigating Scherer for possible Gun Control Act violations, found two Thompson submachine guns in plain view.

Did Fourth Amendment activity occur? Compare the next two problems.

(10) Suspecting narcotics activity, a federal narcotics agent knocked on defendant's door, identified herself as a gas company employee, and said that she was checking for a gas leak. The defendant invited the agent to enter and showed the agent to the basement, which housed a gas meter, a gas furnace, a hot water tank, and a clothes dryer. Pretending to check for a leak, the agent observed a clear plastic bag on a table containing what appeared to be cocaine. The agent then identified herself as a federal officer and arrested the defendant.

What result on the defendant's motion to suppress? Did Fourth Amendment activity occur? Was the deception here legally more significant than that in the last two problems? Why (not)? What if the agent had said that she was there to read the gas meter? What if the agent truthfully identified herself after gaining entry and then obtained the defendant's consent to search? For purposes of determining whether Fourth Amendment activity occurred, would it matter if the police sent a squad of agents throughout the community posing as gas company employees or meter readers?

(11) Officer Don Mattingly applied for and received a search warrant from a judge, to search the defendant's apartment for marijuana and other contraband. In support of the warrant request, Mattingly submitted an affidavit in which he referred to an anonymous tip that defendant lived in a particular apartment and that he may be growing marijuana there. The informant told Mattingly that he had seen defendant and another man carry a carbon dioxide tank and other equipment into defendant's apartment. He also told Mattingly that from the hallway of the apartment building he could smell the odor of marijuana plants emitted from the defendant's apartment. Through defendant's open windows, the informant also had observed a very bright white light, which he described as "growing lights," as well as the tops of the marijuana plants. He also described the defendant as a Caucasian male, five feet eleven inches tall, weighing 180–200 pounds. Mattingly observed defendant's name on the apartment's mailbox, and verified his build via a computer check of arrest records.

In the affidavit, Mattingly asserted that he checked the utility records for the defendant's apartment and two neighboring apartments in defendant's building that were the same size. The records showed the defendant's average kilowatt usage was more than three times that of either of the other two apartments for the preceding year. He also returned to defendant's apartment and aimed a thermal imager at the bedroom area Of defendant's apartment. He did not physically cross any fence lines or enter any curtilage area while using the thermal imager. Based upon his prior training and experience with the imager, he concluded that the surface temperature of defendant's structure was significantly higher than that of similar adjacent structures. The search pursuant to the warrant yielded marijuana plants and seedlings, sprouts, seeds, bagged vegetable matter, and some drug paraphernalia. Defendant filed a motion to suppress the evidence, arguing that the police use of the thermal imager allowed them to gather information regarding the interior of the defendant's apartment which they otherwise could not have gathered without a search warrant. Should the motion be granted?

(12) Two years ago, Detective Murphy began investigating the distribution of child pornography on the Internet. He accessed the Internet by way of United States on Line (USOL), an Internet service provider, and used a private chat-room to find individuals who were distributing child pornography. He started a computer program that generated a list of screen names being used by individuals in the chat-room, and he received e-mail messages from persons who had been in the chat-room. Two messages were received from a chat-room user identified as Ci921. Each message attached a photograph of a nude child with a nude adult in a sexually suggestive pose.

After receiving these images, Detective Murphy prepared an affidavit and presented it to a judge who found probable cause to issue a warrant for the USOL subscriber information for Ci921 and several other screen names. Murphy served the warrant on USOL at its headquarters where the subscriber records were maintained. USOL complied with the warrant and provided Murphy with the requested subscriber records. Those records revealed that Ci921 was Brian Simpson of Louisa, Kentucky. Local police soon received Detective Murphy's information, prepared an affidavit, and successfully sought a search warrant for Simpson's house. Louisa police immediately seized Simpson's computer, notes, papers, pictures and other items. The search of his computer revealed several files containing depictions of child pornography. He was indicted for distribution of matter portraying a minor in a sexual performance.

Simpson filed a motion to suppress the evidence seized. Does he have standing to challenge the seizure of the matter from his computer?

3. ACTIVITY THAT CONSTITUTES A SEIZURE

(13) While riding in their unmarked car, plainclothes Officers Kane, Atkinson, and White received a radio report that a narcotics sale was taking place in the 2400 block of Kermit Court. Walking to the designated area, they found two males, Scott and Calvin, conversing. When Scott observed the three officers, he started to walk away. Kane immediately identified the three as police officers and said, "Come here." At this, Scott started to run, but Calvin stayed put. During their several minute chase, Atkinson and Kane observed Scott run behind some houses and drop a "medicine type vial." After apprehending Scott, the two officers returned to the area where the drop had occurred and retrieved the vial, which contained valium. In the meantime, White asked Calvin how much dope he had sold, and Calvin responded by claiming that he was not a dealer, that Scott was his only customer, and that he had sold a little valium to Scott to help out a friend in need.

Finding that illegal Fourth Amendment activity had occurred, the trial court suppressed the valium in Scott's case and Calvin's statements in his case. Pursuant to statute, the prosecutor has filed an interlocutory appeal. What result? Did Fourth Amendment activity occur? If so, when and as to whom? What result if an officer had shot at Scott during the chase?

(14) At a suppression hearing, Officer Crooke testified that three Drug Enforcement Agency officers approached Wilson as he was leaving Washington National Airport carrying two coats and a carry-on bag. After the officers identified themselves, Crooke asked whether Wilson would speak with them. Wilson agreed. Crooke then requested identification, and Wilson produced a check cashing card.

After explaining DEA's purpose, Crooke obtained Wilson's permission to search his bag. Wilson also volunteered to let Officer Prince pat him down. Both searches proved unproductive. Wilson then angrily refused to allow a search of his coats. Questioned about this refusal, Wilson said that he wanted some things to remain private.

When Wilson then asked why the agents were stopping him, Crooke responded that Wilson was free to leave. Walking beside Wilson, Crooke asked whether he would at least let a trained dog sniff his coats. Wilson agreed but refused to go to a police station for this purpose. Crooke then noticed a large bulge in the brown coat. Following Wilson to the taxi area, Crooke again asked why he would not permit a quick pat-down of the coat. Wilson responded that he was late for an appointment; Crooke replied that a pat-down would take only a second. As the exchange continued, Wilson's voice got loud, and he complained of being harassed. In Crooke's words, "he had to be asked numerous times by myself and Officer Rogers to please quiet down."

"[E]ventually," Crooke added, "he agreed to allow us to search the coat." When Crooke went straight to the bulge, Wilson snatched the coat and leaped over the taxi railing. Although Rogers was able to grab Wilson's foot, Wilson broke away. While running, he tossed his brown coat in the air. Shortly thereafter, the officers caught Wilson and retrieved the coat from where he had thrown it. The bulge was a package of crack cocaine.

What result? Was Wilson "seized" at any point before the officers apprehended him? If so, when? Before his apprehension, did Wilson submit to the officers' authority or did they otherwise restrain him? Was Wilson seized when Rogers grabbed his foot? (Consider also problem 57.)

B. PROBABLE CAUSE: THE TRADITIONAL MEANING

To be constitutional, most searches and seizures require probable cause, as that term has been traditionally defined. (Those that may be based on some different standard of cause, such as reasonable suspicion or administrative guidelines, are considered in Section C.) Even in its traditional sense, however, probable cause has been an elusive concept. For example, it still is not clear whether probable cause requires the necessary inferences to be more probable than not. Courts often speak of probable cause in terms of a fair probability, a substantial possibility, or even a substantial chance, but they generally have not indicated how, if at all, these terms reflect quantitative considerations and how, if at all, they differ from each other.

To complicate matters further, some commentators have suggested that the standard of probability may differ depending on the aspect of probable cause under consideration. To illustrate, an arrest requires probable cause to believe both that a crime has been committed and that the person to be arrested committed the crime. Even if a lower standard applies to the suspect part of the inquiry (thus allowing two suspects to be arrested in a one-person crime when the odds are at best 50–50 for each), these commentators would argue that the more probable than not standard applies (or should apply) in determining whether a crime has been committed. Similarly, some would apply the more probable than not standard in determining whether the suspect possesses evidence of a crime but not in determining whether the evidence is in the suspect's home rather than, say, the suspect's office. Others would question whether a more probable than not standard applies to any aspect of the inquiry.

Whatever the standard, the probable cause inquiry requires difficult judgment calls. The problems in Subsection 1 are intended to demonstrate the difficulties in determining how much cause is enough. The problems in Subsection 2 involve the separate issue of determining whether hearsay reports (tips from informants) are sufficiently trustworthy to be considered in evaluating whether probable cause exists.

1. THE REQUISITE QUANTUM OF CAUSE

(15) Two men, described by witnesses as Hispanic and in their twenties, committed two armed robberies early one evening in Chicago. In the process, they also murdered four people, wounded two others, and abducted a twelve-year-old girl. Witnesses told police that the robbers had escaped in a light-colored, four-door Ford, with primer on the door and trunk. The witnesses also described part of the car's license plate number.

About an hour after the second robbery, an officer on patrol observed a car meeting the description. After a short high-speed chase, the suspects' car crashed. Shots were then exchanged, and both the officer and Garcia, one of the car's occupants, were wounded. Other officers, who had been summoned to the scene, then arrested Garcia and rescued the kidnapped girl. The car's other occupant escaped.

Running a license plate check, the officers discovered that the car was registered to Vilma Llaguno at an address two miles from the crash. One of the robberies had occurred between this address and the crash; the other robbery, in the officers' words, was within the "proximity." The car had not been reported as stolen.

Relying on this information, several officers went to the disclosed address, entered without consent or a warrant, and searched for an Hispanic male in his twenties. They found the home occupied by Gloria Llaguno, Gloria's husband, and several children and grandchildren. Vilma, Gloria's daughter-in-law, was not at home. When David, one of Gloria's adult children, claimed that he owned the car in question, the officers arrested him.

In the meantime, and unknown to the arresting officers, other police found and killed the person who had fled the crash. He was Roger Llaguno, Gloria's son and David's brother, who did not live with the family. The police never charged Vilma or David with any role in the crimes.

The Llaguno family has now brought a civil rights action against the officers who entered their house. Assuming that the circumstances were sufficiently exigent to justify a warrantless entry to arrest if the police had probable cause, what result? Do exigent circumstances have any bearing on the probable cause issue? Was there a "fair probability" that the second robber was in the home? Was it more probable than not that he was there? Does probable cause require such a high standard? Should the standard be lower in this case because of the certainty that a crime was committed? If the officers lawfully entered the house, did they then have probable cause to arrest David? (Reconsider this problem when you study the warrant requirement.)

(16) Routinely patrolling Washington, D.C., in an unmarked car late one afternoon, two plainclothes police officers observed Campbell and Cooper walking together. Campbell was carrying a screwdriver and Cooper was carrying a television. Aware that burglars often steal televisions, the officers made an abrupt U-turn and approached the two men. As the officers left their car, Campbell dropped the screwdriver. Identifying themselves as police, the officers recovered the screwdriver and attempted to give it to Campbell, who denied that it was his. One of the officers then asked where the two men had obtained the television. Campbell responded that he had just purchased it from Cooper's cousin, who had driven them to a point one block away. After ascertaining the cousin's name, the officers took both Campbell and Cooper to the station for "investigation."

At the station, the officers placed the men in an unlocked room. An hour later, they located Cooper's cousin, who denied having sold a television. Shortly thereafter, the officers learned that the television had been stolen from a house only twenty-five feet from where they had confronted the suspects. They then formally arrested the men and uncovered other stolen items in a search of their persons.

Assuming that Campbell and Cooper were arrested for Fourth Amendment purposes when they were taken to the station, what result on a motion to suppress the evidence seized from them? At what point, if any, did probable cause exist for arrest? If probable cause was lacking, what should the officers have done? (Were Campbell and Cooper "seized" when the officers first confronted them?)

(17) At 8:30 p.m. on December 22, San Francisco police officers Povey and Hunt observed defendant, who is white, a black woman, and three black men leave an elevator in a residential complex and walk toward a stairway leading to the parking lot, where the officers were sitting in a marked car. When the five people observed the officers, they stopped, walked back, and formed a "huddle of some sort" in front of the elevator, which had closed. The officers decided that "something was wrong," probably "either narcotics or weapons due to the hour and a white male being in the [predominantly black] projects." Upon the officers' approach, the group immediately fragmented, the defendant heading toward the street in a "very quick walk, almost a run." The officers then seized the defendant and, in a subsequent search, uncovered a gun.

At a suppression hearing, Povey, who had patrolled the area for more than three years, testified that he had "never observed a white person in the projects on foot in the hours of darkness for an innocent purpose." He indicated that he had made 500 arrests in the area, including twenty of whites for narcotics. The only other whites he had encountered were robbery victims.

What result? Did the officers have probable cause to arrest the defendant? How relevant is the group's "flight"? Is it permissible to take account of the defendant's race? Why (not)? If probable cause was lacking, was there at least "reasonable suspicion" for a stop? See the problems in Section C.

2. PROBABLE CAUSE BASED ON HEARSAY

(18) Arizona police learned from the New Mexico State Police and the United States Drug Enforcement Administration [DEA] that Clarence Romero was suspected of being a major seller of heroin. Some time later, a DEA agent notified the Arizona police that she had received a tip from an anonymous informer. The informer stated that Romero had flown that morning from Albuquerque to Tucson to purchase a half-kilo of heroin and that he would probably ask a second person to return the heroin to Albuquerque on T.W.A. flight 239 at 2:50 p.m. the same day.

An Arizona police officer went to the Tucson International Airport, where he learned that "C. Romero" had a reservation on the described flight. The officer then observed defendant, whom he knew to be Romero's associate, board the plane. The ticket clerk informed the officer that defendant's ticket bore the name "C. Romero." Boarding the plane, the officer arrested the defendant, searched him, and found heroin.

How would you rule on the defendant's motion to suppress the heroin? Consider your answer under both the old two-pronged test and the test that has replaced it. Is this a case in which strength in one prong compensates for weakness in the other?

(19) After arresting Linson for selling narcotics, the police offered to reduce the charge from a Class C to a Class E felony, with a promise of probation rather than imprisonment, if Linson would reveal his source. Accepting the offer, Linson identified Reivich as his supplier for the past few years, provided Reivich's phone number, and stated that Reivich resided in the area of 59th and Troost streets. The police then ascertained that the phone number Linson provided was listed to a person at a certain address in the vicinity of 59th and Troost Streets. Checking the license plate number, they also learned that the car in the driveway was registered to Reivich.

Relying on the above information, the police have applied to you for a warrant to search Reivich's house. What is your response under both the two-pronged test and its replacement? Is this a case in which strength in one prong compensates for weakness in the other? Does it help that Linson's statement was arguably against his penal interest? Did the bargain provide Linson a motive to lie, a motive to tell the truth, or both? How, if at all, does the police corroboration affect your decision? What does "common sense" suggest as the right result? What result on a motion to suppress or on a later appeal if you issue the warrant? [To complicate the problem, what result on a motion to suppress if the police failed to mention the bargain in their warrant affidavit?]

C. THE WARRANT REQUIREMENT AND ITS EXCEPTIONS

Black letter Fourth Amendment law states that warrantless searches are *per se* unreasonable unless they fall within one of the supposedly few and carefully delineated exceptions to the warrant requirement. In reality, the exceptions are neither few in number nor always carefully delineated. Indeed, some of the rules in this area are confusing as to both their underlying rationale and scope.

After several problems showing some of the issues associated with executing a warrant, the subsection headings reveal the area or warrant exceptions. This permits students to work with the warrant exceptions as they are studied and to gain an appreciation of their nuances through application. Subsection 11, which provides review problems, presents an opportunity for students to identify and choose the warrant rule(s) that should be discussed.

1. EXECUTION OF WARRANTS

(20) John has moved to suppress the fruits of a no-knock search warrant on the basis that no circumstances existed to justify a no-knock search. He was staying at the home of his friend Julie in rural Frazier County. The home had been searched successfully for weapons and drugs under a warrant six weeks prior to the current search. A reliable informant bought drugs from Julie at her home two days before the search. The next day, based upon the information from the informant, a sheriff's deputy applied for a search warrant for Julie's property, vehicle and Julie herself. A judge signed the warrant and it was executed two days later.

Prior to executing the warrant, officers parked about a quarter of a mile from Julie's house. Before entering, they observed Julie and John sitting at a table playing what appeared to be a word game. When one officer tried the front door and found it unlocked, the officers, in camouflage, helmets and masks, entered with their guns drawn, shouting, "Police." Julie did not move other than to raise her arms above her head. John, stunned by the entry, tossed the dictionary he was holding into the air and attempted run from the room. He held his fist closed and then appeared to shove its contents down the front of his pants. Officers subdued him, finding a knife in his belt and drugs and an inhaler in his pants.

When the warrant issued, what basis existed for an unannounced entry to execute the warrant? Is the suspected crime relevant to your answer? If no justification for a no-knock search exited at the time the warrant issued, did it exist at the time the warrant was executed? Were the officers in danger or was there any concern about the destruction of evidence?

(21) State police obtained a warrant authorizing an unannounced entry to search Gathright's home for Gathright and her husband. Both of them had criminal records for violent crimes, and she had escaped from a penitentiary. An informant had told the police that they had explosives and rifles stored in a bedroom in the rear of the house. During execution of the warrant, one of the state officers broke a window in that bedroom and stuck his weapon through the opening to prevent any occupant from gaining access to the firearms he believed were stored there.

The Gathrights moved to suppress the fruits of the search due to the property damage during execution of the warrant. They claim that, when property is damaged during a no-knock entry, police must establish more information about exigent circumstances than during a damage free entry. Do you agree?

(22) Police executed a search warrant on Salsman's home after a long investigation revealed a broad based drug distribution conspiracy. They suspected that Salsman stored and distributed large quantities of methamphetamine at his residence. Twenty minutes after execution of the search warrant began, a local television reporter arrived and accompanied police officers for the remainder of their time inside Salsman's home. After police found more than a pound of methamphetamine, prosecutors indicted Salsman for conspiracy to traffic in a controlled substance. Salsman has moved to suppress the fruits of the search by alleging that the involvement of the news media violated his Fourth Amendment rights. Do you agree?

2. WARRANTLESS ARRESTS

(23) Responding to a domestic disturbance call, two police officers went to the complainant's home and were admitted by her. The officers then observed what appeared to be the continuation of an extremely loud and bitter argument. The woman complained that her husband had just hit her, and the officers observed a red mark on her face. Because of the husband's intoxicated condition, his previous record of violent assaults on his wife, and the wife's statement that she called the police after her husband had threatened to "do worse" to her, the officers decided to arrest the husband for battery, a misdemeanor. A search of his person then revealed narcotics.

What result when the husband moves to suppress the narcotics?

(24) After a previously reliable informant purchased heroin from the defendant in his wheel alignment shop, two plainclothes officers went to the shop, entered through the open customers' entrance, and asked for the defendant. An employee then called into the back room for the defendant. When the defendant entered the customers' area, the officers arrested him for illegally selling narcotics, a felony. A search incident to the arrest disclosed heroin. The officers did not have a warrant.

What result on the defendant's motion to suppress? What result if after learning who the officers were, the defendant ran back into the rear room with the agents in pursuit?

(25) Federal agents developed probable cause that Colombian nationals in room 106 of a local motel were co-conspirators in a drug buy that they had just witnessed on a docked Panamanian vessel. After the agents arrived at the motel without a warrant, one agent phoned room 106 and, without identifying himself, stated in Spanish that there had been trouble at the vessel. The agent also said that arrests had occurred and that the occupants should leave the room and the area. Within minutes, three men, carrying light luggage, emerged from the room. After the men were well into the corridor, the agents arrested them and, in a search of the luggage incident to the arrests, found a large quantity of cocaine.

What result on a motion to suppress? What interests are protected by requiring a warrant for nonconsensual entries to arrest? Were those interests implicated by the agent's deception here? Did the agents' conduct differ significantly from that in the previous problem? What result if the agents surrounded the room and ordered the occupants out?

(26) On July 14, an informant reported to the FBI that he would be meeting Chandler and Cravero at a restaurant. FBI agents, who had been looking for the two men pursuant to arrest warrants on narcotics charges, staked out the restaurant but refrained from making an arrest because of concern about revealing the informant's identity. Instead, the agents followed the men, absent the informant, to Marianne Cook's apartment, where they conducted a four hour surveillance. During this time, the agents learned from headquarters that the informant had called to report that Cravero suspected both the presence of surveillance teams at the restaurant and the informant's duplicity. The agents then knocked on Cook's door, identified themselves, and announced their purpose. Cook opened the door and upon seeing the agents shouted inside, "Hey you guys, the police." The agents then entered without permission and arrested Cravero in the living room and Chandler in the bathroom.

Both Cravero and Chandler seek to suppress cocaine taken in searches incident to their arrests. What result? You should assume that the arrest warrants were valid. (Is there a standing issue in this problem?) If the defendants lose their suppression motion, would Cook have a basis for a civil rights action against the agents?

3. SEARCHES: GENERAL EXIGENT CIRCUMSTANCES

The most accepted justification for a warrantless search is the existence of exigent circumstances—that is, circumstances in which having to obtain a warrant would threaten valid law enforcement interests. In fact, an exigent circumstances rationale may be seen as underlying some or perhaps most of the specific exceptions. The automobile exception, of course, is an anomaly in this regard. In any event, exigent circumstances can excuse the warrant requirement even when a more specific warrant exception cannot be found.

(27) Charged with aggravated bank robbery in St. Peters, Mississippi, defendant Golden filed a motion to suppress $12,000 in bank currency seized from his hotel room. The evidentiary hearing disclosed that at 2:00 a.m. one Saturday morning, someone in the hotel reported a serious fight to the police. The police arrived within minutes and found a person lying on the floor with a fatal gunshot wound. The desk clerk advised the officers that Golden had gone upstairs with a gun, apparently wounded. The officers and clerk went to Golden's room, knocked on the door, and received no answer. At the officers' request, the clerk unlocked the door. Inside, the officers observed a blood-stained shirt on the bed. After looking under the bed and in the closet and bathroom, they concluded that Golden was not in the room. Continuing to search the room, the officers opened a suitcase that was in the closet and discovered $12,000

under some clothing. Golden was arrested after bank employees subsequently identified the money as stolen.

Be prepared to argue both sides. What did the officers expect to find after determining that Golden was not present? Could the officers have satisfied their goals by posting a guard and returning with a warrant?

(28) Pursuant to undercover agent Gay's request to purchase cocaine, Gieber directed Gay to a parking lot at about 4:00 p.m. and left "to make a phone call" about a shipment that he claimed had just come in. In reality, as police surveillance detected, Gieber walked a few blocks to Michael Blake's home, talked to Blake outside, and returned alone to Gay, telling him that he had seen a pound and a half of the best cocaine anyone had seen in a long time. Gay then gave Gieber $2,400 in marked money, whereupon Gieber again went to Blake's home, returned to the lot, and gave Gay an ounce of cocaine.

When Gay said that he would be interested in purchasing an additional ounce at a later time, Gieber responded that the cocaine, being so good, would probably be gone before the next day. Gay then left Gieber and reported to his superiors. In the meantime, the surveillance team reported that they had observed heavy vehicular and pedestrian traffic at Blake's home and that they knew some of Blake's visitors to be drug users.

Having decided to secure Blake's home while obtaining a search warrant, several officers went to the home about 5:30 p.m., entered without consent when no one answered the bell, and ordered Blake, his wife, his preteen daughter, and four other men into the living room. They then arrested Blake, searched his person, and found a small quantity of cocaine. While some of the officers removed Blake and the other men from the scene, others stayed in the home with Blake's wife and daughter to await the search warrant. When the warrant arrived five hours later, the officers searched the home for another five hours and found a large quantity of 94% pure cocaine, thirty pounds of marijuana, several guns, and most of the marked money that Gay had given to Gieber.

What result when Blake moves to suppress all the evidence? Should the police have done (a) nothing until they obtained a search warrant, (b) an immediate search of the home without a warrant, (c) exactly what they did, or (d) none of the above? When it comes to homes, rather than cars, can we generally tell whether a warrantless seizure is a greater or a lesser intrusion than a warrantless search? What if it took ten hours to obtain the search warrant?

4. SEARCHES INCIDENT TO ARREST

(29) Two armed men robbed the Nashville City Bank and escaped with over $10,000 in white sacks. According to witnesses, both robbers wore long leather coats and hats, and one wore a ski mask.

Four days later, several police officers obtained valid arrest warrants for two men who lived in a nearby apartment. After lawfully gaining entry, the officers, who carried shotguns, arrested and handcuffed the two defendants in the living room and placed them against the living room wall. An immediate search disclosed six bullets in one defendant's pocket. One officer then seized a leather jacket, ski mask, pistol, and fur cap in plain view in the living room. By lifting the flap and bending down, another officer found three bank sacks of money and a pistol under the living room couch. A third officer, who had gone into an adjoining bedroom to look for additional people, seized money, a pistol, and a leather coat, all in plain view. She also seized money from a closed paper bag on a shelf in the bedroom closet. Finally, one officer seized money from a closed paper bag between a water heater and an adjoining wall, about four feet from the defendants. At the time, a police officer stood in the hallway that separated the defendant and the heater. The closet-like depression behind the heater contained a number of items in addition to the bag.

Should any of this evidence be suppressed? Are you satisfied with the analysis necessary to solve this problem? If not, what doctrinal change(s) would you make? Does the holding or rationale of *New York v. Belton*[b] have any bearing on this problem?

(30) Two police officers staked out an apartment building hoping to execute an arrest warrant on Geraldo Hernandez for violating his parole. After a while, the officers observed Hernandez and two unknown men emerge from a Cadillac. The officers observed that Hernandez "kept pulling up his belt, like something was falling," and this, along with Hernandez's prior conviction for trafficking in weapons, led them to conclude that Hernandez was armed.

After Hernandez and the other men had entered the building and backups had arrived, the officers entered the building, knocked on Hernandez's apartment door, and announced their purpose. Receiving no response, they broke down the door and immediately arrested Hernandez in the living room. Meanwhile, as part of a protective sweep, an officer discovered a woman on a bed in the bedroom that was immediately to the right of the front door. The officer handcuffed the woman and temporarily placed her on the floor. Because the officer intended to place the woman back on the bed where she would be more comfortable and easy to observe, he searched the drawers of a dresser next to the bed and ran his hand both over the mattress and between the mattress and box spring. In the latter place, the officer discovered a .357 magnum revolver.

Indicted for illegal possession of a firearm, Hernandez has moved to suppress the gun. What result?

5. PRETEXT ARRESTS

(31) In the early morning hours of February 20, Nemes was pulled over for speeding by state Trooper Wilkinson. At the spot where Nemes was

b. 453 U.S. 454, 101 S.Ct. 2860, 69 L.Ed.2d 768 (1981).

pulled over, another police officer, Detective Prizant, happened to be present with his drug-detecting dog, Beepers. As Trooper Wilkinson began to write Nemes a citation, Detective Prizant walked Beepers around the exterior of Nemes's Isuzu Trooper. Beepers indicated that the odor of narcotics was emanating from the Isuzu.

The officers searched the vehicle and allowed Beepers to enter it. Beepers alerted to an area in the back of the Isuzu where he had alerted when he was outside the car. The officers found a bag with large amounts of cash in it. Beepers then alerted to an area in the middle console of the car. The console was taken out and the officers found a load of methamphetamine.

Although Trooper Wilkinson had probable cause to believe that Nemes was violating the speed limit, her real interest in Nemes's car had nothing to do with enforcing the state's traffic laws. It was also no coincidence that Detective Prizant happened to be waiting with his drug-detecting dog in the exact spot where Trooper Wilkinson pulled Nemes over. In fact, the whole incident had been planned hours in advance in coordination with DEA agent Nichols.

In the years preceding Nemes's arrest, the DEA was conducting an investigation into a number of groups who were manufacturing large quantities of methamphetamine in the Seattle area. Local police were notified that an Isuzu Trooper was driving through the state and the DEA suspected that it was carrying methamphetamine. Detective Prizant was informed by agent Nichols that the Isuzu would be driving through Medford where Prizant and Beepers were located. Prizant talked with several federal and state officials about a plan to intercept the Isuzu driven by Nemes. The officials decided to follow the Isuzu when it entered the Medford area and wait for it to violate a traffic law. The car would then be pulled over by Trooper Wilkinson. Detective Prizant would be present at the scene with Beepers. Everything went according to plan.

Nemes moved to suppress the evidence obtained by the search. Did the officers have probable cause to search the car? Was the fact that the stop was pretextual relevant to the reasonableness of the initial seizure? If a stop yields no evidence in support of the more serious offense, can the police nevertheless seek the driver's consent to search all or part of the vehicle?

(32) Portland, Oregon police officers Bell and Jones observed two young men ride their bicycles through a stop sign. Because of their manner of proceeding and because one of the two had a laundry basket on his bicycle that contained an object, the officers became suspicious that the young men had engaged in criminal activity unrelated to the traffic infraction. The officers then stopped the two bicyclists and observed that the item in the laundry basket was a television set. The officers also observed that one of the young men, who appeared "nervous, as if he might run," had a bulge in his pocket. The officers then formally arrested both young men for failing to obey a stop sign, and in a search

incident to the arrest, uncovered a gun on the individual with the bulge. Later, at the station, the officers learned that the bicycles and television had been taken in a recent burglary.

Assuming that the two young men actually ran the stop sign and that this constitutes a violation of a local traffic ordinance, what result when they challenge the admissibility of the gun, television, and bicycles? Should limits in this area be placed on (a) the decision to arrest, (b) the decision to search, (c) both, or (d) neither? If an officer has probable cause, why should the officer's motive matter?

6. SEARCHES INCIDENT TO ARREST: AUTOMOBILES

Students must understand the difference between this exception and the automobile exception. Students also need to understand, however, that the presence of an automobile has an impact on the application of the search incident to arrest doctrine. (Do we really expect the police to sort this all out?)

(33) Police officer Mertel observed Stoffle and Shaw standing at the rear of a car in a city park and drinking beer in violation of a local ordinance. Mertel approached the two men, asked for and received identification, and ascertained that the car belonged to Stoffle. He then ran a warrant check in accordance with standard police department procedure. Within three or four minutes, Mertel learned that Stoffle had outstanding warrants for traffic offenses. Mertel then arrested Stoffle, handcuffed him, and placed him in the rear seat of his patrol car.

After doing this, Mertel examined the front seat area of the car. In the driver's seat, he observed a black film canister. Pulling the lid off the canister, Mertel discovered cocaine. A further search of the car revealed various items of drug paraphernalia. Mertel later indicated that he knew from experience that film canisters are often used to carry contraband.

Now charged with drug offenses, Stoffle has moved to suppress the cocaine and the other evidence found in the car. What result? Would the automobile exception (see infra) justify the initial search that uncovered cocaine? If not, is it clear that search incident doctrine would allow this search? (For review, don't forget the issues raised in problem 31.)

(34) Acting with reasonable suspicion of illegal narcotics activity, Detectives Berti and Martin stopped two men, Maldonaldo and Arango, after they parked and emerged from a jeep. Both men denied owning the jeep, and only Maldonaldo produced identification. While Berti went to the jeep to look for ownership papers, Martin asked Arango if the police were still looking for him in connection with a drug shooting. Arango responded by pushing Martin to the ground, breaking his kneecap. Both men then fled the scene, with Berti in pursuit.

Two uniformed officers apprehended Arango a block away. After formally arresting him, Berti took Arango back to the scene of the assault, where Martin was in need of medical attention. Berti then searched the jeep and discovered a large quantity of cash behind the passenger's seat and a package of cocaine in a camera case on the rear seat. Continuing to search, Berti discovered a secret compartment underneath the carpet behind the jeep's rear seat. The compartment contained a large quantity of cocaine.

What result when Arango moves to suppress all the evidence? Assume that Arango has standing, that the initial stop was lawful, and that probable cause to search the jeep was lacking after Arango's arrest. (Was it?) Even if the search that produced the money and the first quantity of cocaine can be upheld without relying on the automobile exception, will the prosecutor need to rely on this exception at some point in the analysis?

(35) Sean and his schoolmate Jason went for a drive in Sean's Ford pickup truck to meet a friend at a local roadhouse. On the way, they pulled into a city parking lot in a small village. They had with them a 12 pack of beer, which was ripped open and now contained both empty and full bottles. Sean grabbed a bottle of beer from the pack as he was pulling into the lot, opened and drank half of it as he stepped from the truck. Village police officer Trudy was parked in the same lot in his marked squad car. When he saw Sean take two drinks from the beer bottle as he approached Sean's truck, he pointed his flashlight at Sean. In the village of Nyland, separate ordinances prohibit open intoxicants in public and in motor vehicles.

Officer Trudy directed Sean to hand over the bottle. Sean complied, and the two of them walked to the back of the truck where the officer asked Sean for identification. The officer then asked Sean whether there were any open beer bottles in the truck, and Sean responded affirmatively. The officer then took Sean to the squad car and seated him there. As Officer Trudy returned to Sean's truck to conduct a search, he noticed that Jason, the passenger, followed him by walking parallel to the officer along the opposite side of the truck. Jason then stood by the passenger door. Jason put his hands on a zippered duffel bag resting on the middle of the front seat. When Jason nervously said that he wanted to remove the bag, the officer told him to leave it on the seat, because he planned to search all the containers inside the vehicle. The search of the bag yielded personal items, an open box of clear sandwich bags, often associated with narcotics, and a large vial of white powder. Later laboratory analysis showed that the powder was cocaine.

Jason has moved to suppress the cocaine found in the duffel bag. Does it matter whether Officer Trudy arrested Sean when escorting him to the squad car? If Sean was arrested, can the belongings of a presumably innocent passenger be searched incident to the driver's arrest? Was there any reason for the officer to fear for her safety or for the destruction of evidence?

(36) Members of the local Drug Investigation Unit noticed Fenzel's car backed into a driveway on a street where a reliable informant had told police that Fenzel often distributed controlled substances. As the police pulled into the driveway, they noticed Fenzel reach into the vehicle and

hand another person a clear plastic bag containing narcotics. Both Fenzel and the other person immediately walked away from the vehicle at a fast pace, and both were arrested minutes later at a nearby grocery store. Fenzel's wife had been in the car during the transaction and drove away, but she was found in the car fifteen minutes later at her mother's house. One officer took the keys from her, and conducted a cursory search of the car while it was still parked in the driveway. Under local law, vehicles used to transport, sell or conceal drugs are subject to forfeiture by police. Pursuant to that legal authority, one officer drove the car to the police station where it was immediately searched and drugs and drug paraphernalia was seized. Following his indictment for drug trafficking, Fenzel moved to suppress the items found in his car. Was the search of the car incident to Fenzel's arrest? In the alternative, was the search permitted because the car was subject to forfeiture?

7. THE AUTOMOBILE EXCEPTION

This exception, as already indicated, does not require true exigent circumstances. Given the general rule favoring warrants, what rationale supports this exception? Does this exception mean that a warrantless search of a car is always permissible as long as probable cause is present?

(37) Using the automobile exception, reconsider problems 33 and 34.

(38) Officer Dean lawfully arrested Osban for driving with a suspended license. He then searched the passenger compartment of Osban's car and found three "Black Mollies"—a controlled substance—and $3,000 in cash. Dean then took the keys from the ignition, unlocked the car's trunk, and found several stolen guns.

What result when Osban moves to suppress the drugs, money, and guns? Can the automobile exception salvage the initial search? If not, can any other doctrine? Given that no apparent exigency justified a warrantless search (did it?), what rationale supports the automobile exception?

(39) At 3:30 p.m., Truman Langfield observed a man in a golf course parking lot roll a new tire toward an old car and place it in the trunk. Langfield then drove around the lot and observed two cars with holes punched in their trunk lids; he did not see any cars on jacks or otherwise in the process of a tire change. Langfield then described the old car he had seen to police officers, who immediately issued an all points bulletin for an old maroon Oldsmobile with extensive right side damage. Shortly thereafter, Officers Clark and Jones, who had received the bulletin and were approximately four miles away, observed a car fitting the description. The officers then stopped the car, arrested the two occupants for larceny from an automobile, and searched the passenger compartment of the car. Unable to find the trunk key, the officers did not search the trunk. They then took both the men and the car back to the police station.

Sometime after 7:00 p.m., the owner of one of the two cars with trunk lid holes finished playing golf and discovered that a tire had been stolen from his trunk. He immediately telephoned the police, pursuant to a note that the police had left on his windshield. The next morning, Detective Rautio, who had just been assigned to the case, had the Oldsmobile towed to a car dealership to open the trunk. When several master keys failed to unlock it, Rautio forced the trunk open with a screwdriver and discovered three new radial tires. This warrantless search occurred approximately 18 hours after Officers Clark and Jones first stopped the car.

What result when the defendants move to suppress the tires? What if the search of the trunk occurred two weeks later?

(40) On appeal from her drug possession conviction, Darlinda has moved to suppress the crack cocaine found in her purse. She was a passenger in a vehicle stopped for making a turn without a proper signal. At the same time that Officer Stroud asked the driver, Lassiter, for his license and proof of insurance, the Officer Mattingly approached the passenger side of the vehicle and obtained identification from Darlinda. She retrieved her identification from her purse on the floorboard. When Lassiter appeared nervous, Officer Stroud asked him to exit the vehicle. Lassiter consented to a search of his person, and nothing illegal was found there. Lassiter then consented to a search of the vehicle. Officer Mattingly asked Darlinda to get out. She reached for her purse to take it with her but Officer Mattingly told her to leave inside the vehicle. As Officer Stroud began searching the passenger area, he found a crack pipe in the center console ashtray. He then searched Darlinda's purse sitting on the floorboard and found a plastic bag containing crack cocaine.

Did the officers legally request the occupants to exit the vehicle? Once the crack pipe was found, was there probable cause to believe that drugs would be found in the vehicle, including Darlinda's purse?

8. CONTAINERS CONNECTED AND NOT CONNECTED TO VEHICLES

Because no container exception as such exists, the subheading may seem confusing. Yet, to understand the difficulties encountered when a container is in a car that is subject to search under the automobile exception, one needs to understand the rule that governs containers that are not in automobiles. Students should see that as long as automobiles are subject to different rules than other containers, there will be *no* satisfactory answer as to what approach should govern when a container gets placed in an automobile. The following problem, which is presented with four factual variations, also provides an opportunity to explore further the search incident to arrest rule in the automobile context.

(41) "Variations on a Theme"

Facts Common To All Variations: An unidentified female called the Fort Worth police dispatcher and claimed that she had driven two males, Banner and Johnson, from California to Fort Worth. She also reported that the two males were currently on their way to the Trailways bus station, where they intended to retrieve two suitcases filled with drugs from lockers 17 and 20 and transport them to Houston. The caller detailed the appearances of both men and one of the suitcases.

In response to the call, police officers went to the station and observed two men go to the designated lockers and retrieve two suitcases. Both men and one suitcase matched the descriptions the caller had given.

Variation #1: The men then proceeded to a counter where they checked the suitcases and purchased tickets for Houston. Thereafter, a Trailways employee placed the suitcases on rollers, which carried them to the rear of the station, out of public view. At that point, the police, with the help of a porter, seized and opened the suitcases, finding crack. They then went to the station platform and arrested the two men, who turned out to be Banner and Johnson, where they were waiting to board the bus for Houston.

What result on the defendants' motion to suppress?

Variation #2: Same initial facts except that the officers went to the station platform where the bus for Houston was waiting. After the luggage was brought out some time later, the bus driver loaded it into the luggage compartment under the bus. The driver then permitted the passengers to board the bus. When the driver started to back the bus out of its parking space, the officers signaled the driver to stop, boarded the bus, arrested and handcuffed the two men, and directed the driver to retrieve the suitcases. The officers then opened the suitcases, finding crack. What result on the defendants' motion to suppress?

Variation #3: Same basic facts as in variation #2, except that the officers learned about a valid fugitive warrant on felony charges for both men before boarding the bus. Assuming now that the woman's tip did *not* provide probable cause, what result on the defendants' motion to suppress?

Variation #4: Same basic facts and assumptions as in variation #3, except that the luggage was on the luggage rack over the men's seat and the men, in handcuffs, were escorted off the bus before the search. What result? Considering all four variations, what would it take to bring doctrinal coherence to this area?

9. INVENTORY SEARCHES

Inventory searches are one kind of administrative search, but unlike many of the others, they are typically performed by law enforcement officials and frequently turn up evidence of crime. It should be noted that inventory searches require neither traditional probable cause nor a warrant. Would a warrant requirement make sense as long as inventory searches require no more cause than administrative reasonableness?

(42) Police officers lawfully arrested the defendant for driving without a valid license and with an expired registration from a different car. After the defendant had been removed from the scene, Officer Straub, following departmental procedure, impounded the car, searched it, and found a dagger, a blackjack, and an ignition device. Five hours later, after he returned to the station, Straub filled out the department's inventory form.

The inventory form, a copy of which is given the person, directs police to list only those items that they seize and retain. The form does not provide space for the police to list items that were either left in the car or given back to the person, and the police do not ask the person to sign a receipt for such items. Straub later testified regarding what is retained rather than left in the car or returned:

> "It depends. Contraband or weapons, we voucher that. Money or valuables, the defendant will usually take them. If there is a radio to be removed, they can take it."

On cross-examination, Straub said he had received on-the-job training for how to conduct an inventory. The following exchange then occurred:

Q. Do you have particular standard instructions?

A. No, we don't have instructions.

Q. Nothing written anywhere?

A. Not that I recall.

Q. They leave it to your judgment on the scene?

A. That's correct.

Now charged with criminal possession of a weapon and unlawful possession of master keys for motor vehicles, defendant has moved to suppress the evidence taken from his car. What result?

(43) As the defendant walked into a hospital, police officers lawfully arrested him for a shooting incident that had occurred some months before. The defendant then asked the police to park and close the windows of his car, which he had left partially blocking the ambulance approach to the emergency room. An officer responded, however, that the police would take the car to the City Garage for safekeeping. After they had done so, the police discovered stolen goods in an inventory search that complied with the department's written and detailed guidelines.

What result on the defendant's motion to suppress?

10. PLAIN VIEW SEIZURES

The most important thing to keep in mind here is that plain view is not a exception to the search warrant requirement, i.e., it is not a warrantless theory standing alone. If the police have a prior justification for being where they are and items seized are incriminating on their face, police may seize those items.

(44) David Burns told Officer Malone that someone, whom he suspected to be the defendant, stole a tool box from his pickup truck while it was parked outside a bar. Malone and Burns then went to the defendant's house and knocked on the door. While standing on the front porch waiting for the door to be answered, the two men looked through the front window and observed a tool box, which Burns identified as his, on the kitchen floor. When the defendant answered the door, Malone immediately entered the house, proceeded to the kitchen, and seized the box.

What result when the defendant moves to suppress the box? If the plain view exception cannot justify Malone's conduct, can any other exception? If the tool box must be suppressed, can Malone still testify as to what he observed from the front porch?

(45) Acting with consent but without probable cause, Baltimore police officers lawfully took Riddick into an interview room at a train station. When an officer asked whether he was carrying drugs, Riddick opened his duffel bag, pulled out a sweat shirt, and proclaimed that he did not have anything. Without touching the open bag, one of the officers was able to see a spoon in the bag. She then reached inside the bag, removed a quarter-gram silver spoon, and identified heroin residue on the spoon. The officers then arrested Riddick and a search of his person revealed other incriminating evidence.

What result on Riddick's motion to suppress? What if the officer had seen a white residue on the spoon while it was still in the bag?

(46) Acting with probable cause, North Dakota police officers obtained a warrant to search the defendant's home for narcotics. Before applying for the warrant, Officer Maixner attempted to contact Officer Lennick to inquire whether the warrant should also authorize a search for stolen goods. Although Lennick had previously indicated to Maixner that he suspected the defendant of being involved in a burglary, he had not indicated the basis of his suspicion. Because of his inability to reach Lennick, Maixner did not include stolen goods in the warrant application.

Officer Dever, who accompanied Maixner to execute the warrant, later testified that the search provided an opportunity to discover stolen goods that could connect the defendant to burglaries. Indeed, in the basement, Dever observed a microwave oven on a cooler. Without moving the microwave, Dever observed the serial number on the back and called it into the police station, where officers ran a computer check through the National Crime Information Center. When they learned that the microwave was stolen, the officers notified Dever, who seized the microwave. Subsequently, the police used the microwave to obtain a warrant for stolen goods, and a search pursuant to this warrant proved successful.

What result when the defendant moves to suppress the microwave and the fruits of the subsequent search?

11. REVIEW OF WARRANT EXCEPTIONS

(47) Trooper Rogers and Johnson chased a car at speeds exceeding 100 miles per hour after trying to stop the car for having a broken taillight. During the chase, the fleeing car slid off the icy highway into a ditch.

The defendant driver then fled on foot, leaving his wife in the disabled car. Rogers pursued the defendant while Johnson placed the defendant's wife in her patrol car. During the two hours that Rogers was gone, Johnson conducted an "inventory" of the defendant's car, including a closed but unlocked suitcase. When Rogers returned without the defendant, Johnson informed him that she had seen an ammunition belt in the suitcase. The officers then ordered a tow truck for the car and took the suitcase to the station, where they conducted a more careful inventory that uncovered credit cards bearing the name of Lucille Collins. Subsequent investigation disclosed that Ms. Collins had been murdered, and the defendant is now charged with the murder.

Assuming that the police have a standard procedure for conducting an inventory of impounded cars, what result on the defendant's motion to suppress? Consider all arguably relevant legal doctrines.

(48) King County Officer Jansen stopped Michael Vasey after observing him speeding. As Jansen approached the car, she observed Vasey appear to push his hand between the front seats and handle something "furtively" on the right rear floorboard. (Vasey claims he was unfastening his seat belt and reaching for his wallet.) Jansen obtained Vasey's license and in a warrant check learned that an arrest warrant for possession of narcotics was outstanding against Vasey. Jansen then arrested Vasey, handcuffed him, and uncovered $1,128 in a search of his person. After being placed, still in handcuffs, in the rear seat of Jansen's patrol car, Vasey refused to consent to a search of his car.

Responding to a call for assistance, Officer Lane arrived on the scene, looked in the window of Vasey's car, and saw a pill bottle with a printed label that he could not read from where he was standing. Asked about the bottle, Vasey described the pills as a food supplement that he sold, and he gave the officers the name and phone number of his employer. Suspicious of drug-related activity, the officers told Vasey that they were going to impound and inventory his car.

Ignoring Vasey's request that the car be locked and left by the side of the road, the officers then entered the vehicle and in an "inventory" search discovered $5,000 and a gold watch under the driver's seat. This search occurred about forty-five minutes after Vasey's arrest. The officers then decided to get a search warrant before continuing their search. In a subsequent search pursuant to a warrant based on all the preceding facts, the officers uncovered $71,111 and a small quantity of cocaine.

The King County Public Safety Manual provides that vehicles should be impounded as a last resort. It also provides that an officer should tell an arrestee that his or her car will not be towed if the arrestee signs an impoundment waiver form exonerating the county from liability for leaving the vehicle unattended. Jansen and Lane did not comply with this directive.

What result when Vasey moves to suppress all the money and the cocaine? Consider all arguably relevant legal doctrines.

D. CONSENT SEARCHES

1. REQUIREMENTS OF VALID CONSENT

(49) On August 2 at Union Station in Washington, D.C., Officer Beard and four other members of a drug interdiction squad observed Maragh with two other persons exit the gate where a train from New York had arrived. The squad then "deployed." Beard approached Maragh while another officer approached one of the other men. Both officers faced the gates; both interviewees faced the station exit. Officer Hansen stood as a backup about five feet behind the two interviewees, thus forming a triangle with the two interview pairs. The other two officers caught up with and questioned the third individual nearer to the station exit, but at a point still visible to Maragh.

Following his usual routine, Beard introduced himself and asked whether he could see Maragh's ticket. When Maragh complied, Beard asked if Maragh was carrying drugs. When Maragh answered that he was not, Beard asked if he could search Maragh's tote bag. Maragh answered that he had no problem with that. In the pocket of swimming trunks inside the bag, Beard found cocaine.

Maragh's suppression hearing revealed these additional facts. Maragh, who was born in Jamaica, was a twenty-year-old electrical engineering student at Brooklyn College. At the time of the search, he had been in the United States five years. Beard estimated that in his three years on the interdiction squad, he had conducted about 1,500 interviews like this one, and in approximately two-thirds of these he had asked for consent to search. Beard also claimed that no person had ever walked away from him on his initial contact and only eleven had refused consent to search. Beard said that squad members wear plain clothes, speak in a conversational tone, and do not block an interviewee's path. Beard also estimated that about twelve percent of interviews result in an arrest.

What result? Can Maragh still prevail if the court concludes he was not seized for Fourth Amendment purposes? Are the issues of what constitutes a "seizure" and the voluntariness of consent searches conceptually related? (Consider also problem 14.)

(50) Officer Rudolph stopped twenty-year-old David Crenshaw for failing to obey a stop sign. Rudolph noticed that Crenshaw wore expensive clothing and jewelry and that he had a pager at his belt. While writing a citation, Rudolph asked whether she could search the car and its trunk for drugs, and Crenshaw said that she could.

Crenshaw opened the trunk for Rudolph, who found nothing inside. When Rudolph turned her attention to the car's interior, she saw that "the screw that was securing the plastic vent to the door post had striation marks"; it "looked like someone had been tampering with the screw." Using a screwdriver, Rudolph removed the vent and took an automatic weapon and cocaine from the interior of the door post. These items were not visible before the vent was removed.

What result on Crenshaw's motion to suppress? What if Rudolph found these items by slashing the car's spare tire?

2. THIRD PARTY CONSENT

(51) Brandon leased an apartment for six years before Silva moved in with her. Although they were not married, the couple then took out a lease in the names of "Mr. & Mrs. Silva." Silva paid the rent, and the couple lived in the apartment more than two years, before a quarrel on New Year's Day.

On New Year's Day, Silva punched Brandon in the face. Brandon's nine-year-old son then ran from the apartment screaming that he intended to call the police. Silva directed Brandon to fetch the boy, but after doing so she called the police instead of returning home. Brandon told the police not only that Silva had hit her but also that he was a convicted felon with guns in a closet in their apartment.

When Brandon subsequently tried to let the police into the apartment, she found the door had been locked. She then put her hand through the jalousie and unlocked the door from the inside. Once inside, she told the police that the guns were in the hall closet. Silva forbade the police to enter the closet, but relying on Brandon's permission, the police entered the closet, searched it, and found two guns. Besides the guns, the closet contained only Silva's belongings. Brandon occasionally entered the closet to clean; her son entered it once in a while.

Charged with illegal possession of firearms, Silva has moved to suppress the guns. What result? What if Silva had given strict instructions for Brandon and her son not to use the closet and Brandon had lied to the officers about having joint use of it? What if Brandon no longer lived with Silva but falsely stated that she did? What if Brandon's son had called the police and consented to a search of the closet?

E. THE BALANCING APPROACH FOR DEFINING THE REQUISITE LEVEL OF CAUSE

In *Camara v. Municipal Court*,[c] a case involving the right of city health inspectors to make warrantless inspections of homes, the Supreme Court indicated that the level of cause required for such inspections could be determined only by balancing the need to search against the scope of the invasion. The Court went on to conclude that "probable cause" in this context exists "if reasonable legislative or administrative standards for conducting an area inspection are satisfied with respect to a particular dwelling." In recognizing the concept of area probable cause, the Court for the first time indicated that the meaning of probable cause can vary with context.

The Court relied on the *Camara* balancing approach in *Terry v. Ohio*,[d] its first stop and frisk case. The Court in *Terry* held that street stops and limited searches

c. 387 U.S. 523, 87 S.Ct. 1727, 18 L.Ed.2d 930 (1967).

for weapons only required what later cases labeled reasonable suspicion. Interestingly, however, the Court did not follow *Camara*'s lead and state that probable cause in this context means only reasonable suspicion. Rather, the Court suggested that the new standard is an exception to the probable cause requirement. The difference is not just a semantic quibble. For example, the Fourth Amendment's warrant clause requires warrants to be based on probable cause. If reasonable suspicion is an exception to probable cause, it cannot support a warrant; if reasonable suspicion *is* probable cause in this context, it can support a warrant. Since *Terry*, the Court has frequently (and unfortunately?) spoken of "exceptions" to the probable cause requirement.

1. "STOP" AND "FRISK": THE REQUISITE STANDARD OF CAUSE

(52) At 4:00 p.m., a uniformed police officer on duty in Washington, D.C.'s, downtown shopping district observed the defendant among a group of people at a bus stop on the southeast corner of 13th and F Streets. When the defendant saw the officer, he withdrew his hand from his coat pocket and nervously began rubbing his face. To the officer, it "seemed that something was wrong." The officer walked one block south on 13th Street and, periodically looking over his shoulder, noticed that the defendant was watching him. The officer walked back, but as he approached the bus stop, the defendant crossed F Street and began walking north on 13th Street. The defendant walked one block north, crossed to the west side of 13th Street, and started back toward F Street. The officer followed and, placing his hand on the defendant's elbow, said, "Hold it sir, could I speak with you a second?" The defendant immediately responded, "It's registered, it's registered." When asked what was registered, the defendant answered "my gun." The officer then patted down the defendant, finding a gun.

The government now appeals from the court's suppression order. What result? Did a seizure occur before the patdown? If so, was it lawful? If no constitutional violation occurred before the patdown, was the patdown lawful?

(53) On October 27, at approximately 1:00 p.m., two police officers responded to a "burglary in process" call. At the designated address, the officers discovered that the rear door to a first floor apartment had been forced open. After a fruitless search for clues, the officers left the apartment. Outside they noticed a man walking down an alley behind the building. When the man observed the officers, he began running in the direction he had been walking. The officers pursued in their vehicle. After temporarily losing the man, they rediscovered him walking a

d. 392 U.S. 1, 88 S.Ct. 1868, 20 L.Ed.2d 889 (1968).

couple of blocks away. Stopping their vehicle, the officers called for the man to approach them, which he did. One officer asked the man his name and then immediately conducted a "patdown." Finding a knife, the officers arrested the man and more fully searched his person. This search produced a number of items taken from the burglarized apartment.

What result on a motion to suppress the evidence? Did a seizure occur before the patdown? If the officers had sufficient cause for a seizure, did they also have sufficient cause for a "frisk"? What would you have done in the officers' shoes?

(54) An anonymous person telephoned Officer Lewis of the Pinellas County, Florida, Sheriff's Department and told her that Arthur Howard had arrived from Atlanta, Georgia, with seventeen ounces of cocaine. The informant, who would not reveal his name because he was "deathly afraid" of Howard, indicated that Howard was staying at a Best Western Motel, probably under an assumed name, and that he planned to stay in the area a few days. Lewis, who during the past four years had been investigating Howard in connection with pornography, summoned another officer and promptly began to search for Howard. At the second Best Western Motel the officers visited, a desk clerk identified a picture of Howard as that of a person who had registered under another name. The room registration listed a Georgia license plate number for the occupant's automobile.

When Howard arrived a short time later, the officers stopped him with their guns drawn, and Lewis immediately conducted a frisk. Feeling a hard object, Lewis reached inside Howard's coat and retrieved an envelope. Opening the envelope, Lewis discovered a vial of white powder, which turned out to be cocaine, and two plastic straws.

What result on defendant's motion to suppress the cocaine? What is the test for evaluating an informant's tip in the stop and frisk context? Can the defense persuasively argue that an arrest rather than a *Terry* stop took place?

(55) Fifteen year police veteran Lt. Holland received a telephone call at his office on a private line used only by confidential informants. The caller, without identifying himself, asked for Sgt. Caldwell who was not present. But the informant proceeded to inform Lt. Holland that two guys from Newark were "running our pockets," a term he understood to describe armed robberies of drug dealers. The caller reported that two black males were involved and were driving a gray BMW with tags in the rear window up and down Jersey Drive in a high crime area. Lt. Holland immediately broadcast the information to all officers in the area, as well as going out to pursue the call himself.

Biggs and another black man were standing next to a gray BMW with tags in the window on Jersey Drive during the early morning hours, when Sgt. Caldwell and another officer pulled up in a police cruiser within an hour after the call. The noticed that Sgt. Caldwell approached Biggs on the passenger side of the vehicle and noticed a gun protruding from Biggs's pants. As Caldwell asked Biggs his name, Biggs ran. Caldwell caught him, patted him down, handcuffed him, placed him under arrest and read him his rights. Biggs was on parole and had been convicted of several armed robberies.

Biggs moved to suppress the gun that formed the basis of his conviction for possession of a firearm by a convicted felon. Did Lt. Holland have sufficient reason to view the tip as reliable and issue the bulletin to the other officers? If the caller had not referred to the armed robberies, would reasonable suspicion still have existed? Did Sgt. Caldwell act reasonably in relying on the information in the radio broadcast? If Sgt. Caldwell had never received the broadcast about what the informant had reported, would there have been sufficient grounds to stop Biggs if he had tried to run away from Sgt. Caldwell? How should the trial court rule?

(56) A confidential informant met Kendra at his home and purchased cocaine from Kendra. Four days later, at about 3 p.m., Kendra was arrested at his job site for the cocaine transaction. Shortly after the arrest, a police dog responded positively to drugs at the doorway of Kendra's apartment. Several officers left to obtain a search warrant. Because they knew that Kendra shared the apartment with Marjorie Oliver, two officers remained at the apartment building to prevent her or anyone else from entering the apartment and destroying evidence. Three hours later Oliver arrived at the apartment. Officer Ellis explained to her that Kendra had been arrested and that the officers were securing the apartment while others obtained a search warrant. Ellis told Oliver that she was not under arrest and was free to come and go. However, if she entered the apartment an officer would have to accompany her to prevent destruction of any evidence. After the search warrant issued at 11 p.m., it was executed immediately, resulting in the discovery of a pound of marijuana in the refrigerator. Kendra and Oliver were both charged with drug trafficking. Oliver moves to suppress the admission of the marijuana against her, because she argues that the police had no right to impound her apartment and deny access to her. How should the trial court decide the motion? Was Oliver subjected to an unlawful seizure? Did the police respect her right to privacy? Was the seizure of the apartment far longer than necessary?

2. SCOPE OF PERMISSIBLE DETENTION

(57) On Friday, July 29, at 2:04 a.m., the burglary alarm sounded at a business in Savage, Minnesota. Heading toward the scene in response to a radio dispatch, Officers Andrews and Stevens observed a car with three men going in the opposite direction. The officers did not observe any other car in the area, which was located about a mile from the burglary.

After stopping the car at approximately 2:15, the officers observed that the men were sweating profusely, that two were wearing tennis shoes, and that one had muddy bare feet. The men claimed to be on their way to visit a friend, but they failed to provide a name. The officers then ordered the men out of the car and placed them in their squad cars.

The officers then called Officer Brandt at the crime scene and learned that the police had detected what appeared to be tennis shoe prints. Under orders to do so, Andrews and Stevens directed each man to give them one shoe. This occurred at about 2:45. Asked by the men if they were under arrest, Andrews responded, "No, you're being detained."

At about 3:00, Officer Randall, whom the police dispatcher had aroused from sleep at 2:20, arrived at the scene of the stop, picked up the shoes, and took them to the crime scene, where a match was made with the shoe prints. Informed of this by phone, Andrews and Stevens arrested the men at 3:16. A subsequent search of the car uncovered evidence of the burglary.

What result on a motion to suppress? Do not forget to analyze the initial stop. How many Fourth Amendment intrusions need justification? For Fourth Amendment purposes when did full probable cause develop? When was it needed? What result if Andrews and Stevens could have saved some time by transporting the men to the crime scene? Contrast the next two problems.

(58) Members of the police drug and weapon interdiction unit (DWIU) are trained to observe certain characteristics in people. Dressed in casual clothing and without displaying weapons, three DWIU members boarded a westbound bus in Lexington. Fifteen people already were randomly seated on the bus. Two people caught their attention. Detective Hamilton walked up to the defendant, Miller, identified himself by showing his credentials, and asked to speak with him. In response to a question about weapons, Miller said he had none. But his hands were shaking and feet were tapping on the floor of the bus. Detective Hamilton then asked Miller if he could look in the duffel bag on the seat next to him. Miller said, "I really don't see the reason for that." The detective asked Miller why he was acting so nervous, and he told Miller that he thought Miller had something illegal in the bag. As Miller reached into the duffel bag, he told the detective that he had a weapon and drugs in the bag. Detective Hamilton immediately arrested him. Miller moved to suppress the evidence taken from the bag. Should the motion be granted? Was Miller free to leave the bus? Is that the correct focus of the Fourth Amendment analysis? What additional circumstances should be considered by the trial judge?

(59) After observing an automobile proceeding improperly on a one-way street, Officer Thomas signaled the driver to pull over. As Thomas did this, she observed the front seat passenger turn, lean over the back seat, and appear to move an object onto the rear floor. Thomas then approached the driver, explained why she had stopped him, and asked both men for identification. Both men produced driver's licenses and explained they had become lost while looking for a facility, which Thomas knew to be miles away. Thomas then returned to her car and made a radio check for outstanding warrants. After about ten minutes, the radio dispatcher indicated that outstanding arrest warrants existed for both men. Thomas then arrested the men and in a search incident to the arrest uncovered stolen items.

At a subsequent suppression hearing, Thomas testified that she made a warrant check because (1) the men were not local residents, (2) the men were near a local high school but were not high school age, (3) the high school area had considerable drug traffic, and (4) the passenger made a furtive gesture. What result? Did Thomas need any separate cause to detain the men while making a warrant check? If so, what degree of cause? What if the radio check took two minutes rather than ten? What if a "down" computer caused it to take twenty minutes rather than ten? How strong is the state's interest in making routine warrant checks on stopped motorists? Was the state's interest greater in this case than in a routine case?

3. SCOPE OF PERMISSIBLE SEARCH

(60) From their unmarked van in an area of Des Moines known for drug dealing, Officers Batts and Anderson observed a Buick and a Ford Tempo pull over and stop about 150 feet away from their van. Through binoculars, Batts observed two men leave the Buick, approach the Ford, and give the driver money. The driver of the Ford, Wayne Brown, then reached to the area of the glove compartment, retrieved a white bag, and handed it to the men. The cars then drove off in different directions. After following Brown's car a short distance, Batts and Anderson stopped it, ordered Brown and his two passengers to step out, and frisked the three men without finding anything. Opening the glove compartment with a key that was on the front seat, the officers then found and retrieved a bag containing cocaine and $931 in cash.

What result on Brown's motion to suppress? Assume that the facts do not establish the full probable cause needed to invoke the automobile exception. (Do they?) Were there sufficient grounds for a limited weapons search? Was this such a search? What result if you conclude that the officers reasonably suspected only that narcotics were in the glove compartment?

(61) Detectives Huttick and O'Flaherty developed reasonable suspicion but not full probable cause that defendant, who turned out to be Farah Riggs, was flying from New York to Detroit with a quantity of narcotics for distribution. The detectives also had reason to believe that Riggs was really Cynthia Joyce Griggs, also known as Betty Jackson, who was free on bail on a narcotics charge. The officers knew that three handguns and a shotgun had been found in Griggs's home when she had been arrested.

Seeking to confirm their suspicions, the detectives stopped defendant Riggs at LaGuardia Airport and directed her to produce her plane ticket. In response, Riggs produced a ticket in the name of "F. Riggs." Asked for identification, Riggs removed a leather camera case from her shoulder, placed it on the floor, and took a utility bill from her purse. The bill was in the name "Farah Jackson." Asked for better identification, Riggs opened her purse wider, revealing a plastic bag with white powder. She retrieved from her purse a utility company letter addressed to "Farah Jackson." O'Flaherty then flipped open the top of the camera case and observed two plastic bags containing white powder. The detectives also observed money both underneath and on the sides of the bags. At this point, the detectives placed Riggs under arrest.

What result on Riggs's motion to suppress the contents of the camera case? Assume that the state would not prevail under the search incident to arrest doctrine. (Would it? Does it matter that the search preceded the arrest?) Can the search be justified as a limited search for weapons? For purposes of the latter, is it important that the officers first saw the bag of white powder in Riggs's purse?

4. ROADBLOCKS

(62) At 10:00 p.m., Indiana State Police officers Cox and Fox received a radio dispatch indicating that two men, one with a shotgun, had robbed a motel in West Lafayette, Indiana, within the past seven minutes. Based on statements from witnesses, the dispatch further reported that the robbers were two black men, both about six feet tall, who had fled in a car traveling toward the northwest. At the time of the dispatch, the officers were located on State Road 18, four miles east of U.S. Highway 231, and fifteen miles northwest of the robbery. Knowing Highway 231 to be a major link-up between Highway 52 and Interstate 65 (the most direct route to Chicago), the officers immediately proceeded to the intersection of Highways 18 and 231. Their hope was to intercept the robbers traveling northbound on Highway 231. As Officer Cox later testified, "We knew from the time element that the individuals we were looking for had time to be at this location at about this time."

The officers established a roadblock at the intersection. They then stopped two cars, which they immediately released after observing that the occupants were white. After stopping a third car, driven by a black male, Officer Cox asked to see a driver's license. Officer Fox in the meantime looked into the car with his flashlight and observed another black male lying on the rear floor with a shotgun in open view. The officers then arrested the men, and a further search of the car uncovered items taken in the robbery.

What result when the defendants move to suppress the shotgun and the robbery proceeds? Can the reasonableness of Fourth Amendment activity ever be established without individualized cause? What result if the officers discovered the second man by ordering the driver to open his trunk? Does such an intrusive search always require individualized cause?

(63) In May, the motorcycle squad of the city police set up a roadblock on the main highway as a part of "Operation Street Sweep," which was aimed at general crime control. Miller's car stopped at the roadblock, where Officer Mattingly asked him for his license and insurance card. Miller was unable to produce his license and appeared to have difficulty locating his insurance card. Officer Mattingly detected an odor of alcohol on Miller and noticed that he had bloodshot eyes, a flushed face, and slurred speech. Miller admitted that he had been drinking. Officer Mattingly then asked Officer Runyon, a member of the DUI counter-measures team for assistance in administering a field sobriety test. Officer Runyon had specialized training DUI and intoxilyzer training. Officer Runyon led Miller through the nine-step walk and turn test, and the one-leg stand test. Based on these tests, Officer Runyon determined that Miller was intoxicated to the extent that he was an unsafe driver and placed Miller under arrest. Was the use of the roadblock illegal in this instance, thereby invalidating Miller's arrest?

(64) Nall was stopped at a roadblock set up by an intergovernmental task force to arrest six individuals named in two federal indictments. The plan called for arrest "teams" to arrest the persons either at their homes or places of employment. The roadblock was one of six set up to catch any of the six if they were in transit at the time of the police operation and to prevent their escape if any attempted to flee.

Nall was not named in the federal indictments, but he was known to police officials for his involvement in drug trafficking and for trying to flee the scene when police attempted to stop his vehicle. At the road-block, Officer Ramirez looked inside Nall's vehicle and noticed the handle of a shotgun. The weapon was secured and Officer Rector ran a computer check on Nall's driver's license and serial number of his shotgun. While Nall was still detained at the roadblock, but before the shotgun had cleared, Rector noticed a propane tank and clear plastic tubing inside the vehicle. Both items are commonly associated with drug manufacturing. Narcotic detection dogs were brought to the scene to sniff for the odor of drugs, but they did not appear to detect the odor of drugs. Officer Ramirez then noticed two bags in the back seat containing an off-white powder. The officers then entered the vehicle, seized the contraband and arrested Nall. Was the roadblock legal under the Fourth Amendment?

5. SPECIAL NEEDS SEARCHES

(65) Thomas, a firefighter for the City of Mesa, challenges the constitutionality of a proposed random drug testing program for firefighters. The purpose of the city's testing program is fourfold: 1) to provide firefighters with a safe work environment; 2) to ensure the safety of the general public; 3) to ensure that firefighters receive information on substance abuse; and 4) to provide necessary employee assistance for victims of substance of abuse.

All firefighters must submit to unannounced and random breath or urine testing, within thirty minutes of random selection. Employees use private bathroom stalls to collect urine samples. Anyone who refuses to submit to a test is terminated from employment. Anyone who once tests "positive" for one of several drugs is put on inactive duty and evaluated by a drug counselor. A second positive test results in termination. Drug testing records cannot be released to anyone outside the fire department without the employee's consent. Does the employee drug testing program violate the firefighters' Fourth Amendment rights?

(66) Defendant abducted a 24–year old woman he met while she was working as a bartender of a hotel which he had been patronizing. Several hours after he left the bar, the victim also left and walked to her car in a nearby parking lot. Defendant jumped on her back, hurled her to the ground, wrapped duct tape around her mouth, face and head, and bound her hands and feet. During the next three days, he sexually assaulted her several times in the sleeper compartment of his truck. Upon arriving at a truck stop three states away, the victim managed to remove the plastic cuffs which bound her hands and feet and obtain the aid of a security guard, who arrested defendant. After his federal indictment for kidnaping and following his guilty plea, defendant opposed the prosecution's motion for an order requiring him to furnish a blood sample that could be tested for the presence of the HIV virus causing AIDS. Is there a "special need", without probable cause or a warrant, for the court to grant the motion?

(67) On July 14, a confidential informant told the police that a Puerto Rican female was running a drug vending operation at a certain apartment in a multi-family building. The following evening, at about 1:00 a.m., the police drove the informant to the apartment to make a controlled buy. The informant returned with a packet of powder, which a field test confirmed to be cocaine. The informant described the male who sold him the drugs, disclosed that six or seven people were in the unit, and indicated that the group was about to go to a "speakeasy" to get rid of the remaining drugs.

Several officers then converged on the apartment building, some going to the rear and some to the front. Officers Mehring and MacBride, who went to the front, saw three Hispanic females on the steps of the building entrance. When asked if they "lived here," one of the three, Joanne Rodriguez, indicated that she did.

After knocking, announcing their purpose, and getting no reply, the police entered the apartment in question by forcing the door. Mehring, who remained outside during the entry, then directed the three women at gunpoint to accompany him inside the apartment. Once inside, Mehring took Rodriguez's purse and gave her *Miranda* warnings. Opening her purse "to look for possible weapons," Mehring discovered a large quantity of cocaine.

What result when Rodriguez moves to suppress the drugs taken from her purse? Was the detention a mere *Terry* stop, an arrest, or something in between? Does Fourth Amendment doctrine acknowledge an intermediate step? If not, do the cases in practice seem to require more suspicion the more intrusive the detention? Was something more than reasonable suspicion present in this case? Even if Rodriguez could be detained during the warrantless search of the apartment, was the search of her purse legal?

(68) Police discovered the bodies of Wallace Marshall, his wife Constance, and Beatrice Williams, all killed with knives by one or more left-handed persons who, police theorized, had access to the Marshall home. Examination of the scene disclosed strands of a fourth person's hair and traces of semen over two of the bodies. Shortly thereafter, the prosecutor's office requested a warrant to detain defendant for blood and hair samples. (Blood type can be ascertained from semen.) The supporting affidavit averred that defendant, a left-handed male, was Wallace Marshall's son and Constance's stepson. The affidavit further averred that defendant had a history of assaultive conduct, that he had been having serious arguments with his father, and that anonymous callers had implicated him in the crime. The judge concluded that the affidavit did not quite establish probable cause, but he nevertheless issued a "temporary detention order" authorizing a brief detention for the purpose of taking blood and hair samples. The judge's order required a physician to take the blood and granted the defendant the right to have counsel present. The order specifically prohibited any interrogation.

Pursuant to the order, the police took custody of the defendant and obtained the desired samples, which proved incriminating. What result on defendant's suppression motion? Do all station house detentions require traditional probable cause? If not, can some station house detentions be based on mere reasonable suspicion? Does this problem illustrate an intermediate step between a street stop and an arrest? Compare problem 67.

Chapter 2

POLICE INTERROGATION
AND CONFESSIONS

Although *Miranda*'s[a] Fifth Amendment doctrine dominates the law of confessions, other legal doctrines that affect this topic remain important. In particular, the voluntariness doctrine, which is the focus of Section B, deserves more classroom attention than it usually receives. Of lesser importance, but not to be ignored altogether, are prompt arraignment requirements and the possibility that courts will use an exclusionary doctrine to enforce them.

The Sixth Amendment right to counsel, which entered the confessions arena before *Miranda*, still plays a limited, somewhat strange, but sometimes important role in this area. As was the case in the last edition of this book, it still is unclear whether Sixth Amendment study should precede *Miranda* study or vice versa, and neither choice is completely satisfactory. Whatever the instructor's choice, students should know that Sixth Amendment rights may sometimes apply when *Miranda* rights do not and that, more often, *Miranda* rights may apply when Sixth Amendment rights do not. (Of course, sometimes both doctrines will be applicable; sometimes neither will be.) Students must learn to identify and work with the different triggering events for the two doctrines, and they must learn why it is important to know which doctrine is applicable. Do the doctrinal differences make sense in view of the different purposes underlying the Fifth and Sixth Amendments? Even if the differences are theoretically sound, do they have the appearance of being formalistic?

A. PROMPT ARRAIGNMENT REQUIREMENTS

The Supreme Court created the *Mallory*[b] exclusionary rule to enforce the federal prompt arraignment requirement in an exercise of its so-called supervisory authority over the federal courts. Whether such a power, especially when used to control the executive branch, can be squared with the Constitution's separation of powers has been questioned. It seems well-established, however, that even if such authority exists, Congress can overturn supervisory power decisions by

---

a. Miranda v. Arizona, 384 U.S. 436, 86 S.Ct. 1602, 16 L.Ed.2d 694 (1966).

b. Mallory v. United States, 354 U.S. 449, 77 S.Ct. 1356, 1 L.Ed.2d 1479 (1957).

statute. Whether Congress rejected or only modified *Mallory* in 18 U.S.C. § 3501 is still the subject of dispute.

Because the Supreme Court clearly lacks supervisory power over state courts, *Mallory* does not apply to the states. (Could the Court apply *Mallory* to the states by recharacterizing its rule as "prophylactic"?) A few state courts, however, have chosen to follow *Mallory* as a matter of state law. Is this a wise decision?

(1) On December 2, at about 8:40 a.m., FBI agents arrested the defendant for shooting a woman the previous day. Questioned after waiving his *Miranda* rights, the defendant at first denied the shooting but then said that it had been an accident. At 12:40 p.m., the defendant signed a written statement, and around mid-afternoon, he re-enacted the events for video tape. At 11:20 p.m., the agents issued the defendant a citation, told him to appear in court for arraignment on December 4, and released him.

Now charged with the federal felonies of assault resulting in serious injury and wanton endangerment in the first degree, the defendant has moved to suppress his oral statement, his written statement, and his re-enactment of the shooting. What result? Assume both that federal jurisdiction is proper in this case and that the defendant does not challenge the voluntariness of his statements.

(2) Pine Bluff, Arkansas, police officers arrested Samuel Duncan around noon on Wednesday, March 5, for the murder of a police officer the previous day. Shortly thereafter, detectives interrogated Duncan for two and one-half hours, but he insisted that he was innocent. The police then took Duncan to a cell, where he remained, unable to make a phone call, until Friday night. Late Friday night, the detectives questioned Duncan again, this time successfully. On Saturday, the police permitted Duncan to see his girlfriend, who was also in custody, but they refused to allow him to have other visitors or to use the phone. On Sunday, the detectives asked Duncan to repeat his statement on videotape, which he did. An Arkansas rule of criminal procedure provides that an arrested person "shall be taken before a judicial officer without unnecessary delay."

What result when Duncan moves to suppress his Friday and Sunday statements? Assume no *Miranda* violations occurred. Is it relevant that Duncan, an eleventh grade dropout, was classified as mildly retarded? If so, to what issue? (Is there a Fourth Amendment basis for suppression in this problem?)

B. THE VOLUNTARINESS DOCTRINE

The voluntariness doctrine warrants more attention than it often receives. First, the voluntariness doctrine governs those noncustodial contexts in which *Miranda* does not apply. Second, even if the police comply with *Miranda*, they may engage in subsequent conduct that renders a statement involuntary. Third, involuntary statements may not be used for impeachment, but voluntary statements, even if taken it violation of *Miranda*, may be so used. Fourth, involuntary statements and statements taken in violation of *Miranda* receive different fruit of the poisonous tree analysis.

Courts have largely ignored the question whether the concept of voluntariness varies in meaning depending upon whether the issue is due process voluntariness or Fifth Amendment (self-incrimination clause) voluntariness. The question is relevant, of course, to a critique of *Miranda*.

(3) Searching for two suspected bank robbers who had fled into the woods, police officers employed the services of Kino, an 88–pound German shepherd trained in tracking and apprehending suspects. After the first suspect had been caught, Kino followed the scent of the other suspect, Stauffer, to a large spruce tree. Unable to see into the tree's thick branches, and concerned that Stauffer might be armed, the officers commanded Kino to go into the branches to apprehend him.

Kino obeyed, in the process biting Stauffer on the neck, arm, and legs. (Stauffer was later treated in the hospital for severe bite wounds.) As Kino dragged him into the open, Stauffer screamed: "You caught us. You caught us. Get this dog off me. We shouldn't have robbed the bank. You caught us. Get the dog off." Still concerned about their safety, the officers did not call Kino off until they had Stauffer in handcuffs.

Now charged with bank robbery in state court, Stauffer has moved to suppress his incriminating statement. What result and why? Does it matter that the statement obviously was reliable, given that the officers had not mentioned the robbery before Stauffer's outburst? Is it relevant that the officers were not trying to elicit a response? Does the issue turn on whether the police were justified in their use of Kino? Can a claim of involuntariness ever prevail without a showing of police misconduct?

(4) At approximately 8:40 p.m., defendant Carl's wife phoned the police and reported that their daughter had been abducted about forty minutes earlier from the family car that they were packing in a motel parking lot. When the police arrived, they asked to examine the car. After expressing some initial reluctance, Carl agreed to open the trunk; when he did so, the officers discovered two large stacks of money. The officers then accompanied Carl to his motel room and gave him *Miranda* warnings. Counting the money on a bed, Carl responded, "Don't bother me." When the officers turned to Carl's wife, Carl told her not to answer because he could handle the matter.

At 11:00 p.m., Carl received the first of several threatening phone calls concerning his daughter. Between calls, the officers encouraged Carl and his wife to relate all the circumstances surrounding the kidnapping. Finally, following another call and further entreaties by the officers and his wife, Carl told the officers what had happened.

According to Carl, two individuals had owed him money for a previous narcotics transaction. Carl had subsequently agreed to sell the men some hash, but when the men arrived, Carl and some accomplices robbed them at gunpoint of more than $15,000 to make up for the past debt. Carl added that the men were threatening to kill his daughter unless he returned the money to their apartment.

After rescuing the child, the police charged Carl with aggravated robbery. What result on Carl's motion to suppress his motel statement?

Should the court evaluate the degree of pressure on Carl, the propriety of the police behavior, or both? Did the police "exploit" the pressure created by others? In an improper way? Would it be "unfair" to use Carl's statements against him? *Constitutionally* unfair? Why (not)?

(5) Police arrested *A* and *B* for burglary. Knowing from prior experience that neither was likely to confess, the police nevertheless took *A* and *B* to an interrogation waiting room, where a secretary was typing. A detective then called *A* into the interrogation room. When, as expected, the interrogation failed to elicit an admission, the detective made *A* and *B* exchange places. Again, as expected, the detective failed to get an admission.

While *B* was still in the interrogation room, the detective returned to the waiting room and, in front of *A*, asked the secretary to come into the interrogation room with a pencil and notebook. After an appropriate time in the interrogation room, the secretary, who had been coached for this role, returned to the waiting room and began to type from what appeared to be shorthand notes in the notebook. At one point during the typing, the secretary looked up and asked *A* how he spelled his name. The secretary then took the typed pages to the detective in the interrogation room.

Following this, the detective made *A* and *B* switch rooms again. Asked what he had to say for himself, *A*, thinking that *B* had confessed, asked what *B* had said. The detective responded, "Never mind that. I want it from your own lips." *A* then confessed.

Assuming full compliance with *Miranda*, what result on *A*'s motion to suppress? From a policy standpoint, was the trickery in this case unfair or unjust, or was it simply clever police work? Whatever your policy views, would use of *A*'s confession violate the Constitution? Why (not)?

(6) Barbara Welch reported to the police that her estranged husband had confessed to her that he had committed an unsolved, five-year-old murder. He had been worried, she added, that God would not forgive him. In response to this new lead, two homicide detectives asked defendant Kerry Welch to come to the station for questioning. After complying with this request, Welch received and waived his *Miranda* rights and denied being involved in the murder.

Officer Easley, a professed born-again Christian, then replaced the two detectives in the interrogation room. After identifying himself as a police officer, Easley expressed concern that Welch did not understand the nature of divine forgiveness. During the next three hours, Easley and Welch prayed together and discussed forgiveness and salvation. In the process, Welch made a number of incriminating statements. When Easley left the interrogation room, the two detectives returned and asked Welch whether he wanted to make a statement. Welch said that he did. Welch then made a full and detailed confession to the murder.

In Welch's subsequent trial, the prosecutor, over defense objection, introduced into evidence Welch's statements to Officer Easley and his confession to the detectives. Following his conviction, Welch unsuccessfully exhausted his appellate rights. What result when he now seeks a writ of habeas corpus from the federal district court? What if instead of identifying himself as a police officer, Easley had pretended to be a member of the clergy?

(7) Shortly after midnight, homicide detectives arrested Jose Amaya–Ruiz, a Spanish-speaking, undocumented alien from El Salvador with an I.Q. of 75, for the murder of his employer's pregnant wife the previous day. At the station, the detectives observed blood stains on Amaya–Ruiz's clothing. They then provided him a blanket, confiscated everything but his jockey shorts, and placed him alone in a room with a bench, on which he could have slept.

Some nine hours later, after he had been offered food, and while he still was clad only in his shorts and the blanket, the detectives used an interpreter to advise Amaya–Ruiz of his *Miranda* rights in Spanish. Unable to write, Amaya–Ruiz placed his mark on a waiver of rights form that the interpreter read to him. Asked whether he would answer questions, he replied, "I don't know if I will answer. Ask me something." In response to questioning, Amaya–Ruiz denied even knowing the victim's family. Although further questions quickly prompted Amaya–Ruiz to admit that this statement was a lie, he continued to maintain his innocence regarding the murder.

One detective then said untruthfully that two witnesses had seen him run from the victim's truck. When Amaya–Ruiz still denied his guilt, the detective urged him to tell the truth:

> "We can forgive your lies, but the United States court system will not. If you want any forgiveness, you should tell the truth. This is your only opportunity to tell the truth. If you lie to us now, it will be on the record for the rest of your life that you lied, and then you'll never be able to say you're sorry."

Amaya–Ruiz then said, "I didn't do it, but I was drugged." A few moments later, he said, "I took her life."

Convicted of murder, Amaya–Ruiz now appeals. Assuming no Fourth Amendment issues, what result and why? What factors are relevant to your analysis?

C. THE SIXTH AMENDMENT RIGHT TO COUNSEL

Sixth Amendment "interrogation" cases raise a number of difficult issues pertaining to the attachment of Sixth Amendment rights, the existence of deliberate elicitation, the validity of a purported waiver, and the applicability of the rigid, prophylactic rule that sometimes precludes an otherwise valid waiver. As at least some of the next six problems reveal, these issues frequently overlap.

Depending upon the order of study, students may also want to address the Miranda issues that are present in some of these problems. If the order of study precludes this, these problems should be revisited when *Miranda* is studied. The problems should help to illustrate the important and sometimes confusing differences between Fifth and Sixth Amendment doctrine in this area.

(8) Following a shooting early Sunday morning, police arrested Lale for attempted murder. Pursuant to a valid warrant for the handgun used in the shooting, they also searched Lale's house and seized a handgun, a short-barreled shotgun, and a machine gun. (The legality of the seizures is not in issue.) At a bail hearing the next morning, with Lale represented by retained counsel, the prosecutor asserted that the state had not yet completed its investigation. Nevertheless, the prosecutor asked the court to take into account that the state soon would be charging Lale with attempted murder. The court released Lale on a $10,000 recognizance bond. In the courthouse corridor after the hearing, Lale's lawyer exacted a promise from the prosecutor that Lale would not be questioned.

On Friday, the prosecutor filed a written complaint with the court charging Lale with illegal possession of a sawed-off shotgun and a machine gun. Later that day, detectives urged Lale's girlfriend to persuade him to cooperate before they filed the attempted murder charge on Monday. In response to her entreaties, Lale went to the police station and agreed to talk without his lawyer. Shortly thereafter, he confessed to the shooting. On Monday, the prosecutor filed a complaint with the court charging Lale with attempted murder.

Facing trial for attempted murder and for illegal possession of the shotgun and machine gun, Lale has moved to suppress his confession. Assuming that Lale was not in custody for *Miranda* purposes (he was not, was he?), what result and why? What if the prosecutor delayed filing the attempted murder complaint specifically to give the police a chance to obtain a statement relating to the shooting? What if Lale had used his illegally possessed shotgun in the shooting?

(9) At 9:00 a.m. on March 22, police lawfully arrested Pack and seized clothes belonging to a store that had been burglarized a few hours earlier. After Pack received *Miranda* warnings and invoked his right to silence, the police filed a complaint in court charging Pack with theft and receiving stolen goods. The judge released Pack on bail and appointed the Public Defender to represent him.

On April 1, with a prosecutor's approval, the police obtained a judicial warrant authorizing them to arrest Pack for the burglary of the store. After arresting Pack and taking him to the station, the police gave him *Miranda* warnings and obtained a voluntary waiver. Pack then admitted that he had broken into the store and stolen the clothes; he also admitted that he had committed an earlier, unrelated burglary. Withdrawing the previous complaint, the prosecutor then filed a new complaint in court adding the two burglaries to the other charges.

What result when the defendant moves to suppress his admissions on Sixth Amendment grounds? (Would suppression be required under *Miranda*'s Fifth Amendment doctrine? If you conclude that the results would differ under Sixth and Fifth Amendment analysis, what policies justify such a difference?)

(10) Eighteen-year-old David Smith, accompanied by his lawyer, voluntarily went to police headquarters but left after learning that Sergeant Jordan, who wanted to question Smith about a recent murder, was away. Shortly thereafter, Jordan obtained an arrest warrant for Smith and pursuant to the warrant arrested Smith. At the station, Smith waived his *Miranda* rights, stating specifically that he did not need a lawyer because he was innocent. When Smith continued to maintain his innocence, Jordan placed him in a holding cell and ordered him lunch.

In the meantime, other officers had arrested and were questioning an additional suspect, Michael Werner. Jordan entered Werner's interrogation room, told Werner that the police had a solid case against the two suspects, and, stating that they believed Smith had done the actual shooting, offered to "go easy" on Werner if he cooperated. Werner then agreed to be placed in Smith's cell with a hidden radio transmitter. Jordan instructed Werner not to ask Smith any questions and to let Smith choose the topics of conversation.

Shortly after Werner appeared in the cell, Smith asked him whether he had confessed. When Werner denied that he had, Smith said, "Good. They can't prove we did it without a confession. My lawyer says that she can win any case as long as there's no confession." Smith also warned Werner not to fall for any tricks, such as the police telling him that Smith had already talked. After these remarks, Smith did not talk about the murder, and Werner did not attempt to return to the subject. Some two hours later, the police arraigned both men on murder charges.

What result when Smith moves to suppress his overheard holding cell statements? Should Smith have had a Sixth Amendment right to counsel when Werner did not? If (a big if) Smith's Sixth Amendment rights had attached, did the use of Werner violate these rights? Why (not)? What result under *Miranda*? Are any other constitutional arguments available to Smith?

(11) In response to an investigation by the Bureau of Alcohol, Tobacco, and Firearms, a grand jury indicted York for mail fraud and arson. The indictment alleged that York blew up his bar and killed his business partner to collect on insurance policies. York's subsequent conviction was overturned on appeal, but he remained in Terre Haute Penitentiary to await retrial.

In the interval between York's trials, federal officials transferred Beaman, who was serving a forty-year sentence for bank robbery, from Alabama to Terre Haute. For the previous four years, Beaman had been a prison informant for the FBI under instructions to report what he heard about crimes such as murder, official corruption, and drugs. In return, the FBI promised to notify the parole board of Beaman's assistance. Although the FBI did not know of York at the time of Beaman's transfer (the transfer had occurred because of safety concerns), Beaman continued to meet regularly with the FBI in Terre Haute under the same arrangement he had maintained in Alabama.

Working in the recreation department at Terre Haute, Beaman saw York almost daily, and the two frequently conversed. In one conversation, Beaman told York about his son's troubles with the law. After responding by telling of his own son's troubles, York added that his son suspected that York had killed his mother. When Beaman said, "You must have been pretty mad at the bitch," York said, "Mad enough to put a bullet behind her head." In a later conversation, York mentioned that he was going to make some money on a building he had blown up and on a woman he had killed. When Beaman asked whether York was really going to make any money out of it, York responded that he wouldn't have done it otherwise. York went on to explain how he blown up the bar and killed his partner.

Because Beaman thought York's assertions were "rubbish," he did not bring them up in his subsequent meetings with the FBI. Several months later, however, after another inmate read Beaman a news story about York's first trial, Beaman decided to report the conversations to the FBI. York wants to suppress these statements from his second trial. What result? (Assume that the admission relating to his wife's murder would be otherwise admissible as "other crimes" evidence.)

(12) Epstein broke into the Feed and Seed Store in February and stole seven leather-studded spiked dog collars. A month later, he broke into the Pet Shop and stole a pet python snake and lamp to keep the snake warm. Entry into both shops was gained by throwing a rock through the glass front door. In April, he was arrested for the Pet Shop break-in and was arraigned the following day and remanded to the jail. In May, detective Murphy took Epstein from the jail to the detective bureau for questioning about other burglaries that had occurred in the city. At that time, Epstein had not been arrested on the Feed and Seed burglary. Before he began to question Epstein, Murphy did not know that Epstein had an attorney on the Pet Shop charge. During the interview, Epstein waived his *Miranda* rights and confessed to the Feed and Seed burglary. He was indicted and counsel was appointed on that charge.

Epstein has filed a motion to suppress the Feed and Seed confession. He claims that once he had counsel on the Pet Shop charge, the right carried over and extended to the Feed and Seed charge, with the result that the detective could not question him unless he initiated the contact with the police. The trial court denied the motion. On appeal, how should the court rule? Were the police required to contact Epstein's counsel about either burglary before questioning began? How does the Sixth Amendment right to counsel differ from the Fifth Amendment privilege? Are both amendments offense-specific?

(13) At his initial appearance (preliminary arraignment) on state firearms charges in March, Martinez requested appointment of a lawyer and completed a form entitled "Affidavit of Indigence and Order for Appointment of Counsel." The state, however, dismissed the charges before counsel was appointed. Nevertheless, Martinez remained in state custody because his arrest had led the authorities to revoke his pre-existing parole. (The legality of the parole revocation is not challenged.)

In September, federal authorities filed a complaint in federal court alleging that Martinez's conduct that had led to the state charges violated federal law. Two days later, state officials released Martinez into federal custody. Federal agents then advised Martinez of his *Miranda* rights, which he waived. In response to questioning, Martinez confessed to the federal charge.

The government has now brought an interlocutory appeal from the trial judge's order suppressing the confession on Sixth Amendment grounds. What result? (Should the trial judge also have suppressed the statement on *Miranda* grounds?)

D. *MIRANDA* AND THE FIFTH AMENDMENT[c]

1. THE CUSTODY AND INTERROGATION REQUIREMENTS

Black letter law indicates that both "custody" and "interrogation" are necessary for *Miranda* to become applicable. Whether they always are sufficient is not altogether clear. Arguably, to have a nexus to the Fifth Amendment's compulsory self-incrimination clause upon which it is based, *Miranda*'s holding, at least outside the station house context, should be limited to "inherently compelling" situations, or at least to situations with the same potential for compulsion as is present in station house interrogation. The Supreme Court on occasion has factored *Miranda*'s rationale into its analysis, but the relationship of rationale and black letter holding remains unclear. In any event, even in straight black letter terms, the precise meanings of the custody and interrogation requirements are not that clear. The problems in this section explore these and other issues.

(14) Responding to an inmate's fatal stabbing, two prison guards followed a trail of blood to James Conley, another inmate, who exhibited a fresh two-inch wound on his wrist. The guards then placed Conley in handcuffs and escorted him to a small conference room to await transfer to the infirmary. In the conference room, one of the guards, who knew Conley on "friendly terms" and always addressed him by his nickname, asked how he had been injured. Conley answered that he had been stabbed when he tried to stop a fight between the deceased and two other inmates. In response to another question, Conley said he could not identify the inmates because they wore ski masks. Asked if he was up to the same old stuff again, Conley replied that he and the deceased were "cool" (i.e., friends) but that the deceased had a bad attitude.

Conley was convicted of murder after a trial in which the prosecutor introduced his statements. What result on appeal? What if standard prison procedure required handcuffs on an inmate being transferred to the infirmary? Would it matter if the prison guards had interviewed

c. In all the *Miranda* problems that involve federal cases, students should consider the impact, if any, of 18 U.S.C. § 3501 on the suppression issue.

Conley as a witness rather than as a suspect? (Was Conley actually compelled to become a witness against himself?)

(15) On Thursday, October 15, Philadelphia police discovered the sexually assaulted body of fifteen-year-old Doris Shenk. Investigation disclosed that the defendant, another boy, and three girls, all juveniles, had been with Ms. Shenk on the night of the murder. According to the others, the defendant was the last of the group to be with Ms. Shenk.

At 11:00 p.m. the next night, three police officers made the hour-long drive to a home outside the city, where the defendant was staying with relatives. Without indicating whether he had a choice, and without mentioning anyone's death, the officers asked the defendant whether he would accompany them back to Philadelphia to answer some questions about drinking with Ms. Shenk. The defendant and his uncle agreed to go.

At the beginning of the drive, with the defendant's uncle present, one of the officers asked the defendant whether he knew Doris Shenk, whether he had been with her on Thursday night, and whether he had been drinking with her. The defendant answered yes to each question. No other questioning occurred in the car.

What result when the defendant moves to suppress his automobile statements? Does either the intent of the officers or the belief of the defendant regarding the defendant's choice about returning to Philadelphia have any bearing on whether *Miranda* was applicable? What would a reasonable person have thought, and what relevance does this have to *Miranda*'s Fifth Amendment concern? Should the uncle's presence in the squad car affect the analysis? (Was the defendant actually compelled to answer the three questions?)

(16) Suspecting David Griffin of involvement in a recent bank robbery, two FBI agents went to Griffin's home at 7:00 p.m. and were admitted by Griffin's stepfather, who owned the home. Griffin was not home, but his stepfather permitted the agents to wait for him in the living room. When they heard Griffin approach a little over an hour later, the agents moved to the hall near the front door. As soon as Griffin entered, the agents identified themselves, indicated that they were investigating a bank robbery, and said that they needed to speak with him. Griffin immediately said, "The gun wasn't loaded."

After explaining to his parents that they needed to talk in private, the agents asked Griffin to step into the dining room. Griffin's parents then went upstairs, where they remained the rest of the night. The agents did not draw their guns, handcuff Griffin, or place him under formal arrest, but neither did they inform him that he was not under arrest or that he was free to leave without speaking to them.

During the two-hour interview that followed, Griffin on two occasions asked to obtain cigarettes from other places in the house. Telling Griffin that he had to remain in their view at all times, one of the agents escorted Griffin each time he went to get cigarettes. After Griffin implicated himself and another individual in the robbery, the agents arrested him, transported him to their office, and for the first time gave him *Miranda* warnings.

What result when the government appeals to the district court the magistrate's suppression of Griffin's hallway and dining room statements?

(17) Late one evening, Franchell Rosse drove Sam Masson to an apartment building. At the building entrance, Masson was arrested by police who had learned about his plan to sell narcotics to the apartment's occupant, whom they already had arrested. Two unmarked police cars then blocked Ms. Rosse's car. With guns drawn, two officers directed Ms. Rosse and a male passenger in the back seat to exit the car, patted-down both for weapons, and put handcuffs on the passenger. Finding both "clean," the officers put their guns away. Not having found the narcotics in question on Masson's person, the officers then searched Rosse's car, also to no avail.

Officer Luey, one of the seven officers present, then requested Rosse to sit in his car. Luey told Rosse that she would be free to go "once we figure out exactly what is going on." After some brief questioning, Luey said, "I believe you know more than what you have stated about driving Sam to drop off some money." In response to further questioning, Rosse made incriminating statements. After about fifteen minutes, the police released both Rosse and her passenger.

Rosse was subsequently charged with violations of the Controlled Substances Act. After a trial in which her statements were admitted as evidence, a jury found Rosse guilty. The intermediate appellate court reversed, finding a *Miranda* violation. What result on the state's appeal? Was Rosse arrested or only subject to a *Terry* stop? Would it matter on these facts? Why (not)? (Do not discuss possible Fourth Amendment violations. Were there any?)

(18) After customs agents at Miami International Airport decided that the defendant, a seventeen-year-old girl who had just returned from Colombia, might be carrying drugs, they directed her to a secondary room and conducted an unproductive strip search. (The search is not in issue.) The agents then left the defendant alone in the room while they again inspected her luggage. After dressing, the defendant began to read a booklet of newspaper clippings that, along with other magazines, was on a table in the room. The clippings described deaths that had resulted from drugs hidden in body cavities. When the agents returned, the defendant said, "I have drugs in my body." She then removed the drugs.

What result when the defendant moves to suppress both her statement and the drugs? Is the answer necessarily the same for both? What if such a story was in a news magazine on the table? Would the agents' knowledge of the story's presence be relevant? Do your answers to these questions have anything to do with whether the defendant was compelled to reveal the drugs?

(19) Police arrested the defendant for murdering his two-month-old son and brought him to the station. To console the defendant, who was visibly upset, a detective said, "Don't worry. God takes care of little babies, and your baby is probably already in heaven." The defendant then asked the detective whether he was religious, and the detective replied, "Not as religious as I should be." Without the detective saying anything more, the defendant then described why and how he killed his son.

What result on the defendant's motion to suppress?

(20) Police arrested the defendant for the murder of a young man and the rape and stabbing of the man's female companion. At the station, a detective introduced himself and stated, "I just want to tell you where we stand." The detective then stated that the police had arrested the defendant's accomplice, which was true, and that the surviving victim had identified the defendant from a photograph, which was false. The defendant then said, "I can't keep this to myself any longer. I'll tell you what happened." The detective then read the defendant his *Miranda* rights, and the defendant agreed to talk without a lawyer.

What result on the defendant's subsequent motion to suppress his confession? Is the truth or falsity of the detective's statements relevant to the *Miranda* issue? (Was the defendant actually compelled to become a witness against himself?)

(21) On Tuesday, September 9, Weedon's lawyer summoned the police to Weedon's home. When two detectives arrived, Weedon and his lawyer invited them to search Weedon's car. In the trunk, the detectives discovered Weedon's wife, who had been shot twice in the head. The detectives then arrested Weedon and read him *Miranda* rights. In response, the lawyer stated that the police were not to question Weedon about "any aspect of the investigation." The lawyer did agree, however, that Weedon could answer questions from the arrest register, which one detective described as including such things as name, address, date of birth, social security number, and driver's license number. Relying on this understanding with the police, the lawyer did not accompany Weedon to the police station.

At the station, a homicide division booking officer asked Weedon questions from the "arrestee data" and the "offense data" sections of the arrest register. Responding to questions from the latter section, which included items such as the date and time of the offense, Weedon indicated that the shooting had occurred on Sunday, September 7, at 10:00 a.m.

The state now wants to introduce this statement in Weedon's murder trial. What result? (Assume that the statement is relevant.)

2. INVOCATION OF *MIRANDA* RIGHTS

Miranda's minor directives and abundant dicta continue to trouble the courts. The directive pertaining to a suspect's invocation of the *Miranda* right to remain silent and the quite different directive pertaining to a suspect's invocation of the *Miranda* right to counsel stand out in terms of difficulty of application and frequency of litigation. (Does it make constitutional or common sense to have two different rules in this area? Does either rule have any bearing on whether the defendant was actually compelled to become a witness against himself?) The problems in this subsection explore some of the issues that these directives have produced. Students should continue to be alert for issues that were explored in the previous subsection.

(22) Relying on Portland, Oregon, arrest warrants in connection with two thefts, police officers in Lynnwood, Washington, lawfully arrested Richard Grooms. At the request of the Portland police, the arresting officers did not tell Grooms that he was also wanted for questioning in Portland about a robbery-murder. They did, however, read Grooms his *Miranda* rights, and when Grooms declined to answer questions, the officers terminated their attempt to interrogate him.

Four hours later, at 11:00 p.m., two Portland detectives arrived in Lynnwood. With one of the Lynnwood arresting officers present, the detectives read Grooms his *Miranda* rights, obtained a signed waiver, and questioned him about the two thefts. When Grooms confessed shortly thereafter, the detectives turned to the robbery-murder, and Grooms soon confessed to that crime as well. The Lynnwood officer did not mention that Grooms had earlier declined to talk. The interrogation by the Portland detectives took place in the same room that the Lynnwood officers had used in their attempt to interrogate Grooms.

What result when Grooms moves to suppress both confessions?

(23) Police arrested Michael Trapp in connection with a robbery and kidnapping. At the station, Detective Gazaway gave Trapp *Miranda* warnings, and Trapp replied that he understood his rights and that he would not answer questions. Gazaway immediately terminated the discussion, but he remained in the room with Trapp tending to other work.

A minute or so later, Trapp asked, "How did you find out where I would be?" Gazaway responded that he could not talk about the investigation because Trapp had originally refused to discuss the matter. Gazaway added that he could talk to Trapp only if Trapp voluntarily requested that he do so. Trapp then said he would discuss his role in the crimes as long as he did not have to implicate anyone else.

After calling another officer to join them, Gazaway recited that Trapp had both received his rights and acknowledged that he understood them, that Trapp had exercised his right to remain silent, and that only moments later Trapp had voluntarily requested to talk to Gazaway as long as he was not asked to implicate others. Trapp confirmed the accuracy of Gazaway's recitation and said he was willing to talk. The other officer then left the room, and in response to Gazaway's questions,

Trapp made incriminating statements, which he now wants to suppress. What result?

(24) Arrested and taken to the police station for murder, Nate Harvey responded to *Miranda* warnings by saying he would talk but not until he had spoken with his father. While officers went to get Harvey's father, other officers obtained lunch for Harvey and chatted with him in general. When Harvey's father arrived, the two spent fifteen minutes alone together. After Harvey's father left, more than three hours after Harvey had requested to see him, the interrogating officers came back into the room. Without repeating the *Miranda* warnings or reminding Harvey of the warnings he had received, they questioned him and obtained an incriminating statement.

What result on Harvey's motion to suppress?

(25) Drug Enforcement Agents lawfully arrested Paul Porter for trafficking in narcotics, took him to their headquarters, gave him *Miranda* warnings, and asked whether he would like to make a phone call. In the presence of DEA agent Pasquarello, Porter then called his attorney's office. Because his attorney was out of the office, Porter simply left a message that he had called and that the DEA had arrested him.

After Porter made his phone call, DEA Supervisor Garidotto, who was unaware of the phone call, entered the interrogation room and asked the other agents whether Porter had been advised of and understood his rights. When they answered affirmatively, Garidotto asked Porter whether he understood his rights, and Porter answered that he did and that he would answer questions. Garidotto then proceeded to interrogate Porter, and Porter made inculpatory statements.

The trial court found that Porter knew of his rights and voluntarily waived them. On appeal after conviction, what result? (Was Porter actually compelled to become a witness against himself?)

(26) On January 24, Eric Wright pleaded guilty to the armed robbery of a pharmacy. At the plea hearing, Wright's lawyer said that she wanted to be present during any interviews of her client. At a subsequent interview by a probation officer who was preparing a presentence report, Wright's lawyer was present.

On February 8, FBI agents investigating a bank robbery visited Wright in jail and gave him *Miranda* warnings. At the time, Wright still had not been sentenced on his guilty plea to the pharmacy robbery. Wright agreed to talk without a lawyer, and he soon confessed to robbing the bank.

What result when Wright seeks to suppress his confession in his bank robbery trial? Does it matter whether a state or the federal government prosecuted the first robbery charge? (Does Wright have a valid Sixth Amendment claim?)

(27) Eldred Ikaika voluntarily came to the police station at 11:25 a.m. after learning that the police were looking for him as a person who had witnessed a murder a year earlier. When Ikaika denied knowledge of the crime, the police gave him *Miranda* warnings, obtained a waiver, and asked whether Ikaika would take a polygraph test. After the test indicated deception, the police said they were going to hold Ikaika for further questioning.

At 1:55 p.m., Detective Tomas repeated the *Miranda* warnings, and Ikaika said he wanted a lawyer. Tomas then told Ikaika that he would not be interviewed any further and that he would be taken to the booking area of the station. Alone with Ikaika at booking and preparing to take his fingerprints, Officer Bartolome said, "What's happening Eldred? Must be heavy stuff for two detectives to bring you down here?" Ikaika responded that he had been detained for questioning about a murder. Starting to cry, he then said, "Bartolome, I can't lie to you, you've been too nice to me. I shot the haole." Until this point, Bartolome, who was an acquaintance of Ikaika, knew nothing about the case. Ikaika then said he would talk without a lawyer, and Bartolome returned him to Detective Tomas. At 2:35 p.m., Detective Tomas again read Ikaika his *Miranda* rights. Ikaika agreed to talk without a lawyer present and then gave a detailed confession.

What result on Ikaika's motion to suppress? What if Ikaika had asked for a lawyer before he took the polygraph test?

(28) Police officers arrested the defendant at 8:00 p.m. for shooting another individual in a bar. At 9:40 p.m., a detective took the defendant to an interrogation room and advised him of his rights. When the defendant responded that he wanted a lawyer present, the detective left him alone to telephone a lawyer he had retained in a previous case. During the next two hours, the defendant made several unsuccessful attempts to contact his lawyer. At midnight, the detective called a public defender, but after a short conference with her, the defendant declined her services.

At 3:00 a.m., the detective transported the defendant to another room for fingerprinting. The detective's suppression hearing testimony described what happened:

Q.   Then what occurred?

A.   Then on our way down in the elevator he told us he would tell us what happened. He returned to room 104 and we started taking a statement from him.

Q.   Let's get into this "on the elevator on the way down." Had you asked him anything? What was going on in the elevator that he made this statement that he would tell you what happened?

A.   We were talking in general and I told him we didn't have to have a statement from him because witnesses had identified him but we would like to hear his side of the story. At this time he said, "take me back up and I will tell you what happened."

The detective then returned the defendant to the interrogation room. After again being warned of his rights, the defendant agreed to talk without a lawyer and, in response to questioning, gave a statement admitting guilt.

Should the court suppress the confession?

3. OTHER *MIRANDA* ISSUES

(29) A half block before reaching a bank in response to a silent alarm, Officers Jan Montgomery and Valerie Dentherio observed Don Adams holding a gun on Joe Fleming, who was kneeling in a field. With guns drawn, the officers ordered Adams to drop his gun. As he did so, Adams said that Fleming was a fleeing bank robber. Not even sure that a bank had been robbed, the officers told both men to put their hands in the air. Adams complied, but Fleming said he could not comply because he had been shot.

When Montgomery, who observed a gunshot wound in Fleming's arm, then asked who had shot him, Fleming responded, "The guard at the bank." When asked who had been with him, Fleming said that he had been alone, which turned out to be untrue. Montgomery followed this response by asking where Fleming's gun was, and Fleming claimed that he had dropped it. Montgomery then asked whether Fleming had robbed the bank. Fleming said that he had and added, "I didn't shoot the guard. I didn't even get any money." Shortly thereafter, the officers arrested Fleming and gave him *Miranda* warnings. They never found the gun.

What result on Fleming's motion to suppress his statements in his trial for robbery? (Does Fleming have a viable voluntariness claim?)

(30) Robert Provost walked into a police station and asked to be locked up because he had "burned" Barbara Lawson, his wife. Seeming quite agitated, he also demanded that they help her "fast." Smelling gasoline on Provost and noticing that the hair on his neck was singed, the officers with whom he was speaking asked where Barbara was. Because Provost seemed unable to give coherent directions, the officers asked him to show them where Barbara was. When Provost agreed, they handcuffed him and placed him in a police car. As they drove along, the officers asked for directions and asked how and why he had burned Barbara. When they found Barbara's badly burned body, the officers gave him *Miranda* warnings.

Now charged with murder, Provost has moved to suppress all the statements he made in the police car and all physical evidence that the police found with his help, including the body. What result?

(31) After taking eighteen-year-old Edward Dailey into custody for a sex offense, the police read him his *Miranda* rights. Coming to the third warning, the officer said,

> You have the right to talk to a lawyer before we ask you any questions and to have him with you during questioning. You have the same right to the advice and presence of a lawyer even if you cannot afford one. If you decide to answer questions now without a

lawyer present, you will still have the right to stop answering at any time. You also have the right to stop answering at any time until you talk to a lawyer.

Dailey, who has an I.Q. of 71, a word identification level just below second grade, and a reading level below third grade, said that he understood and signed a waiver.

What result when Dailey moves to suppress his incriminating statements?

(32) Undercover officer Julio Valez arrested Jose Cruz in connection with drug offenses. He then gave him the four *Miranda* warnings, adding at the conclusion of the fourth warning that if Cruz decided to answer questions without a lawyer, he had a right to do so. After acknowledging that he understood his rights, Cruz asked Valez what was going on. Valez responded by asking questions, to which Cruz gave incriminating statements.

What result on a motion to suppress?

Chapter 3

EYEWITNESS TESTIMONY AND PRETRIAL IDENTIFICATION PROCEDURES

Not much has happened in this area in the last several years. The issues, moreover, are not that difficult. Indeed, the Sixth Amendment problems in the last chapter laid the foundation for some of the Sixth Amendment problems in this chapter. Accordingly, this chapter, unlike the first two, has relatively few problems for consideration.

A. THE RIGHT TO COUNSEL

1. THE SUBSTANTIVE RIGHT

(1) Police discovered a stolen car in a ditch beside the road. They arrested the defendant near the scene after obtaining the driver's description from witnesses. They then brought the defendant before a judge, who issued an arrest warrant for larceny. Approximately thirty minutes later, two witnesses identified the defendant as the car's driver in one-man showups at the police station. The defendant was not represented by counsel.

A state statute provides that, except when waived, no person may be tried without a grand jury indictment or presentment. A second statute governs the procedure for warrantless arrests:

> A person arrested without a warrant shall be brought forthwith before an officer authorized to issue criminal warrants in the county or city where the arrest is made, unless such person is released on summons as provided by law. The officer before whom such person is brought shall proceed to examine the officer making the arrest. If the officer before whom such person is brought has reasonable grounds upon which to believe that a criminal offense has been committed, and that the person arrested has committed such offense, he shall issue such a warrant as might have been issued prior to the arrest of such person.

The defendant now moves to suppress the out-of-court identifications. What result?

(2) Police arrested the defendant for car theft after finding him in a stolen car. At a preliminary arraignment held shortly thereafter, the magistrate appointed counsel to represent the defendant, continued the arraignment for two weeks, and released the defendant on bail. During the two week interval, the arresting officer notified Detective Glen that the defendant fit the description of one of two men who had recently robbed a woman in her apartment. Glen then requested that the woman attend the defendant's arraignment on the stolen car charge.

When the defendant's theft arraignment subsequently resumed, the detective and woman sat together in the courtroom. Glen instructed the woman to observe the men who were arraigned and to tell him "when you see the fellow who did it." During a twenty-minute period, the woman observed eight men, several the same race as the defendant, stand up for arraignment. When she next observed the defendant, she immediately told Glen that he was one of her assailants. After the arraignment, Glen arrested the defendant for robbery, and a grand jury subsequently indicted him for that offense.

During a suppression hearing in the robbery prosecution, Glen testified that he did not inform defendant's counsel, who was present at the theft arraignment, of the planned identification. Both Glen and the woman denied that Glen had called attention to the defendant at the arraignment, and the woman testified that she did not hear the defendant's name called before she identified him. What result?

(3) During a recess in the defendant's robbery trial, a witness, at the prosecutor's urging, walked through the courtroom and observed five people, including the defendant. The witness then returned to the witness room, where she had been sequestered while other witnesses testified, and informed the prosecutor that the defendant resembled the robber. Defense counsel was in a rest room when the witness observed the defendant.

When trial resumed, the defendant notified counsel of the witness's presence in the courtroom. Counsel then objected unsuccessfully to the witness making any identification of the defendant. During her testimony, the witness stated that the defendant strongly resembled the robber, but she added that she could not be "absolutely sure" about her identification.

What result on appeal? What if the witness had accidentally encountered the defendant in the hall before testifying?

(4) After the defendant's arraignment on bank robbery charges, an Assistant United States Attorney placed him in a five-person lineup attended by four witnesses from the two victim banks. Before the lineup began, the prosecutor denied defendant's lawyer an opportunity to interview the witnesses, and she also refused to disclose any descriptions the witnesses had previously given of the robbers. The prosecutor then instructed the witnesses not to say anything or point to anyone during the lineup, and she required the witnesses, each accompanied by an FBI agent, to stand approximately fifteen feet apart. After the viewing, defense counsel repeated her earlier requests. Following an angry exchange of words, the prosecutor ejected defense counsel from the premises. Thereafter, with the lineup participants no longer present, the prosecutor questioned the witnesses about the lineup, and three of them identified the defendant.

What result on the defendant's motion to suppress?

(5) An indictment charged the defendant with murder and robbery. In a subsequent police interview, the defendant waived his *Miranda* rights and agreed to stand in a lineup without counsel. Without notifying defendant's retained lawyer, the police then conducted a lineup, and a witness to the robbery identified the defendant.

What result when the defendant moves to suppress the witness's out-of-court identification? What if the defendant was not yet represented by counsel when the lineup occurred?

2. THE EXCLUSIONARY REMEDIES

(6) About 4:15 a.m., Dale Kuecken, who had just returned home from work, observed several men scurrying about a Laundromat across the street. After calling the police, Kuecken heard glass breaking and an alarm ringing and saw two men running toward his house. Taking his shotgun, Kuecken went outside and stopped one of the men. He also observed a second man, with sandy blond hair and a white T-shirt, running to his left. While Kuecken's attention was momentarily diverted, the first man struck him over the head with a tire iron and fled. When the police arrived shortly thereafter, Kuecken pointed to a car driving away. The police pursued the car and apprehended three men, including the defendant Hutton. After the men were arraigned on burglary charges, Kuecken observed them through a one-way mirror at the police station. He identified one as his assailant and the defendant as the person he had seen running. The defendant, who was wearing a white T-shirt, did not waive counsel.

At a suppression hearing Kuecken positively identified the defendant. When asked about his certainty, Kuecken responded,

> A. I said it before and I probably say it again that's the fellow they had down at the police station.

> Q. Right, that's the only reason you know as far as his identification, is that he was at the police station, is that correct?

> A. Yes, and that they picked him up in the car and he was one of the fellows that ran across the street.

> Q. As far as your identification goes you're sure that Mr. Hutton was in that police station?

> A. He was in the police station, yes.

Q.   But you are not sure that he was involved in a crime?

A.   I am very sure, yes.

Q.   How are you so sure?

A.   By the description.

Q.   In other words, you are basing your sureness on a white T-shirt?

A.   Yes.

Q.   How long did you see Mr. Hutton?

A.   Briefly.

Q.   So you saw Mr. Hutton out of the corner of your eye?

A.   I looked at him.

Q.   And he got as close as thirty feet?

A.   I would say.

Q.   And you saw him from five to ten seconds?

A.   Yes.

Q.   And that is what you are basing your identification on?

A.   That is the same man I saw across the street.

Should the court suppress Kuecken's identification testimony? In deciding an independent source issue, should the court consider the witness's claim that his in-court identification is not based on the illegal out-of-court confrontation? Should the court automatically prohibit the in-court identification when the witness admits relying exclusively on the out-of-court identification? Is it relevant to consider external factors that minimize mistake, such as the defendant's apprehension in the fleeing car?

B.   DUE PROCESS LIMITATIONS

(7) In the pre-dawn hours of February 1, a seventy two-year-old widow, who had cataracts and always wore glasses, awakened to the sounds of an intruder. Using a flashlight but without her glasses, she attempted to call her son on the telephone. At that point, the intruder entered her bedroom. Before being attacked and raped, the woman observed the intruder momentarily with her flashlight and determined that he was white. Afterwards, the woman remained in bed about ten minutes until the man apparently fell asleep. She then crept downstairs, dressed in a bathroom, slipped out the rear door, and walked to her son's house a quarter mile away.

In response to subsequent police questioning, the woman estimated that the rape had occurred at 4:30 a.m. Her son reported that she had arrived at his house around 7:00 a.m. At 7:30 A.M., police officers discovered the defendant in the woman's bed and arrested him. After routine booking procedures, two uniformed officers then escorted the defendant in handcuffs to a doctor's office where the woman, who was being treated, identified him.

At his suppression hearing, the defendant testified, denied guilt, and said that he had been drinking with friends until 2:30 a.m. He further claimed to have picked up an older hitchhiker as he was driving home in his truck. According to the defendant, the hitchhiker left the truck when the defendant pulled off the road to sleep. The hitchhiker returned a while later, awakened the defendant, and took him to a house with an empty bed. The defendant claimed that he followed the hitchhiker into the house through the front door.

Police investigation disclosed that the assailant had broken into the woman's house through a second-story window. The woman remembered locking the doors before going to sleep, but she did not check the front door before escaping to her son's house. The police found the defendant's truck in plain view outside the house. A police chemist detected semen stains on the woman's linens, but not on the defendant's shorts, which he was wearing when awakened by the police, nor on his handkerchief.

According to the doctor who treated her, the woman described her assailant as resembling a certain fifty-year-old man in the community. The defendant was twenty-six. The woman described the assailant to her son as slender and long-faced, but "other than that, she really didn't have too much of a description." The police, who never investigated the hitchhiker story, explained that one-person showups were standard procedure because their community of 1,000 citizens could not provide a pool of non-suspect lineup participants.

Should the court suppress the woman's out-of-court and in-court identification of the defendant?

(8) Two weeks after a bank robbery, which lasted only a matter of minutes, bank tellers informed Louis Kotzen, the only customer in the bank during the robbery, that police had arrested two suspects. Some two weeks later, an FBI agent showed Kotzen a six picture photo display that included the defendant's picture. When Kotzen identified someone other than the defendant, the agent told him his selection was wrong. Kotzen then selected the defendant's picture.

At a subsequent suppression hearing, Kotzen identified the defendant and indicated that he based his identification upon his observations during the robbery and not upon the photo display. Kotzen testified that he had observed the robbers from a distance of twenty-five feet and that the defendant had worn a straw hat and sunglasses. On cross-examination, Kotzen said that he really could not be sure that the robber had worn sunglasses. Kotzen also testified that he selected the two pictures from the photo display because the men in those pictures had prominent noses that resembled the shorter robber's nose. On cross-examination, Kotzen admitted that he had not mentioned the prominence of the robber's nose in a description previously given the FBI, even though the description sheet contained a space expressly designated for noting unusual features.

What result on the motion to suppress?

(9) Following a robbery, a department store cashier described the robbers as neatly dressed, rather good-looking, and identical enough to be brothers. She could not, however, remember any details concerning their facial or physical characteristics. Several days later the cashier identified the defendant at a twelve-man lineup, which the police photographed.

Sometime later, researchers showed the photograph of the lineup to twenty female subjects and asked them to rate each lineup participant on an eleven-point scale: (1) extremely good-looking, (3) very good-looking, (5) somewhat good-looking, (7) about average, (9) not good-looking, (11) definitely not good-looking. The defendant averaged 5.95 on the scale, while the eleven other lineup participants averaged between 7.20 and 9.40. The researchers then compared each subject's rating of the defendant with her rating of each other lineup participant. In the 220 comparisons, the defendant rated more attractive than the other participant 179 times, the two rated equally attractive 23 times, and the defendant rated less attractive 18 times. In a second test, the researchers showed the same photograph to twenty-one different female subjects and instructed each to imagine herself a witness to a crime who only remembered the criminal as rather good-looking. They also instructed the subjects to imagine themselves at a lineup where the police believed they had captured the guilty person. The researchers then asked each subject to identify the guilty man. Eleven women chose the defendant; four others rated him their second choice.

Using these results, would you conclude that the lineup was unnecessarily suggestive? (A non-witness to the crime at a perfectly unbiased lineup would have a $1/n$ probability of identifying the defendant, where n constitutes the number of people in the lineup. By chance, therefore, fewer than two of the twenty-one non-witnesses should have chosen the defendant at an unbiased lineup.) Do witnesses experience psychological pressure to identify someone at a lineup? Do witnesses experience pressure to identify someone who matches descriptions they have given to the police? How can the law assure fairness when remembered characteristics are not physically measurable, as are height, weight, race, and hair color?

(10) A man with shoulder-length hair, a full beard, a bright shirt, and a headband entered a bank in Pasadena. Renfro, a teller, observed the man writing at a table for three or four minutes. When the man began walking toward Kelly's window, Renfro, who was not busy, asked whether she could assist him. The man mumbled something and joined the short line at Kelly's window. Upon reaching the window, the man handed Kelly a note that read, "Hand me your money. I am not kidding. I have a bottle of nitroglycerine." Kelly handed the man $300.

Prior to trial, defense counsel requested that the court either conduct an in-court lineup or permit the defendant, who was beardless and in short hair, to sit with the spectators. The court refused both requests. Kelly testified that she was "ninety percent but not one hundred per cent sure" that the defendant was the robber. Renfro related that the defendant's appearance, with a few differences, seemed "very close" to the bank robber's. The government produced no other testimony connecting the defendant with the crime.

After conviction, the defendant appeals. What result?

C.   SPECIAL JURY INSTRUCTIONS AND EXPERT TESTIMONY

(11) After being robbed, a white victim could tell the police only that his black assailant concealed a gun under a trench coat that he carried. Six months later the victim identified the defendant in a police station lineup. At trial, defense counsel asked the court for the following jury instruction:

> In this case the identifying witness is of a different race than the defendant. In the experience of many, it is more difficult to identify members of a different race than members of one's own. If this is also your experience, you may consider it in evaluating the witness's testimony. You must also consider, of course, whether there are other factors present in this case that overcome any such difficulty of identification. For example, you may consider whether the witness has had sufficient contacts with members of the defendant's race that he would not have greater difficulty in making a reliable identification.

Should the trial judge give the instruction? Is such a instruction prejudicial and divisive? Should the prosecutor be permitted to argue that an identification is more reliable when the victim and the defendant belong to the same race?

(12) On February 17, at about 10:45 p.m., a man entered a Mac's Milk Store, threatened and struck an employee, Robert Paxton, and fled with $372. Paxton could only describe the offender as "wearing a hat" and "having a small beard, like a goatee." Another witness, Shirley Brennan, stated that the robber had a reddish goatee, black suede shoes, and a tattoo that looked like "love" across his knuckles.

On February 18, Brennan viewed fifty police photographs but failed to identify anyone. On February 20, she viewed an additional sixteen photographs, from which she tentatively identified the defendant. The defendant was beardless in the photograph. The police then arrested the defendant, and Brennan identified him at a ten-man lineup, again with some reservation. The next day she stated unequivocally that the defendant had committed the robbery.

At trial, Brennan provided the only positive identification of the defendant. She described his black suede shoes as similar to those worn by the robber. A policeman next related that the defendant shaved his goatee after the robbery and before his arrest. The prosecutor pointed to the defendant's hands: one tattooed "luck," the other "help." Finally, the prosecutor introduced two incriminating statements that the defendant gave to the police.

The defendant denied making the statements and presented four witnesses to corroborate his alibi defense. The judge instructed the jury to exercise caution before convicting solely on eyewitness identification, but she also specifically referred to evidence that the jury could deem corroborative. The judge refused defense counsel's request for a special instruction concerning the unreliability of human observation and recollection. She also refused to caution the jury that the photographic identification may have influenced Brennan's in-court identification.

What result on appeal and why?

(13) Your state is considering whether to require the following jury instruction when eyewitness identification evidence is a critical part of the prosecution's case:

> In weighing the reliability of eyewitness identification testimony, you should first consider the extent to which any of the following factors, if present, would affect the accuracy of the identification: (1) the opportunity the witness had to observe the defendant at the time of the crime (time, lighting, obstructions, etc.); (2) the emotional state of the witness at the time of the crime; (3) whether the witness had observed the defendant on earlier occasions; (4) the time that elapsed between the crime and any later identification; (5) whether the witness ever failed to identify the defendant or made any inconsistent identification; (6) the degree of certainty demonstrated by the witness; and (7) any other circumstances that may have affected the accuracy of the identification.

Would requiring this instruction be a good idea? Would you add or subtract anything? Should the defendant be able to control whether or not the instruction is given?

(14) The government's proof at the defendant's robbery trial consisted primarily of testimony from two eyewitnesses who identified the defendant. After the government rested, the defendant offered a psychologist, with special training in memory and eyewitness identification, as an expert on the unreliability of identification evidence. In a written offer of proof, defense counsel indicated that the expert would not comment on the testimony of the two eyewitnesses but instead "would confine her recitation to such scientific facts as limited perception given limited opportunity to observe, rate of memory decay, and the source of memory given limited opportunity to observe followed by review of mug shots." After receiving the offer of proof, the trial judge sustained the prosecutor's objection to such testimony and precluded the psychologist from testifying.

What result on appeal?

Chapter 4

EAVESDROPPING AND ELECTRONIC SURVEILLANCE

A. SURVEILLANCE COVERED BY FEDERAL LAW

Congress regulated both private and governmental interception of oral and wire communications in Title III of the Omnibus Crime Control and Safe Streets Act of 1968. In 1986, Congress enacted the Electronic Communications Privacy Act, Title I of which incorporated, with some modification, most of Title III and subjected additional forms of surveillance to regulation.[a] In addition, Congress in 1978 enacted the Foreign Intelligence Surveillance Act (FISA).[b]

The problems in this section concern questions about the kinds of surveillance that are covered by Title I (formerly Title III). While the problems do not deal with FISA, that statute has sometimes influenced courts in interpreting the provisions of Title I. See, for example, problem #4. Nevertheless, to analyze these problems (and those in the next section), students need only have access to Title I. The problems are designed to illustrate some of the statutory regulations and to hone skills in statutory interpretation.

(1) The FBI arrested Charles Harrelson and charged him with murdering a federal judge. While Harrelson was in jail awaiting trial, his wife, Jo Ann, visited him several times. During these visits, John Spinelli, a career criminal in an adjoining cell, secretly recorded their incriminating conversations with a tape recorder disguised as a radio that the FBI, without judicial approval, had given to him for this purpose. Before each of his wife's visits, Charles, who on a previous occasion had secretly recorded the conversations of a fellow inmate for the government, examined his cell for possible recording devices.

What result when the Harrelsons move to suppress the tapes? Did the tape recording implicate the Fourth Amendment? Was it covered by federal statutory law pertaining to electronic surveillance? What result under the Fourth Amendment and federal statutory law if Spinelli recorded Harrelson's conversations with his attorney?

a. The 1986 statute still can be found at 18 U.S.C. §§ 2510–21.   **b.** 50 U.S.C. §§ 1801–11.

(2) Armed with a valid warrant to arrest Samuel Passarella for narcotics offenses, federal agents lawfully entered his house and learned from other occupants that he was expected to return shortly. While waiting for Passarella to return, special agent Moultan answered the phone several times. In two of the calls, the caller assumed that Moultan was Passarella, although Moultan did not so identify himself. In one of the calls, Moultan identified himself as Passarella. Each of the three callers provided incriminating evidence against Passarella.

What result on Passarella's motion to suppress evidence of the calls? Did Moultan's actions implicate the Fourth Amendment or federal statutory law? Would your analysis be different if, instead of having had an arrest warrant, the agents had possessed a warrant to search Passarella's home for drug paraphernalia?

(3) When Richard arrived in Kennedy Airport from Panama, Customs officials lawfully searched his luggage and discovered 155 pounds of heroin. Richard, who had reserved a three-room suite at the Hotel McAlpin, agreed to cooperate with the agents by permitting them to "bug" his telephone and monitor it from an adjoining hotel room. The next day, Gonzalez arrived in New York and took a cab to the McAlpin. Gonzalez immediately went to Richard's suite and telephoned San Martin at another hotel to discuss delivery of the heroin. The agents in the adjoining hotel room monitored the call using their electronic equipment.

What result when Gonzalez and San Martin move to suppress the contents of their phone conversation? Was the use of the bug a Fourth Amendment search? Was it covered by federal statutory law? What result if Richard had permitted the agents to listen by using an extension phone from another room in the suite?

(4) Suspecting that defendants were laundering drug money, federal law enforcement officials obtained a court order to install hidden microphones and silent closed circuit television cameras in their business premises. The surveillance produced silent video tapes of the defendants receiving, counting, and packaging large amounts of cash, which they later deposited in local banks. The government maintained that this money was eventually funneled to companies owned by Colombian drug dealers.

Charged with various drug and money laundering offenses, the defendants have moved to suppress the video tapes. What result? You may assume that the application to install the microphones complied with 18 U.S.C. §§ 2510–21, that the application to install the video cameras did not, and that both applications satisfied Fourth Amendment requirements. (Is the Fourth Amendment satisfied as long as its probable cause and particularity requirements are satisfied?) Does the federal statute prohibit video surveillance, leave it unregulated, or do something in between?

B. STATUTORY LIMITATIONS

The following problems illustrate only a few of the restrictions that Congress has imposed on electronic surveillance.

(5) Under state law, state courts may issue electronic eavesdropping orders for investigations relating to several crimes, including the crime of sexual abuse. Sexual abuse is defined as including voluntary sexual activity with a person under fifteen.

Acting on probable cause that the defendant was engaging in sexual activity in his home with teenage prostitutes, a state prosecutor, conforming to all the requirements of the state wiretap statute, obtained a judicial order from a state judge to tap the defendant's phone. Pursuant to the tap, police learned that the defendant planned to bring two young teenagers to his house for sexual activity. The police then obtained a search warrant for the defendant's home and, executing it at the appropriate time, found the defendant and two thirteen-year-old boys nude in bed.

What result when the defendant claims that the evidence should be suppressed because the wiretap order violated § 2516 of the federal wiretap statute? Assuming that such a violation occurred, did Congress have the authority to impose such a restriction on the states? If the federal statute was violated, is suppression a mandatory remedy?

(6) Suspecting defendant Petti of engaging in money laundering and currency reporting violations, federal agents in San Diego, with the approval of an Assistant Attorney General, obtained a judicial order permitting them to intercept Petti's telephone conversations. In their application for the judicial order, the agents alleged that they had obtained telephone toll records of calls that Petti had made, but that these records did not provide the information necessary to prosecute Petti. The agents alleged further that they had tried to wire an informant, but that Petti was cautious not to incriminate himself in front of others. Because of the informant's criminal record, the agents also alleged that he would not make a credible witness at trial without corroborating evidence.

The wiretap application further alleged that Petti had used, was using, and in all likelihood would continue to use "various and changing pay telephones" in connection with his offenses, and the judge found probable cause to this effect. Accordingly, as requested with the Assistant Attorney General's explicit approval, the judge authorized a wiretap of Petti's conversations over various and changing pay telephones in San Diego County.

What result when Petti moves to suppress incriminating conversations intercepted by this "roving" wiretap? If statutory violations occurred, is suppression a required remedy? Do the facts present any Fourth Amendment issues?

(7) With probable cause to believe that defendant King was involved in a scheme to smuggle marijuana into the United States on a vessel, the *Mercy Wiggins*, Justice Department officials obtained a court order authorizing a tap on King's phone. The Department indicated that it wanted to know where in Mexico the vessel would be loaded, where and when it would arrive in the United States, and the identities of King's confederates.

Following the original twenty-day order, the government obtained extensions of fifteen, seven, and seven days respectively. In progress reports supporting each extension order, the government reported that it had not obtained all of its desired information and that only 75% of its interceptions had been helpful. In obtaining the extensions, the government relied solely on the progress reports and on the affidavit attached to its original application.

Defendant King subsequently moved to suppress evidence gathered by the wiretaps. During a hearing, a government supervisor admitted instructing his agents to monitor all conversations except those between an attorney and client. The agents, who obeyed, produced 1,156 pages of transcribed conversation. Defending this conduct, the government attorney cited fifty pages of transcribed conversation between King and an unidentified girl. Two pages in the middle of the otherwise innocuous transcript contained highly relevant information. The attorney also argued that re-examination had disclosed that 85%, rather than 75%, of the government's interceptions had evidentiary value.

What result? Do you have enough information to decide the problem? If the government violated one or more provisions of the federal wiretap statute, is suppression a mandatory remedy?

(8) On February 17, in connection with their investigation of a major international narcotics conspiracy, federal agents obtained a court order authorizing them to tap defendant Shmuel David's telephone. Anticipating that many conversations over David's phone would be in Hebrew, the agents indicated in their affidavit that they were in the process of locating interpreters. Through law enforcement agencies in Israel, the government then arranged to borrow Israeli police officers for this purpose. The Israeli officers arrived in the United States on March 1, and after briefing from the federal agents, began to work as monitors on March 5.

Between February 17 and March 5, federal agents taped in full all conversations in Hebrew over David's phone. The federal agents then gave these tapes to the Israeli officers with instructions to stop listening to a conversation once they determined that the conversation was beyond the scope of the investigation.

Charged with several narcotics offenses, David has filed a motion to suppress the evidence uncovered in the Hebrew phone conversations that occurred between February 17 and March 5. What result?

(9) During their investigation of a residential robbery and triple murder, Nevada police developed probable cause that Delores Homick's husband, Steve Homick, was one of the perpetrators. In compliance with the state's wiretap statute, the police then obtained a court order authorizing a wiretap on three phones at the Homick residence. The affidavit in support of the order identified Steve as a likely perpetrator of the crimes; because Delores was not a suspect, the affidavit made no mention of her.

While the tap was in place, police arrested James Scott in an unrelated incident and, in a search of his person, uncovered a ring that had been taken in the robbery-murder. Although Scott insisted that he had owned the ring for more than ten years, a police officer informed him that the police would not return the ring to him unless he provided proof of ownership.

Later that day, police at the Homick residence in Nevada intercepted a phone call from Steve Homick, in California, to Delores Homick. In their conversation, Delores and Steve discussed things that they could do to get the ring back from the police. Finally, Delores agreed to prepare an affidavit saying that Scott owned the ring.

After getting an extension of the original court order, the police intercepted another call between Delores and Steve and a call between Delores and James Scott, both calls relating to the ring. The police also intercepted calls not involving Delores or Scott, but in which one or both were mentioned in connection with the ring. The affidavit for the extension order named Delores as another person whose conversations were likely to be intercepted.

Now charged with wire fraud in federal court, Delores Homick has moved to suppress the conversations that were overheard in the wiretap and that the government wants to introduce against her. Because she was not a target in the murder investigation when either the original order or the extension was obtained, she claims that the police should not have been listening to her conversations. She also claims that the police violated the federal statute by not notifying the court in applying for the extension that they had extended their investigation from murder and robbery to other crimes, such as wire fraud. What result? Assuming that the phone conversations that did not involve Delores or Steve would be admissible against Delores under the co-conspirator exception to the hearsay rule, will Delores have standing to challenge this evidence under the wiretap statute?

(10) On December 31, in connection with a gambling investigation, federal law enforcement officials obtained a judicial order authorizing them to tap the defendant's telephone. During the month that the order was in effect, federal agents intercepted and recorded over 1400 telephone conversations.

The agents used the original tapes to make copies that were known as "working tapes." The agents then transcribed the conversations from the copies. While they were working on the transcriptions, two of the working tapes broke. Fearing that others might break, the agents kept the originals until they could check the condition of all the copies. On March 1, as soon as their inspection of all the copies was done, the agents turned the originals over to the authorizing judge, who promptly sealed them.

Defendant now seeks to suppress the conversations because of the delay in sealing the tapes. What result?

(11) Investigating narcotics offenses, North Carolina police sought and obtained a judicial order authorizing them to install a "pen register type system known as a 'Group Call'" on the defendant's pager, a digital display model that displays the telephone number of someone trying to telephone the person with the pager. In their application, the police requested permission to use a "clone pager," a device that was capable of displaying the same numbers transmitted to the defendant's pager.

Because the clone pager had no capacity to record or otherwise to store the numbers received, police officers wrote the incoming numbers on a pad. Later, with probable cause based in part on information obtained by the clone pager, the police conducted a search that yielded evidence of narcotics offenses.

The defendant has now moved to suppress this evidence because information obtained over the clone pager was not sealed as allegedly required by 18 U.S.C. § 2518(8)(a). What result? If a statutory violation occurred, is suppression a mandatory remedy?

Chapter 5

ENTRAPMENT

Under the United States Supreme Court's approach, which is followed by a majority of states, the study of entrapment may seem more appropriate in substantive Criminal Law than in Criminal Procedure. Nevertheless, because an otherwise innocent defendant usually does not have a criminal law defense if a private person rather than a police officer induces him to commit a crime, concern about the appropriateness of police conduct—a criminal procedure concern—is apparent under even the majority approach. Indeed, private instigation of crime must rise to the level of "duress" to excuse a defendant's behavior. Why should a defendant have a defense when a police officer rather than a private person induces him to commit a crime that he was not predisposed to commit?

Where did the Supreme Court get the authority to create the entrapment defense for federal prosecutions? Where would it get the authority to adopt the minority approach to entrapment? Are there separation of powers problems in both approaches? Does the Constitution mandate that a jurisdiction have some kind of entrapment defense? These basic questions should be considered before and during the analysis of the following problems.

(1) A four-count indictment charged the defendant with sale and possession of narcotics. According to the government, the defendant sold heroin to Henry Sutton, one of its informants, on two occasions. At trial, the government did not call Sutton, even though he was available, but instead relied on the testimony of federal agents who from a distance had observed Sutton meeting with the defendant.

When the government rested, the defendant testified in her own behalf. After describing her close friendship with Sutton and his wife, she explained her involvement in the two narcotics transactions:

A.   Henry Sutton, he called and told me he wanted some stuff, he and his wife was sick, and would I get it for him. I said I didn't know where to get it and I didn't have any money, and he said he would tell me where to get it and bring the money. I told him I would try. He gave me the money and him and me walked down to the coffee shop.

Q.   What did you do with that money?

A.   I gave it to the people I went to get the stuff from.

Q. Did you use any of the narcotics that you say you purchased on those two dates yourself?

A. No sir, I didn't.

Q. Did you make any profit on your alleged purchases?

A. No, sir.

Q. What did you do on each instance after you received those two packages?

A. I carried and gived it to Sutton.

Q. Did you buy any of this contraband on these two occasions for yourself?

A. No sir.

Q. Do you use narcotics now?

A. No sir, I don't.

Q. Tell the Court what you understand the term 'sick' to mean.

A. Well, because I had a habit before I went to the penitentiary and I know what it is, I knew Thelma to be sick and I have seen her sick, and I knew when a person is sick from drugs. He asked me to go and he couldn't go, and that is the reason I got it for him.

Although the government did not rebut this testimony, the trial court convicted the defendant after rejecting both her entrapment and "procuring agent" defenses. What result under the majority and minority approaches on appeal?

(2) It is illegal in Oregon for caterers and restaurants to sell or purchase "sport caught" fish—defined as fish that have not been caught commercially. After hearing that this law was being violated, the state police randomly called 73 caterers and restaurants in Portland and, using assumed names, offered to sell fresh chinook salmon to them at a price well below that of commercially available salmon. The police left a message to this effect on the answering machine at DeAngelo's restaurant. Before making these calls, the police had no information that any of the people they contacted had made illegal purchases of fish.

When DeAngelo returned the call on his machine, he and an undercover officer negotiated a sale. During the conversation, the officer asked for and received assurance that the police would not be present when the salmon were delivered. DeAngelo indicated that the salmon should be carried into his restaurant in a black bag. Before his arrest, DeAngelo made four separate purchases of salmon from the officer.

What result under the majority and minority views of entrapment? What is (are) the minority test(s) of entrapment? What result if DeAngelo supplements his entrapment defense with a due process argument? Are there any legitimate sources for a judicial value judgment that certain conduct is so offensive as to violate due process? Do such judgments present separation of powers problems?

(3) Traveling in their unmarked car, Detectives Hall and Vidalis, who had previously succeeded in developing drug cases against hitchhikers, picked up Bowser, who was hitchhiking. Referring to the cloth bag that Bowser was carrying, Hall said, "Oh, I know what that's for." Bowser denied that liquor or a "stash" was in the bag.

Bowser, whose arm was in a cast, said his doctor had just set his arm and that his arm hurt. He also said that his doctor had given him a prescription for Tylenol III, a codeine pain medication. When Bowser said that he did not have money to pay for the prescription, Hall indicated that he had money. Hall later testified that Bowser also said he would be willing to "party" with Hall and Vidalis if they bought the Tylenol.

After stopping at a Walgreen's store, Hall gave Bowser the $4.09 that it cost to fill the prescription. When Bowser said that Tylenol went well with beer, Hall purchased a six-pack. Back in the car, Bowser asked, "What would be fair?" Hall then gave Bowser three dollars and asked for six of the pills. When Bowser complied, Hall and Vidalis arrested Bowser for sale and delivery of a controlled substance.

What result when Bowser raises entrapment as a defense? What if he makes a due process argument as well? Should the judge or the jury decide these issues? Do these facts establish entrapment as a matter of law even under the majority approach? Consider also the questions at the end of problem 2. In analyzing this problem, assume that Bowser was in his early twenties, that he had not completed high school, that the detectives did not know Bowser when they picked him up, that Bowser did not have a criminal record, and that Bowser's prescription was valid.

(4) DeWitt Duncan, a police informant, asked defendant Irma Perry whether she knew anyone selling drugs and, if so, whether she could get some for a friend of his. At the time, Duncan had known Perry for ten years and had once been engaged to her. Although they both had married other people, they both were now in the process of getting divorces and had been seeing each other again, often at hotels and motels. Duncan had even proposed that they marry after their respective divorces.

When Perry indicated a willingness to get narcotics for Duncan's friend, Duncan brought undercover officer Gilchrist, whom he introduced as "Georgeann," to Perry's home. The trio then drove to an apartment building at Perry's direction. After Gilchrist gave Perry $170, Perry entered the apartment and returned with heroin. Although Perry did not request anything over the purchase price, Gilchrist gave her an extra $20, and Perry accepted it. Duncan had told Gilchrist that Perry would expect the extra money.

What result under the majority and minority views of entrapment? Is it relevant whether Duncan established the relationship with Perry solely to determine whether she was selling drugs? What result if Perry raises a due process defense? Consider also the questions at the end of problem 2.

(5) The sheriff of Levy County, Florida, with the prosecutor's knowledge, entered into an agreement with informant Norwood Wilson. Wilson agreed to sell several hundred pounds of cannabis that the county had seized in prior cases, and the sheriff agreed to let Wilson keep 10% of all forfeitures arising from successful criminal prosecutions relating to his sales. To collect the 10%, Wilson also agreed to testify in the criminal prosecutions.

Pursuant to the agreement, Wilson sold over 100 pounds of cannabis to the defendants. Shortly thereafter, the sheriff's deputies arrested the defendants and seized several vehicles and more than $80,000 in cash, all subject to forfeiture.

What result on the defendants' motions to dismiss the criminal charges and to have their cars and money returned? Do the defendants have any plausible entrapment defense? Any plausible due process defense?

(6) A seven-count indictment charged the defendant with selling and possessing stimulant drugs. After the defendant introduced evidence of entrapment at trial, the government, over objection, introduced rebuttal evidence to prove predisposition. Sergeant Wolfe testified that Lieutenant Burke had suggested to him that the defendant was dealing in hard drugs. Lieutenant Burke testified that two years before he relayed the information to Sergeant Wolfe, an informant had described purchasing morphine from the defendant with stolen goods. Burke never investigated this tip.

On appeal, what result? Should the state be permitted to prove that the officers reasonably believed that the defendant was predisposed to commit the crime? Is such a belief, if relevant, sufficient to rebut a claim of entrapment? What result if the defendant had been convicted of selling morphine to the informant?

Chapter 6

THE INVESTIGATIVE GRAND JURY

The investigative grand jury, our foremost example of an inquisitorial institution, is a powerful law enforcement weapon, particularly in complex cases such as
those involving organized crime, narcotics conspiracies, business fraud, and public
corruption. The investigative role of the grand jury is quite different from the
screening role played by the grand jury in those jurisdictions that require an
indictment before a case can be brought to trial. For example, when performing its
screening function, the grand jury typically relies on one or a few witnesses who
may not have personal knowledge of the facts, and it rarely hears from the
defendant. The investigative grand jury, on the other hand, usually will subpoena
many witnesses, including targets of its investigation. The conduct of a screening
grand jury is typically challenged, if challenged at all, by a defendant seeking to
quash an indictment. See the problems in Chapter 11. The conduct of an
investigative grand jury is usually challenged by a witness, who may or may not
ultimately be indicted, either by a motion to quash or limit the subpoena or by
raising a legal defense when the prosecutor seeks a judicial order to compel
compliance. Because even an investigative grand jury must eventually decide
whether probable cause exists to indict anyone for a crime, the distinction between
the investigating and screening functions of the grand jury perhaps should be
viewed more as a heuristic device than as a rigid demarcation of separate and
independent grand jury roles.

Because the function of the investigative grand jury is similar in many ways to
that of the police, the problems dealing with this topic have been included in the
part of this book dealing with police practices. Students should be alert for
differences in the scope of power possessed by these two investigative institutions
and for reasons that may explain these differences. If you come to believe that
such differences should not exist, would you limit the power of the grand jury or
enlarge the power of the police? (Should we openly recognize and accept, for
example, that police interrogation also is an inquisitorial practice?)

The problems in Section A survey some of the constitutional and nonconstitutional objections that may be raised by a grand jury witness who is served with a
subpoena duces tecum. Although most of these objections may sometimes also
be applicable when a witness is served with a subpoena ad testificandum, the
problems in Section B do not repeat issues and doctrines considered in Section A.
That is, the problems in Section A should provide adequate coverage for the
student to become familiar with most of the defenses a grand jury witness may
raise.

Although practically all the problems involve federal grand juries, students should be alert for state law limitations, such as shield statutes, that might apply if the grand jury were empaneled under the law of their state.

A. THE SUBPOENA DUCES TECUM: POSSIBLE LIMITATIONS

(1) A newspaper article about union corruption prompted the federal government to begin an investigation of Robert "Buddy" Battle, the director of UAW Region I–A. To determine whether Battle was stealing, embezzling, or otherwise converting union assets to his own use, in violation of 29 U.S.C. § 501(c), a grand jury issued a subpoena directing Battle to produce the following material:

> All books, papers, records, memoranda, and data of the "Buddy Battle Convention Fund" and the "Flower Fund" for [a four-year period]. Also, all books, papers, records, memoranda, and data of all subsidiary funds of the UAW Region I–A for [the same period]. Such records shall include, but not be limited to, bank statements, pass books, cancelled checks, voided checks, check stubs, receipts, the disbursement ledger, and minutes of meetings.

Battle moved to quash the subpoena. He argued that the "Convention Fund" was not a union asset within the terms of 29 U.S.C. § 501(c), and, accordingly, that records pertaining to the fund could not be relevant to any possible statutory violations. He also denied ever having heard of the "Flower Fund." Finally, Battle asserted that he failed to see how the records of the UAW subsidiary funds could possibly be relevant to the grand jury's investigation. The court indicated that it was inclined to grant the motion unless the government made a preliminary showing that the bank accounts were union assets under the statute and that the subpoenaed material might be relevant to the investigation. When the government refused to comply with these requests, the court quashed the subpoena.

What result on the government's appeal? What result if the court did not know what possible crimes the grand jury was investigating? What result if Battle alleged that the subpoena was unduly burdensome?

(2) A federal grand jury issued two subpoenas to the Western Union Telegraph Company. The first requested the company's Monthly Summary of Activity Report of wire transactions at its Royalle Inn agency in Kansas City, Missouri, for the preceding thirteen months. The second requested all Telegraphic Money Order Applications for $1,000.00 or more submitted to the same agency over the preceding 24 months. The Royalle Inn is Western Union's primary wire service agent in the Kansas City area.

Alleging violations of its own rights and the rights of its customers, Western Union moved to quash the two subpoenas on Fourth Amendment grounds. In response, the government submitted an affidavit indicating that confidential sources had told government agents that drug dealers in Kansas City frequently use Western Union to transmit drug money to various locations, such as Florida and California, and that recipients of the money often use their real names. The affidavit also alleged that a search of an inner city "dope house" operated by Jamaican nationals had uncovered copies of Money Transfer Applications that had been used to transfer money from the Royalle Inn to Miami and Jamaica.

What result? Does the court have any basis other than the Fourth Amendment to demand more particularity in the subpoenas?

(3) FBI agent Gully appeared at the premises of Nwamu, Inc., and served on David Singler, an officer of the corporation, a subpoena directing the person served to appear "forthwith" before the grand jury with certain corporate documents and two IBM Selectric typewriter balls. When Singler inquired what would happen if he failed to comply, Gully told him he would be in contempt of court if he did not comply immediately. Gully then told Singler that he could go directly to the grand jury or hand the documents and typewriter balls over to Gully rather than appear before the grand jury. Singler immediately surrendered the items, and Gully brought them to FBI headquarters.

What result when the corporation moves for the return of these items? Are "forthwith" subpoenas ever lawful? When? Even if a forthwith subpoena was lawful on these facts, did Gully's actions taint the use of the subpoena?

(4) During its investigation of the local narcotics industry, a federal grand jury in Oklahoma became suspicious that James Coltharp was employing a "crew" to assist him in drug activities. While the investigation was proceeding, four men suspected of being crew members, all represented by retained counsel, were convicted of narcotics offenses. Suspecting that Coltharp may have paid the four lawyers, the grand jury then subpoenaed the lawyers to disclose the amount of their fees and the person or persons who had paid them. The subpoenas also requested all documents relating to the payment or acceptance of the fees, including checks, cashier's checks, deposit slips, receipts, wire transfers, and fee contracts.

After a hearing, the judge denied the lawyers' joint motion to quash the subpoenas. When the lawyers then refused to comply with the subpoena, the judge found them in civil contempt and ordered that they be jailed. What result on the lawyers' appeal? Would it matter whether any of the lawyers were still representing their clients on appeal?

(5) A federal grand jury in New York was empaneled to investigate the activities of the Colombo organized crime family. In particular, the grand jury was looking into a number of crimes, including murder, racketeering, narcotics trafficking, robbery, gambling, and extortion, that Anthony Colombo and his organization were suspected of having committed. During the course of the investigation, the grand jury subpoenaed Barry Slotnick, Colombo's lawyer for the past 18 years, to produce all fee records pertaining to twenty-one named individuals, including Anthony Colombo, in connection with nine enumerated past criminal proceedings.

Slotnick immediately moved to quash the subpoena under Federal Rule of Criminal Procedure 17(c), and Colombo was permitted to intervene. In response, the government indicated that the grand jury was seeking to determine whether Colombo had paid, or otherwise arranged legal representation, for suspected crime family members. The government maintained that this could help establish Colombo as the head of an "enterprise" under the Racketeer Influenced and Corrupt Organizations Act (RICO), 18 U.S.C. § 1961(4). The government conceded that Slotnick's compliance with the subpoena might create a conflict of interests that would preclude him from representing Colombo if the latter were to be indicted.

When the court denied the motion to quash, Colombo filed this appeal. While the appeal was pending, the grand jury indicted Colombo and several other individuals for several offenses, but not for any RICO violations. What result? Should the government be required to show both a need for the information and that the attorney is the only source of it? Does the issuance of the indictment change the answer as to the validity of the subpoena? If the indictment included a RICO offense, would this preclude the court from enforcing the subpoena? For what reason(s)?

(6) A federal grand jury indicted Donald Payden for narcotics offenses and for engaging in a continuing criminal enterprise in violation of 18 U.S.C. § 848. In connection with the latter charge, the indictment sought the forfeiture of all profits and proceeds obtained from the enterprise.

A week later, the government obtained a subpoena from the district court requesting that Payden's attorney, Robert Simels, produce all non-privileged documents relating to payment of fees by Payden. The government attorney argued that the subpoena was needed for "evidentiary purposes," namely to show that Payden had substantial resources the source of which could not be explained by any of his legitimate activities. The subpoena provoked angry protests from Simels, the criminal defense bar, and the local bar association. Three months later, after the grand jury subpoenaed the same material from Simels, the government requested the trial court to withdraw its subpoena.

Simels and Payden have now moved to quash the grand jury subpoena on Sixth Amendment grounds and on the ground that the subpoena's dominant purpose was to gather evidence for an existing indictment. In response, the government maintained that the subpoena offered the possibility that additional charges and defendants would be discovered. Putting aside the Sixth Amendment issue (see problem 5), what result and why?

(7) A federal grand jury investigating local corruption in Birmingham, Alabama, subpoenaed the mayor and directed him to produce his calendar of events and his schedule or agenda for a six-year period. In response, the mayor filed a motion to quash the subpoena, contending that these papers were his personal property and that compulsory production of them would violate his Fifth Amendment right not to be compelled to become a witness against himself.

More specifically, alleging that the investigation was racially and politically motivated, the mayor stated in an affidavit that he had a "deep and abiding concern that the documents will be used to create perjured testimony." Maintaining that the prosecutors had already gotten one witness, Brown, to concoct a story, the mayor added that "if they obtain my schedules, then they will obviously be in a position to meet with Brown and others whom they may coerce to fabricate another story, while using my personal papers to match the story with my schedule."

What result? What if the mayor claims that by producing the documents, he would be admitting their existence and possession and also proving their authenticity?

(8) Investigating possible violations of the federal securities laws, the Securities and Exchange Commission (SEC) focused on John Doe's trading of securities in his personal brokerage accounts. As part of its investigation, the SEC subpoenaed Doe and his personal appointment calendar—a breast-pocket book in which Doe recorded his appointments, social engagements, chores, phone numbers, and other reminders. After first asserting a Fifth Amendment objection, Doe and his lawyer agreed to cooperate. Doe then produced a photocopy of his calendar. (The SEC ultimately brought a civil suit against Doe for insider trading.)

While the SEC's investigation was pending, the United States Attorney's Office requested and obtained from the SEC access to the documents that Doe had produced. After examining the copy of the calendar, assistants in that office became suspicious that Doe had used white-out on the original before making a copy of it for the SEC. Thereafter, a federal grand jury, which had been investigating Doe for possible perjury and obstruction of justice, subpoenaed Doe to produce the original of the calendar.

What result when the government seeks a court order to compel Doe to comply with the grand jury subpoena? What if Doe claims that by producing the calendar, he would be admitting its existence and possession and also proving its authenticity? What result if Doe can establish that the SEC had promised him it would not disclose the calendar to anyone else? If Doe has a valid Fifth Amendment defense, what kind of immunity would the government have to give to compel him to produce the original calendar?

(9) The FBI obtained arrest warrants for two individuals in connection with an armed robbery and murder the previous day. The FBI's investigation disclosed that one of the suspects had been employed by attorney Bauer before the robbery and that both suspects had been in the attorney's office a few hours after the robbery. When questioned by the FBI as to whether he had received any money or firearms from the suspects, Bauer refused to answer. A week later, a federal marshal served Bauer with a grand jury subpoena requesting production of "any and all monies or weapons paid or delivered into your care, custody, or control by [the two named suspects]."

Bauer has filed a motion to quash the subpoena. What result? Can Bauer raise any defense in his own right?

(10) Pursuant to its investigation into alleged schemes to defraud medical insurance companies, a federal grand jury subpoenaed Dr. Gary Pierce, a psychiatrist whose practice is organized as a professional corporation. The subpoena directed Pierce, or an authorized custodian of records, to produce the following records for eighteen named individuals over a two-year period: patient files, progress notes, ledger cards, copies of insurance claim forms, and any other documentation supporting dates of service rendered, length of treatment on each date, and the identities of the patients receiving said service.

Relying on the Fifth Amendment and other arguments, Pierce has now moved to quash the subpoena. What result?

(11) A federal grand jury was summoned to investigate whether Antoni Gronowicz, the author of *God's Broker*, committed mail or wire fraud in violation of 18 U.S.C. §§ 1341, 1343. The investigation was prompted when the publisher withdrew the book from the market after concluding that it was not based on personal interviews with the Pope and other church officials, as Gronowicz and the book had claimed.

Pursuant to its investigation, the grand jury subpoenaed Gronowicz to produce "any and all notes, recordings, or other records containing verbatim, or in substance, the statements of the Pope or other church officials as contained in the book." The subpoena also sought Gronowicz's travel records, passports, and appointment calendar to determine whether he had made the trips to Europe that would have been necessary to conduct the interviews.

The court is now considering the government's motion to have Gronowicz held in contempt for his failure to comply with the subpoena. What result when Gronowicz asserts that the documents are protected by the First Amendment and/or by a federal common law privilege analogous to the journalist's privilege? Do these doctrines at least impose on the government the burden of demonstrating some special need for such a subpoena?

B.   THE SUBPOENA AD TESTIFICANDUM: POSSIBLE LIMITATIONS

(12) Jason Meadows refused to answer grand jury questions about one "Reynal Santana." At a subsequent show-cause hearing, Meadows filed a motion seeking disclosure of electronic surveillance. His motion contained a list of nine telephone numbers that "may have" been bugged. In a supporting affidavit, Meadows claimed that a DEA agent had told him during an interview that he knew what Meadows paid his lawyer and that "we do funny things with telephones." In response, the DEA agent admitted making only the latter statement. The agent said that he was trying to fool Meadows into thinking that the government knew more than it did.

More particularly, the agent denied that the DEA had bugged any phones. Accordingly, he denied that any grand jury questions were based on information learned through electronic surveillance. On cross-examination, the agent admitted that the DEA had received case information from other federal agencies. He claimed, however, that the case had been accepted by the Organized Crime and Drug Enforcement Task Force, which consists of members from all the federal agencies, and that as case agent, he would have been informed immediately if any agency had used electronic surveillance. Admitting that he had not checked the records of the other agencies, the agent expressed confidence that the interagency notification system would have revealed any electronic surveillance.

At this point, what do you rule as the judge?

(13) Several months after a grand jury began to investigate municipal corruption, particularly in the Housing Authority, the District Attorney called the defendants, both building contractors, to her office for questioning about housing fraud. After an interview, the District Attorney expressed dissatisfaction with the defendants' answers, suggested the likelihood of their imminent arrest, and informed them that they would be summoned before the grand jury.

One week later, the defendants were summoned with their lawyers before the judge supervising the grand jury. The judge advised the defendants of their right not to answer incriminating questions, and the judge further indicated that she would resolve disputes over whether a question had to be answered. The judge then denied the defendants' request to be accompanied by counsel either inside or outside the grand jury room. When the defendants appeared before the grand jury, they answered various questions asked by an Assistant District Attorney.

Five days later, the grand jury issued a presentment recommending indictments against the defendants for false pretenses and conspiracy in connection with their renovation of houses for the Housing Authority. The District Attorney then forwarded the presentment to another grand jury, which indicted the defendants.

What result when the defendants move to quash the indictments? What if the defendants seek to exclude their grand jury testimony at their trial?

C. GRAND JURY REPORTS

(14) A state statute authorizes the grand jury to "inquire into all indictable offenses" and to "present them to the court by indictment." During its regular term, a local grand jury investigated allegations of teacher brutality, lack of discipline, and a non-learning environment at a particular elementary school. As part of its investigation, the grand jury inquired into the principal's competence and ability.

Although the grand jury did not indict anyone, it submitted a written report to the Board of Directors and the Superintendent of the School District. The report recommended that the principal be removed. The report also indicated that there would be future investigations, if necessary, including an investigation of anyone who resisted the principal's ouster. Before the grand jury filed its report with the court, parts of it appeared in the local press. Subsequently, individual grand jurors publicly approved the School Board's request for the principal's resignation.

The principal has filed suit seeking damages and a judgment declaring the grand jury's investigation and report invalid. What result?

Chapter 7

THE SCOPE OF THE EXCLUSIONARY RULES

The doctrines pertaining to standing, fruit of the poisonous tree, and impeachment affect the application of the various exclusionary rules that the Supreme Court has recognized. These doctrines themselves may vary depending on the precise antecedent wrong at issue. For example, in the Fourth Amendment context, the Court has suggested that we should not even talk about "standing"; rather, we should focus on whether the defendant's own constitutional rights were implicated. (It is virtually impossible, however, not to conceive of the issue as one of standing.) More significantly, the application of these doctrines may vary depending on whether there has been a violation of what the Court views as an actual constitutional requirement or of a mere "prophylactic" rule. The problems that follow explore these issues. They also provide an opportunity to review material studied in previous chapters.

A. STANDING

(1) Police uncovered an illegally possessed gun in a warrantless search of a home that the defendant's mother owned and that the defendant's cousin, Robert Taylor, leased. The defendant had been staying with Taylor and his wife for about two weeks before the search occurred, but he did not pay rent because, in Taylor's words, he was "just visiting." During his two week-visit, the defendant, who was free to come and go, did not spend every night with the Taylors. He did not sleep at their home the night before the search, and he was not present during the search.

Although Taylor's daughter normally used the defendant's bedroom, she slept in another room with two other children during the defendant's visits. When the defendant was present, he was the sole occupant of the bedroom in question, but Taylor kept some clothing in the bedroom closet in which police found the gun. The defendant kept three or four suits in the bedroom closet, but the rest of his clothing and other possessions remained in his permanent home, where he continued to receive his mail.

Assuming that the search was illegal, what result on the defendant's motion to suppress the gun?

(2) Lorenzo Moreno arrived at his brother's house around 7:00 p.m. to baby-sit for his brother's young son while his brother went to the store. Moreno intended to return home when his brother returned from the store. Around 7:30 p.m., while the boy was asleep in the living room and Moreno was seated on the living room sofa, the police entered without a warrant and conducted a search for narcotics. The police found what they were seeking in one of the bedrooms.

The state has now charged that Moreno conspired with his brother to sell the narcotics found in the bedroom. What result when the state moves to dismiss Moreno's suppression motion? To prevail, must Moreno establish a reasonable expectation of privacy in the searched bedroom? Is it significant that Moreno was related to the person for whom he was sitting and the owner of the house?

(3) Following a report of an underage drinking party at a private home, two sheriff's deputies entered and searched the home without a warrant. They found the defendant and three other teenagers hiding behind a furnace in the basement. When questioned by the deputies, the defendant admitted to consuming alcohol, and she also tested positive for alcohol consumption. At her trial for consumption of alcoholic beverages by a minor, the defendant who was not a resident of the home moved to suppress all evidence gained by the warrantless entry and search. How should the trial court rule? Did the defendant try to conceal her presence in the home and thereby subjectively preserve her privacy? If so, did she have a reasonable expectation of privacy in the home, in order to challenge the warrantless entry and search?

(4) Wyoming police stopped a car that was weaving and that had only one headlight. The driver, Roosevelt Jefferson, had a suspended Colorado license; the two passengers, Jefferson's brother and the car's owner, Earnest Tillis, had valid licenses. Because the brothers gave conflicting accounts of a trip to California, the officers became suspicious. The officers then searched the car and found crack in the trunk.

Assuming that the three men were taking turns driving home from California, what result when all three move to suppress the crack?

(5) After stopping the defendant for speeding, Officer Holt observed him make a movement "consistent with removing an object from his midsection and placing it on the floorboard." Making a radio check, Holt then learned that the defendant had an extensive record, including a felony conviction within the past five years. The radio dispatcher also indicated that the defendant had been known both to carry firearms and to assault officers. At this point, Holt ordered the defendant and his passenger, Ms. Smith, from the car. Holt then searched the car, found a gun under the passenger's seat, and arrested the defendant for unlawful possession of a gun within five years of a felony conviction.

At the defendant's suppression hearing, testimony disclosed that Mr. Bell, the owner of the car, had lent the car to Ms. Smith. Although Smith had a driver's license, she gave the keys to the defendant to drive the car. What result? Would recognition of "standing" for the defendant result in a denial of "standing" for Ms. Smith?

(6) The defendant left his car at a garage for repairs. Although the garage owner estimated that the repairs would cost $180, he later gave the defendant a bill for $345. Unable to pay, the defendant left without the car, but later that night, after the garage had closed, he returned with another key and took the car.

The next morning, a police officer stopped the defendant for speeding, ordered him out of the car, conducted a cursory search of the interior, and discovered a .38 caliber gun under the driver's seat. She then arrested the defendant for illegal possession of a gun.

Under state law, an owner of goods can commit larceny by taking the goods from a person who has a special right of possession, such as a mechanic's lien, with the intention of depriving the possessor of his rights. Charged with larceny of a motor vehicle and with illegal possession of a gun, the defendant has moved to suppress the gun. What result? Must the suppression hearing judge decide whether the garage owner had a valid mechanic's lien and thus whether the defendant committed larceny? Would this finding be binding on the jury?

(7) Defendants Cassell and Owens moved to suppress robbery proceeds seized in a warrantless apartment search. At the hearing, Ms. Googe testified that she gave Owens, with whom she had previously lived, a key to her recently leased apartment so that he could help move her belongings into it. She added, however, that she and Owens had reached an understanding that he was not to come to her apartment after the move unless expressly invited. Googe further testified that she had demanded that Owens return her key, but that Owens claimed to have lost it. Cassell testified that Owens had told him that they could store things in "his apartment," and Cassell added that Owens used a key to let him into the apartment. Both defendants were in the apartment at the time of the search.

What result? Should the result be the same for both defendants?

(8) On November 23, two men and a woman robbed a restaurant and locked several people inside a walk-in refrigerator. The following May, three witnesses identified the defendant at a police lineup. The police then asked the witnesses to peek into a room where Ms. Gordon, the defendant's close friend, sat alone. After the first witness looked into the room, she exclaimed to the others that she had observed the female robber. The other two witnesses then looked, but only one of them could identify Ms. Gordon.

At the defendant's trial, the prosecutor contended that the defendant, a deceased man, and Ms. Gordon had committed the robbery. The defendant claimed an alibi, and introduced Ms. Gordon as his chief witness. Over objection, the judge permitted the two witnesses to describe their out-of-court identifications of Ms. Gordon and to identify her again in the courtroom.

The defendant appeals after conviction. Does he have standing to raise any issues concerning Ms. Gordon's showup?

B. THE FRUIT OF THE POISONOUS TREE DOCTRINE

(9) Unsatisfied by his answers pertaining to a murder, but still lacking probable cause, the police decided to take the defendant to the station for questioning. Within an hour of the defendant's arrival at the station, an officer noticed what appeared to be blood on the defendant's shoe. The police then formally arrested the defendant, gave him *Miranda* warnings, and took the shoe. Scientific analysis subsequently showed that the shoe in fact had blood stains, which were the same blood type as the victim's.

What result when the defendant moves to suppress the shoe and the blood test report? What if the officer had observed blood on the defendant's shirt after forcing him to remove his sweater? What if the police discovered blood on the defendant's clothing only after making him remove it and subjecting it to microscopic analysis? What if the police took the defendant to the station for the purpose of examining his clothing rather than for questioning?

(10) By questioning gang members, police came to suspect that "Pops" Barton and a boy named Tony had been involved in a juvenile gang killing three months earlier. A day or two later, police detained seventeen-year-old Tony Whitaker at the police station, obtained the requisite *Miranda* waivers, and questioned him about the killing. Whitaker said that Barton and he had walked into enemy "turf" on opposite sides of the street, that he had seen Barton attack and stab a rival gang member, and that he had immediately run from the scene. After his mother arrived at the station, Whitaker repeated his statement for transcription. Twelve hours after taking Whitaker into custody, the police released him.

Two days later, the police arrested Barton. Confronted with Whitaker's statement, Barton confessed but implicated Whitaker in the actual attack. Three days after Barton's confession, the police went to Whitaker's home and asked whether he would come to the station for further questioning. Whitaker agreed. At the station, a homicide detective informed Whitaker of Barton's confession and then recited his *Miranda* rights. Whitaker again agreed to talk without counsel and, in response to questioning, quickly admitted, first orally and later in writing, that Barton's account of the killing was accurate.

What result when Whitaker moves to suppress all his statements? How many fruit of the poisonous tree chains does this problem involve?

(11) After being arrested for robbery in Montgomery County, Harvey Sossamon agreed to provide information about a robbery in neighboring Liberty County in exchange for immunity from prosecution there. Subsequently, the Montgomery County police spoke to Liberty County officials, and on the basis of this conversation, they assured Sossamon that he would have immunity for that offense if he cooperated. Relying on this assurance, Sossamon provided a detailed confession to the Liberty County robbery. The Montgomery County police forwarded the confession to the Liberty County officials.

Before Sossamon confessed, the Liberty County officials did not have any evidence, leads, or suspects. After his confession, they were able to arrest two men, who gave statements that coincided factually with Sossamon's confession. In addition, the robbery victim identified Sossamon from a photo display.

Maintaining that the Montgomery County officials had misunderstood their response, the Liberty County prosecutor's office got a grand jury to indict Sossamon for robbery. At trial, the prosecutor called the robbery victim, who made an in-court identification of Sossamon and also referred to his prior photographic identification of him. The victim's wife, who was present at the robbery, also identified Sossamon. The prosecutor refrained from introducing Sossamon's confession and offered no other evidence of Sossamon's guilt.

What result on Sossamon's appeal after conviction?

(12) The defendant was visiting at an apartment that the police searched pursuant to a valid warrant. When the police arrived, they directed the defendant to sit on a living room sofa, frisked him for weapons, and placed him under guard. They also directed the tenant, who was named in the warrant, and her niece to sit in the living room.

After finding glassine bags of heroin in a bedroom, one of the officers stepped into the living room and asked, "Whose are these?" When the defendant claimed the bags, the police formally arrested him, placed him in handcuffs, and gave him *Miranda* warnings. After searching the apartment in vain for another half hour, the police asked the defendant whether he had any drugs on his person. The defendant responded that he had seven glassine bags of heroin in his waistband. One of the officers then seized these bags.

Assuming that the defendant was lawfully detained during the search of the apartment (was he?), and assuming that his pre-arrest admission was in response to "custodial interrogation" (was it?), what result when the defendant moves to suppress his pre- and post-arrest statements and the heroin taken from his waistband? How many fruit of the poisonous tree chains can the defendant assert? What result if before the post-arrest statement, the police told the defendant that he would be strip-searched at the station?

(13) Without telling the defendant the cause of his arrest, in violation of a state statute, police with probable cause and a valid warrant arrested the defendant for murder. At the station, in part to put the defendant "at ease and to gain his confidence," a detective conducted a "background interview" pertaining to the defendant's personal and employment history. During this interview, the defendant confirmed that he had come to the United States from Cuba with a person the police also suspected of being involved in the murder and that he had worked for the victim.

After about an hour and a half, the detective informed the defendant that he had been arrested for murder and, for the first time, read the defendant his *Miranda* rights. The defendant executed a written waiver, and he admitted the killing after about two and a half hours of further questioning. Questioning continued with intervals for breaks over the next four hours, until the defendant gave a version of the facts that the detective fully believed. During the next and final hour of interrogation, the detective and defendant prepared a formal, written statement.

What result when the defendant moves to suppress all his statements?

(14) Police lawfully arrested the defendant, who was seated in the driver's seat of his truck, for selling narcotics. After getting the defendant out of the truck, one of the officers, without giving *Miranda* warnings, asked whether he had a weapon. The defendant responded that he had a gun under the front seat. The officer immediately looked under the seat and seized the gun.

Now charged with a narcotics and a gun offense, the defendant has moved to suppress his statement and the gun. What result?

(15) Acting with probable cause, federal DEA agents arrested Andrade outside a Seattle hotel for various drug offenses. They immediately searched Andrade's person, but they did not immediately search his garment bag, which was on the ground by his feet when he was arrested. About an hour later, while still at the hotel, a DEA agent opened the bag and discovered cocaine.

At a subsequent suppression hearing, a DEA agent testified that it is standard practice to bring persons arrested for drug offenses to the DEA holding facility at the airport, to book them, and to inventory their personal belongings. In fact, the DEA agents followed that procedure with Andrade after the search of his garment bag.

Assuming that the one-hour interval between the arrest and search invalidates the search as incident to Andrade's arrest (does it?), what result?

(16) An informant and an undercover narcotics agent arranged to purchase narcotics from William Drosten. When they arrived at Drosten's apartment, they were greeted by Donald Barrett, whom the informant had previously met, and whose identity and address the informant had given the police. Barrett informed them that Drosten was out, but that they should call his beeper. The informant, who had previously given Drosten's beeper number to the police, went to a phone booth, contacted Drosten by using the beeper number, and arranged to meet him back at the apartment.

As they were returning to the apartment, the agent became suspicious that Drosten "was on to them." He then ordered the surveillance officers to move in and to search the apartment. The officers made a warrantless entry, arrested Drosten, found and questioned Barrett and Howard Gray, and seized a beeper. The officers were unaware of Gray or his presence before entering the apartment.

Alleging that the warrantless entry was illegal, Drosten moved to suppress the beeper and Barrett's and Gray's testimony. He also moved to suppress the testimony of Rubin Stone. Stone, who leased the beeper, allowed Drosten to use it as long as Drosten made the monthly lease payments. The police learned Rubin's identity by tracing the beeper's serial number; they also could have learned his identity by using the beeper number.

What result?

C. IMPEACHMENT

(17) A police officer stopped the defendant and Ethel Riggiola. Lawfully searching their car, he discovered a narcotics injection kit, a small coin purse containing several balloons of heroin, a Camels cigarette package with twenty-one amphetamine tablets, and a briefcase with two unopened packets of balloons. After her arrest, Riggiola informed the police that the narcotics belonged to the defendant.

At the defendant's trial, Riggiola repeated her accusation. She also described how the defendant prepared and packaged heroin in balloons. In response to brief and limited direct examination, the defendant denied that he had ever possessed the purse or the cigarette package. Over objection, the prosecutor asked whether the defendant had previously seen the balloons in the briefcase. When the defendant denied this, the prosecutor asked whether he had ever seen narcotics. The defendant acknowledged familiarity with marijuana and pills called "red devils," explaining that these drugs were common in the lower-class section of town where he lived. Although the defendant also admitted familiarity with heroin bags, he denied ever seeing actual heroin.

The prosecutor then asked whether the defendant at any time in his life had possessed a heroin balloon. After a negative response, the prosecutor asked whether the defendant had ever been arrested with a heroin balloon. When the court overruled defense counsel's renewed objection, the defendant answered affirmatively but implied that the arresting officer had planted the balloon in his pocket.

In rebuttal, the prosecutor called the arresting officer who previously had discovered the heroin balloon. Over objection, he testified that he had observed the defendant crossing an intersection early one morning, apparently "under the influence of something." After stopping the defendant, he patted him down "solely for weapons," reached into his shirt pocket, and removed a balloon filled with heroin. The court cautioned the jury to consider the officer's testimony only as possible impeachment of the defendant's credibility.

The defendant was convicted and now appeals. What result?

(18) Police lawfully arrested the defendant for conspiracy to sell narcotics. According to the defendant's disputed testimony, after giving him *Miranda* warnings, the police told him that he would get probation if he cooperated with them but that he would get seven years in prison if he failed to cooperate. In addition, the police told him that his cars and his parents' house would be subject to forfeiture if he failed to cooperate. When the defendant asked whether he could talk to a lawyer, an officer responded that the police would not consider a request for a lawyer to be cooperation. The defendant then agreed to answer questions without a lawyer, and he made several incriminating statements.

The defendant has now moved to preclude the prosecutor from making *any* use of his statements in his upcoming trial. Assuming that you believe the defendant's testimony, what is your ruling as suppression hearing judge?

(19) The defendant was charged with raping a barroom dancer. At trial, the defendant admitted having sexual intercourse with the woman in his car, but he claimed that the woman had consented. He also testified that a person unknown to him had interrupted them and forcibly abducted the woman, thereby causing the bruises that the police found on her body.

On cross-examination and in rebuttal, the prosecutor brought out that after his arrest, and after receiving *Miranda* warnings, the defendant said only that he "didn't do it," that he would take a lie detector test, and that he wanted protection because he had heard that the woman's husband was a violent man. The prosecutor also asked the defendant, over objection, "Well, do you think it might have been in your best interests to have also told the police this story you're telling the jury?" Although the judge did not strike this question, she stopped further inquiry along these lines.

What result on appeal?

(20) The defendant was tried for kidnapping. On direct examination of a police officer, defense counsel elicited that the defendant had a drug problem, that he was confused about the events when he was interrogated after his arrest, and that he was cooperative and helpful to the extent of doing everything that was requested of him. On cross-examination, the prosecutor asked whether the defendant had done everything he was asked, including giving a written statement. After a defense objection was overruled, the officer replied that the defendant, who had been given *Miranda* warnings, had declined to make a formal statement and had also stopped the questioning by asking for a lawyer.

What result on appeal after conviction?

(21) After the defendant's indictment for the robbery of a federally insured postal credit union, FBI agents arrested him, informed him that he had been indicted, and gave him *Miranda* warnings. When the defendant refused to sign a waiver form and indicated that he wanted a lawyer, an agent said that they only wanted to clarify some things. In response to questioning, the defendant admitted that his mother worked at the credit union. He also said that he visited her there on occasion by hiring the Amigo car service. Using this information, the FBI located Jose Garcia, the Amigo driver who drove the defendant and his friend to the credit union the day and time of the robbery.

The defendant has now moved to preclude the prosecutor from making *any* use of his statements and of Garcia's testimony in his upcoming trial. What result?

D. GOOD FAITH

Although the issue of "good faith" was present throughout the search and seizure chapter, the next two problems focus squarely on that issue.

(22) A telephone caller, who would not give his name, told Detective Murphy that he had observed a large stash of marijuana in the basement of a home in which he had been employed as a tradesman. The caller did not mention the date of his observation, Deciding that the tip needed corroboration, Murphy conducted a surveillance at the residence in question for two hours on two successive evenings, but he observed nothing unusual. Murphy then presented the following affidavit for a search warrant to a judge:

> An anonymous telephone caller stated that he had been hired to do some work at [the home in question.] Upon entering the basement, he smelled the distinct odor of marijuana and observed what appeared to be marijuana in the basement. Questioned about his knowledge of marijuana, the caller stated that he had been a user in his younger days. He further stated that he feels the occupants are engaged in dealing as opposed to possession for their own use. Surveillance was initiated on 4–13 and 4–14, but no undue amount of traffic was observed going to the home.

After a warrant was issued, a search uncovered more than 300 pounds of marijuana. What result on a motion to suppress?

(23) The defendant was charged with possession of cocaine with intent to distribute. Detective Leger's search warrant affidavit indicated that a confidential informant had purchased cocaine from the defendant on three occasions, and that plenty of cocaine remained in the defendant's home. Sergeant Flores testified at the defendant's subsequent trial that he had purchased cocaine from the defendant on one occasion in an undercover capacity in the presence of "Nicky," a person of unknown reliability. Nicky had asserted that he had purchased cocaine from the defendant on other occasions.

On a hearing to clarify the situation, Leger admitted that he had described Flores as his informant to protect his identity during the investigation. What result on the defendant's argument that the evidence should be suppressed because of the false statement concerning the number of the defendant's prior cocaine sales?

Chapter 8

PRETRIAL RELEASE AND DETENTION

The federal Bail Reform Act, which the Supreme Court has upheld against a facial attack, attempted to deal with the two problems that previously had plagued this area: (1) the need for safety reasons to detain certain individuals pending trial, and (2) the need to prevent the imposition of money bail from denying release to defendants simply because of their inability to pay. Whether the statute has succeeded in addressing these problems is subject to debate. Moreover, concern has been expressed that the safeguards surrounding preventive detention are not adequate to prevent abuse. The problems in this chapter should enable students to explore these issues while learning some of the mechanics of the area.

A. EXCESSIVE BAIL

(1) A pretrial release hearing disclosed that the nineteen-year-old defendant, who had no prior criminal record, voluntarily surrendered to the FBI after a federal grand jury indicted him on several counts of mail fraud. Witnesses testified that the defendant worked his way through high school, where he became a member of the National Honor Society, and one year of college in Odessa, Texas, where he had lived all his life. A probation officer, who conducted a background investigation, predicted that the defendant would appear for court whenever requested. Other witnesses informed the court that the defendant's employer and other persons were engaging in activities similar to those that led to the defendant's indictment.

After the hearing, the court released the defendant on an unsecured $5,000 bond and on the conditions that he (1) remain in the Odessa city limits, (2) refrain from attending his employer's meetings, and (3) move from his apartment to his mother's home as soon as she could provide appropriate space. The court explained that it desired to protect the defendant from the consequences of his folly and from the lure of big money, expensive cars, and racy living.

On appeal, the defendant contends that the conditions violate the Eighth Amendment and the federal Bail Reform Act. What result? Can the defendant successfully argue that the court violated the statute by imposing the bond requirement?

(2) A two-count federal indictment in Texas charged McConnell with bank fraud and conspiracy to commit bank fraud in a scheme that involved more than four million dollars. Two days later, McConnell's lawyer attempted to negotiate a plea in return for McConnell's surrender. When the prosecutor declined to negotiate with a fugitive, McConnell flew from Mexico to Houston and surrendered to federal authorities.

At a subsequent bail hearing, a magistrate conditioned McConnell's pretrial release upon his execution of a $750,000 surety bond. In concluding that the bond was necessary to assure McConnell's appearance at trial, the magistrate cited McConnell's criminal record, his lack of ties to the Houston area, his failure to appear in bankruptcy proceedings, his initial response to the indictment, and the maximum potential penalty of five years' imprisonment and a $250,000 fine for each count.

McConnell has filed a motion in district court to amend the magistrate's pretrial release order. He has alleged, without dispute from the government, that he cannot afford to pay for a surety bond in excess of $250,000. What result under both the Eighth Amendment and 18 U.S.C. § 3142(c)(2) ("The judicial officer may not impose a financial condition that results in the pretrial detention of the person.")? What is the standard of review in the district court? In the Court of Appeals? If the statute should not be read literally, what does it mean? If the statute should be read literally, and if McConnell did pose a risk of flight, what should the magistrate (or government) have done?

(3) In an armed robbery case, a federal magistrate conditioned the defendant's pretrial release on his executing a $5,000 appearance bond with an eight percent ($400) cash deposit. Unable to raise more than $200, the defendant petitioned the court for release on his own recognizance or, alternatively, on nonfinancial conditions. At an evidentiary hearing, the twenty-year-old, unemployed defendant, whose most serious prior conviction was for housebreaking, testified that "for the most part" he lived with his parents, "now and then" staying with his girlfriend. The Bail Agency stated that it could not verify the defendant's address, but defense counsel, explaining that the defendant's parents had just moved and still lacked a telephone, offered to confirm the new address by arranging an interview with the defendant's parents. The following colloquy then occurred:

> Court: This was a robbery at gunpoint. He had a gun on him when arrested?
>
> Counsel: Yes, Your Honor.
>
> Court: And he cannot verify any address or any great community ties. I do not think he would likely appear and further I feel he would likely present a danger to the public, and I will deny it.
>
> Counsel: Your Honor, I have confirmed that his parents were at the preliminary hearing and that two days prior to his arrest they did

move from the Oakdale address to the address that the defendant has just given you.

Court: Did you also confirm that he had a loaded gun at the time of his arrest?

Counsel: That is the testimony.

Court: All right. I will not change my mind.

Defendant appeals alleging that the court violated the Constitution and the Bail Reform Act. What result? What is the standard of review on appeal?

(4) An arraignment judge conditioned the defendant's release on his execution of a $25,000 bond on a charge of driving under the influence of alcohol and a $25,000 bond on a charge of failure to appear. The evidence disclosed that the defendant had been living with and caring for his mother for the past three years, that he was disabled and unemployed, and that his only source of income was social security.

What result on the defendant's emergency state court petition for habeas corpus? State law provides that all persons charged with noncapital crimes "shall be entitled to release on reasonable conditions." Does this law provide more hope for the defendant than the Eighth Amendment?

(5) Police arrested Fred Mott and charged him with rape while armed, a Class A felony. Pursuant to Local Court Rule 10, which sets forth a "standard minimum bail" for each class of felony, the judge set bail at $40,000. Even with family help, Mott, an indigent, was unable to raise enough money to secure his release.

At a hearing on a motion to reduce bail, evidence indicated that Mott had lived in the community, with a cousin, for seven months prior to his arrest. Although Mott's mother and sister had lived in the community for four years, Mott had spent most of this time in prison. Mott had an extensive juvenile record, including seven arrests for burglary, theft, gambling, escape from a detention home, and rape. His adult record showed two rape convictions. Even though Mott had a Bachelor of Science degree in human resources, he could not show any employment prospects.

The judge decided that Mott had not sustained his burden of showing that a departure from the bail schedule was warranted. What result on appeal?

(6) After the defendant was charged in state court with conspiracy to sell and with sale of cocaine, the arraignment judge conditioned his pretrial release on a $75,000 secured bond. On the defendant's motion for a reduction of bail, the court reduced the bond to $50,000 secured. The court denied subsequent motions to reduce the bail even further, and the defendant remained in jail pending trial.

What result on the defendant's appeal after conviction? What if the state has a statute similar to the federal bail statute, but the state judges do not make oral or written findings explaining their decisions? (Does the federal statute require the judge to make recorded findings?) Is the defendant entitled to appellate relief if he can establish that the bail conditions violated the Eighth Amendment or such a statute?

B. PRETRIAL DETENTION

(7) The police lawfully arrested the defendant for a series of sniping incidents that killed six people and wounded seven others. Before the defendant's arraignment, a pretrial release agency worker interviewed him. The agency's policy is to recommend release without money bail whenever a defendant scores five points on an interview sheet that seeks information about such things as prior record, family ties, employment, and residence. For example, a defendant receives one point for having no prior criminal record and minus two points for having two or more felony convictions. The defendant received one point for lacking a prior record, two points for having worked at the Post Office for more than six months, and two points for having lived at his present home for more than one year.

Should the agency recommend that the defendant be released on his own recognizance? Regardless of the agency's recommendation, what should the judge do? What should the law provide for cases such as this? If you think the defendant should be detained pending trial, should this be done directly or by setting money bail at an extremely high amount? Why might prosecutors prefer to accomplish pretrial detention through the use of money bail?

(8) A federal indictment charged Contreras with conspiracy to distribute cocaine and with substantive narcotics offenses. Pursuant to 18 U.S.C. § 3142(f)(1)(C) and (f)(2)(A), the government moved for a pretrial detention order. Relying solely on the indictment, the judge at the detention hearing found probable cause to believe that Contreras had committed narcotics offenses punishable by 10 years or more imprisonment. The judge then concluded that Contreras had not rebutted 18 U.S.C. § 3142(e)'s rebuttable presumption, created by such a finding of probable cause, that no combination of conditions would reasonably assure the person's appearance at trial or the safety of the community. The judge then ordered Contreras detained pending trial.

What result on appeal? Consider both constitutional and statutory arguments.

(9) A federal indictment charged Millan, the alleged leader of the "Blue Thunder" narcotics organization in New York City, with several offenses, the most serious carrying a mandatory life sentence. At a properly conducted detention hearing, the prosecutor presented evidence that Millan had earned millions of dollars from Blue Thunder activity, had traveled extensively in South America, had ordered numerous shootings, and had threatened families of witnesses in other cases. Relying on this evidence, and statutory presumptions, the judge found that Millan

posed a danger to the community and a great risk of flight. Based on these findings, the judge ordered Millan detained without bail pending trial.

Largely because of defense requests for adjournments, Millan's joint trial with several co-defendants did not begin until nineteen months after his arrest. Three days after the trial began, the prosecutor revealed that three of the government's agents had been arrested for unrelated narcotics offenses. After holding a hearing, the trial judge determined that the trial could proceed. Two weeks later, the prosecution revealed that Millan's lawyer was about to be indicted. While the prosecutor trying the case did not know about the pending indictment, other prosecutors had known about it for two months.

Millan then requested a mistrial so that he could retain a different lawyer. The judge took this motion under advisement. One month later, after Millan had changed his mind about hiring a new lawyer, the prosecution revealed that $50,000 was missing; the money had been seized by one of the suspect agents from one of the defendants. The judge then granted Millan's motion for a mistrial.

Millan then petitioned for release on bail pending retrial. Two months later, after Millan had been in custody some twenty-four months, the judge set bail at $1,000,000, the amount to be secured by $500,000 in real property and $100,000 in cash. Finding that the evidence still supported Millan's detention, the judge nevertheless concluded that the period of detention, which she estimated would total thirty months before the second trial was completed, exceeded constitutional limits.

The judge stayed her order pending the government's appeal. What result? What is the standard of review?

(10) A federal indictment charged the defendant, a college student with no prior criminal record, with five counts of transmitting threats in interstate commerce to kidnap and injure another person in violation of 18 U.S.C. § 875(c). The indictment alleged that the defendant transmitted to a friend E-mail messages that threatened to kidnap and injure female college students who lived in his dormitory and thirteen and fourteen-year-old girls who lived in his college town. One such message read in part,

> [Your messages] turn me on more and more. I've been trying to think of secluded spots, but my knowledge is mostly limited to the campus. I don't want any blood in my room, though I've come upon an excellent method to abduct a bitch. My room is right across from a girl's bathroom. Wait until late at night, grab her when she goes to unlock the door, knock her unconscious, and put her in one of those portable lockers.

In another message, the defendant stated that all he thinks of before sleep is how he would torture the girl he got his hands on. In another, he described having an orgasm while thinking of torturing "this cute South

American girl'' in one of his classes. In another, he said that he wanted "to do it to a really young girl first. Their innocence makes them so much more fun, and they're easier to control." In yet another, he said that "thinking about it doesn't do the trick anymore. I need TO DO IT."

The government has moved to detain the defendant pending trial. What result? Is this an appropriate case for preventive detention? Is it relevant to the detention issue (a) that the defense disagrees with the government's contention that a specific individual need not be identified as a target of the threat, (b) that the defense plans to rely on a defense based on the First Amendment freedom of speech, or (c) that the defendant has been posting "stories" on a computer bulletin board describing in graphic detail sexual mutilation of young women, some of whom were identifiable as his classmates? Would the government aid its case for detention by indicting the friend and by adding a conspiracy count to the indictment?

C. RELEASE PENDING APPEAL

(11) The defendant, a police officer, was convicted of violating federal narcotics laws after police discovered 17,000 milligrams of sixty-five percent pure heroin and packaging paraphernalia in his apartment. Given a mandatory five-year sentence, the defendant filed an appeal alleging that the trial court had erred in instructing the jury, in admitting hearsay, and in failing to grant a judgment of acquittal.

The defendant then moved for release pending final disposition of his appeal. A hearing disclosed that the defendant had always lived in Washington, D.C., which was also the home of his wife, two young children, parents, and other relatives. During pretrial release, the defendant had worked for his father-in-law and had never missed a court appearance. The father-in-law promised to continue the employment relationship and to provide room in his house for the defendant's family. The defendant had no prior record except for a disorderly conduct conviction, which had resulted in a ten dollar fine.

After hearing the evidence and arguments, the judge denied the motion. The judge stated, "The evidence was more than sufficient to sustain the conviction and the Court can recall no error in that proceeding." The judge also stated that she could not conclude by clear and convincing evidence that the defendant would not flee or pose a danger to any other person or to the community.

What result on appeal from this order? Should the presumption after conviction be in favor of detention or release?

Chapter 9

THE PROSECUTOR'S CHARGING DECISION

A. POLICY CONSIDERATIONS

Many commentators have called for the development of specific guidelines to limit and structure the prosecutor's charging discretion. The reluctance to take up this challenge may reflect several considerations, including fear of judicial review relating to both the substance of the guidelines and their application or nonapplication in a given case, a perceived need to retain flexibility, and disagreement over what factors are appropriate to consider. In addition, many who oppose such guidelines do not believe that abuse is prevalent enough to warrant the formalization of yet another stage in the process. On the other hand, as more jurisdictions are adopting sentencing guidelines to limit judicial discretion, can the lack of guidelines at the initial stage of the process be defended? (Or would you challenge the wisdom of adopting sentencing guidelines?)

The problems in this section are "soft" in that rather than calling for the application of legal standards, they call for students to assume the role of prosecutors who are required to make policy decisions about whom and what to charge. This should not diminish the importance of these problems. Serious thought should be given to the appropriateness of the various considerations raised by the problems and the possibility of addressing these areas by guidelines.

(1) Federal investigators informed the United States Attorney that Jack Burton, an attorney, fraudulently obtained an urban renewal relocation payment from the Department of Housing and Urban Development (HUD). According to the available evidence, Burton obtained $9,700 from the St. Louis Land Clearance Redevelopment Authority (LCRA), a municipal agency under contract with HUD. Jim Roberts, a business relocation specialist for LCRA, arranged the fraudulent transaction, in which Burton sold business furniture to another individual instead of moving it at personal expense as he reported on his request for reimbursement. Roberts received a kickback of $1,000.

If convicted, Burton could be fined an amount not to exceed $10,000 and/or imprisoned for a period not to exceed five years. Although two real estate brokers can corroborate that Burton sold the furniture to another person, the United States Attorney thinks that a foolproof case against Burton can be developed by granting Roberts immunity and by having him testify at Burton's trial. She also feels some sympathy for Roberts because he is chronically ill with sickle cell anemia.

What advice would you give as First Assistant? When, if ever, is it appropriate to grant one defendant immunity to help convict another? Assuming this is sometimes appropriate, can standards be developed both for selection of appropriate occasions and for selection of the person to be immunized?

(2) A federal statute makes it a crime, punishable by up to five years' imprisonment, to send obscene material through the mail. The United States Attorney has learned from the FBI that a husband and wife had themselves photographed in various sexual acts and mailed the film for development to an out-of-state processing firm. The firm developed the film and mailed the negatives and prints back to the couple.

What do you respond when defense counsel asks you not to prosecute the husband and wife and informs you that they have no previous record of involvement with obscene material, that they wanted the pictures for personal use rather than for commercial gain, and that they lack any close connection with young people? Should the processing firm, or its officers and/or employees, be prosecuted? What if the firm, unlike more established developers, regularly developed obscene pictures? (You should assume that the statute is constitutional, that the pictures are obscene, and that the husband and wife are criminally responsible for the firm's action in mailing the pictures back to them. What if the constitutional issue is close?)

(3) Zef Ahmad and his brother own a grocery store in a lower-middle-class neighborhood of a major city. After the store was burglarized twice within the past year, resulting in extensive loss of goods and property damage, both brothers complained publicly about the lack of serious police investigation. In July, the brothers hid in their store after closing time. When an intruder forced the rear door of the store on the fourth night of their vigil, both brothers fired shotguns without warning, instantly killing a seventeen-year-old male who had an extensive juvenile record for burglaries and violent assaults.

Under the Criminal Code, force may be used to prevent an unlawful entry or an unlawful carrying away of movable property only if a request to desist is first made, unless the actor reasonably believes that such a request would be useless, endanger someone, or result in substantial harm to the property sought to be protected. Use of deadly force is permitted only if the actor reasonably believes either that the other person is seeking to dispossess him of his dwelling or both that the other person is attempting to commit arson, burglary, robbery, or some other felonious theft of property and that the use of non-deadly force would expose the actor to a risk of serious bodily harm.

Should the Ahmad brothers be charged with a crime and, if so, what offense? Is it relevant that many grocery store owners have left the city because of burglaries and robberies or that the police, because of limited resources, do not in fact seriously investigate burglaries that do not involve physical violence? Should the prosecutor take into account that the brothers are Chaldean–Americans, that the intruder was black, and that racial tensions between these two groups, and between blacks and whites in general, have been high? Would the appropriate considerations be different if the brothers were black and the intruder white or Korean? Should the racial makeup of the prosecutor's constituency have any bearing on the question? Can specific standards be developed for cases like this?

(4) A woman prostitute complained to a prosecuting attorney that a man, whom she had previously solicited, forced her to have sexual intercourse at knife point and also robbed her. The identified man, who had no prior criminal record, denied the charges. The prosecutor refused to issue a complaint.

The woman then complained to the prosecutor's supervisor. What should the supervisor do? What if the prosecutor believed the man? Should the woman be required to submit to a polygraph examination? What if, aside from personal belief as to credibility, the prosecutor had good reason to believe the man would be acquitted?

(5) Responding to a disturbance-of-the-peace call, the police caught the defendant in the act of hitting his wife. The arresting officers presented their case to the warrant prosecutor, who refused to prosecute. The prosecutor observed that the defendant had been drinking after receiving a layoff notice. The prosecutor also stated that spouses usually change their minds about prosecution and that, in any event, the criminal law is not a proper vehicle to resolve marital difficulties.

Is the prosecutor's decision defensible? Can it be defended for reasons other than those given? Would this be a proper case for pretrial diversion? What guidelines would you adopt to handle these kinds of cases?

(6) Police arrested the defendant for a minor theft of property. Primarily because the victim expressed little interest in prosecution, the warrant prosecutor refused to initiate criminal proceedings. A couple of days later, however, the prosecutor learned that the police suspected the defendant of having participated in a number of robberies with a gang that was terrorizing a local neighborhood. The police had been unable to obtain identifications or other evidence to arrest any of the offenders. The prosecutor then decided to issue a warrant charging the defendant with simple theft, a misdemeanor.

Defense counsel wants the prosecutor's office to review the decision. What should the outcome be?

B. LEGAL CONTROLS ON THE DECISION NOT TO CHARGE

The problems in this section consider whether there are any instances that warrant judicial oversight of the prosecutor's decision not to bring charges. Despite the danger of occasional abuse, should the decision to file criminal charges lie exclusively with a public prosecutor? In jurisdictions with a separation of powers doctrine, must this be the result?

(7) Plaintiffs, members of a militia group, sued in federal court for a writ of mandamus directed to the United States Attorney General, the local United States Attorney, and the local state prosecutor. The complaint charged the defendants with improper refusal to prosecute two police officers for committing civil rights violations during a demonstration against a raid conducted by federal officers against a religious group. Specifically, the complaint charged that the police officers used unnecessary violence against the demonstrators. The complaint also accused the defendants of failing to create adequate procedures to investigate civil rights complaints. The plaintiffs requested an order requiring the defendants to prosecute the two officers and other known violators and to initiate new procedures for investigating civil rights complaints.

What result? What if the plaintiffs can prove that the two police officers violated the law?

(8) A well-known member of the local bar alleged that another well-known member of the bar had sexually assaulted her. Because members of the prosecutor's office knew both parties, Steven Tinker, a prosecutor from a neighboring county, was appointed acting district attorney for the case. After reviewing the sheriff's file, Tinker decided not to prosecute because he did not believe he could prove guilt beyond a reasonable doubt.

The complainant then petitioned the county court to initiate charges against the defendant. After hearing evidence, Judge Swietlik, who was also brought in from a neighboring county, ordered Tinker to reevaluate his decision. Tinker did so but reached the same conclusion. After another hearing at which the local district attorney was allowed input, Judge Swietlik ordered the local district attorney to file charges against defendant.

What result on appeal? Assume, first, that the jurisdiction has no statute dealing with private prosecutions. Assume, second, that the jurisdiction has a statute authorizing such hearings and providing that a judge may direct a complaint to be filed if the judge finds "probable cause to believe that the person to be charged has committed an offense." Would such a statute violate separation of powers notions in your state? Would such a statute be sound as a matter of policy?

C. LEGAL CONTROLS ON THE DECISION TO CHARGE

While the prosecutor's decision not to charge is relatively immune from judicial oversight, the decision to bring charges can sometimes be challenged by a defendant as discriminatory or vindictive. Why should a defendant have more of an opportunity to challenge a decision to charge than an aggrieved citizen has to challenge a decision not to charge? Outside of challenges based on equal protection or due process principles, is there any room for judicial oversight of the decision to charge? Consider problem #14.

(9) The defendant was charged with refusing to complete a census form, a crime punishable by 60 days' imprisonment and a $100 fine. At a hearing on his motion to dismiss because of alleged discriminatory law enforcement, defendant proved that the government had to date prosecuted only four people, including himself, for violating the census law. All four belonged to and played an active role in a census resistance movement. The movement, which claimed that the census was an unconstitutional invasion of privacy, held press conferences, led protest rallies, distributed anti-government pamphlets, used talk-radio to build resistance to the census, and urged the public to resist. In a complaint to the FCC, census officials had described the radio shows as "calculated to incite people to subvert the census law."

Before the hearing, the defendant asked the United States Attorney how many people had failed to complete the census. After the United States Attorney indicated that such information was not available, the defendant on his own located six other people who had failed to complete the census. None of the six belonged to the resistance movement; none of the six had been prosecuted.

Testifying in rebuttal, the Regional Technician for the Hawaii census described the four activists as "hard core resisters." Because they had caused her office so much concern, the Regional Technician had directed her staff to prepare background dossiers on the four men, something she had not done with regard to anyone else. The Regional Technician also testified that her staff was supposed to bring all known violators to her attention. She claimed not to have known of the six violators uncovered by the defendant.

What result?

(10) Charged with violations of the Meat Inspection Act, defendant Cuezze moved for dismissal on the ground that he had been singled out for prosecution based on his Italian ancestry. In a supporting affidavit, Cuezze claimed that the Department of Agriculture referred only 38 of over 800 known cases of Meat Act violations to the Department of Justice, which initiated only 14 prosecutions. Cuezze also maintained in his affidavit that a Special Agent of the FBI, who had no connection with his prosecution, promised to keep him out of jail if he became an informant. The Special Agent described this case as the "good" Italians against the "bad" Italians, the former apparently referring to the Italian–American prosecutor. The agent added that Mussolini knew that the only way to deal with "Mafia people" was to shoot them.

Denying in an affidavit that Cuezze had been selected on the basis of his ancestry, the administrator of the Agriculture Department said that Cuezze was selected for prosecution because he had wilfully violated the Act and because he had actually distributed adulterated meat. The affidavit did not describe the cases that had not been referred to the Justice Department.

What result when the government moves to deny the defendant's motion without a hearing? If the judge holds a hearing, what would have to be shown for the defendant to prevail? Who would have the burden of proof? Would the government win if it could show that Cuezze was singled out for prosecution because of his suspected ties to organized crime, not because of his ancestry? What if organized crime in the meat industry was dominated by Italian–Americans?

(11) New Jersey State Police stopped the defendants for driving 15 MPH over the limit on Interstate 80, searched their car pursuant to consent, and recovered a large quantity of narcotics. Following indictment, the defendants, who are African–Americans, along with four other African–Americans whose criminal charges also stemmed from traffic stops along I–80, filed a consolidated motion seeking (1) logs of all stops along I–80 during the weeks of their arrests, (2) training materials used by the State Police Elite Drug Interdiction Unit, and (3) the names of instructors who taught the troopers in this unit. The defendants claimed that the desired information would help support their claim of discriminatory law enforcement.

Defendants attached to their motion a study done by the Warren County Public Defender's Office showing that in 43 of its cases involving vehicle stops on I–80 over a three-year period, 70% involved African–Americans, 23% involved Caucasians, and 7% involved Hispanics. The office's overall case load over the last eight months involved 76% Caucasians and only 17% African–Americans. Defendants also submitted an affidavit from an ACLU member claiming that many minority persons had complained of stops for minor traffic infractions and intrusive searches.

What should the trial judge do? What are the competing interests? Does the Public Defender's study lack some crucial information? What burden must the defendant satisfy to get discovery? To avoid denial of this defense?

(12) Officers of the United States Park Police arrested some 200 demonstrators outside the White House and charged them in citation forms with the misdemeanor of demonstrating without a permit. The citation forms listed two options for the arrestees: pay a $50 fine or proceed to trial. The maximum penalty for the particular charge is a $500 fine and six months in jail.

Most of the demonstrators elected to pay the $50 fine. At the arraignment of the others, the prosecutor filed informations that added a misdemeanor charge of obstructing the White House sidewalks to the original charge. The additional charge, which the defendants did not expect, carries the same penalty as the original charge. The prosecutor offered to dismiss the new charge and recommend six months of unsupervised probation for any defendant who pleaded guilty to the original charge. Despite this offer, 36 defendants still elected to go to trial, many voicing a desire to litigate First Amendment defenses.

Counsel for the remaining defendants then moved to dismiss the informations on the ground of vindictive prosecution. Counsel also moved for jury trials, which the defendants became entitled to because of the enhanced penalty made possible by the additional charge. The judge granted the jury trial motion and set a date for a hearing on the vindictiveness claim.

At the vindictiveness hearing, the prosecutor moved to dismiss the additional charge. Although defense counsel objected that the prosecutor's purpose was to deprive defendants of the right to trial by jury, the judge granted the motion. Finding that the prosecutor had vindictively added the new charge because the defendants had exercised their right to go to trial, the judge also dismissed the informations, which now contained only the original charge.

What result on the government's appeal? Do the facts support an actual finding of vindictiveness, a presumption of vindictiveness, or neither? Can this case be characterized as one merely involving plea bargaining? If the judge did not err on the merits, was the remedy in this case beyond the pale?

(13) A year before its indictment, Litton Systems, Inc., won $16 million from the Armed Services Board of Contract Appeals in connection with a claim arising from its contract to construct nuclear submarines for the Navy. Shortly before the Board announced its decision, the district court empaneled a grand jury to investigate Litton's claims against the Navy. Toward the end of the grand jury's term, the government attorneys concluded that they had proved the falsity of Litton's claim but not criminal intent. The attorneys also concluded that they could still prove the latter by investigating several promising leads.

Pursuant to earlier requests for consultation, the Assistant United States Attorney in charge of the criminal investigation explained the status of the case to Litton's lawyer. The Assistant said that he saw a way to resolve the controversy but would not discuss it unless Litton's counsel first gave assurances that the proposals would not be taken as a threat. When Litton's counsel encouraged the Assistant to proceed, the Assistant said that the government would terminate the criminal investigation if both Litton and the Navy petitioned the Board of Contract Appeals to reopen its proceedings. The Assistant also said the government would abide any further Board decision. Litton's counsel found the proposal reasonable, "a breath of fresh air."

Subsequent to this conversation, Litton's executive board rejected the proposal and complained to the Justice Department that Litton was being threatened with prosecution for refusing to reopen the Board proceedings. The Justice Department rejected the claim of coercion, and the government investigation continued before a new grand jury. After hearing further evidence, the grand jury indicted Litton.

Litton has now moved to dismiss the indictment. What result? Do the plea bargaining cases have any bearing on this case?

(14) The defendant, a twenty-year-old with no prior record, surrendered to police and confessed that he had robbed a 7–11 Market. According to the defendant, overdue rent and the need to improve his appearance before seeking employment had prompted him to commit the robbery. During the robbery, the defendant carried an empty pop bottle in his pocket to suggest the presence of a gun. After the robbery, the defendant paid his rent, improved his appearance, and secured a job. He informed the police that he had saved enough money to make restitution.

The prosecutor's information charged the defendant with robbery, an offense carrying a minimum sentence of five years' imprisonment. After first pleading not guilty, the defendant entered, and the court accepted, a guilty plea. On the day set for sentencing, the court *sua sponte* declared a one-week continuance and, speaking to the prosecutor, suggested that the charge be reduced to grand theft, which carries only a one year minimum. The following week, the prosecutor refused to lower the charge, and the court postponed sentencing another six months. At the subsequent hearing, the prosecutor again refused to lower the charge even though the defendant's conduct had been exemplary during the six-month interval. With dismay, and referring to several less meritorious cases in which the prosecutor had reduced similar charges, the court then set aside the plea and dismissed the charge with prejudice. Justice, said the court, would be better served by freeing the defendant than by convicting him of robbery.

What result on the prosecutor's appeal? If the judge had acquitted the defendant, would double jeopardy law deny the prosecutor any recourse? Is this what the judge should have done? Once the defendant has entered a plea, can the judge permit the defendant to withdraw the plea if the prosecutor objects?

Chapter 10

THE PRELIMINARY HEARING

Although agreement exists that the preliminary hearing's purpose is to screen certain cases from the criminal justice system rather than to provide defendants discovery, little agreement exists about the appropriate standard for screening. Should the preliminary hearing test the police decision to arrest, determine the probability of actual guilt, or assess the likelihood of conviction? The latter function, of course, would result in the most screening because "guilty" defendants may not be convictable. Other issues, such as the applicability of rules of evidence, the defendant's rights to cross-examine witnesses and to present evidence, and the judge's authority to make credibility decisions, all depend to some extent on how this basic question is answered. Problem 1 explores the foundational issue; the remaining problems explore these other issues. They also explore whether relief from preliminary hearing errors should be granted after either indictment or conviction.

A. THE BINDOVER STANDARD

(1) An information charged state Senator Francis Lynch with bribery, which is defined as accepting or agreeing to accept any pecuniary benefit as consideration for a decision, recommendation, vote, or other exercise of discretion. At Lynch's preliminary hearing, the state called Samuel Biener, who testified that he had agreed to take $15,000 from Dr. Goldenberg in return for getting the latter's son admitted to a state dental school. Biener testified that he then called Senator Lynch and told him, "I have a boy who wants to get into dentistry and I can get ten thousand dollars." After promising to get back to him, Lynch called Biener two weeks later to request the boy's transcript, which Biener subsequently hand-delivered to Lynch. Two weeks later Lynch again called Biener and asked for the boy's first name, which Biener also supplied. Lynch then told Biener that he would again get back to him.

Shortly after these events, Dr. Goldenberg informed Biener that the dental school would be accepting his son solely on the basis of his college record. Biener, according to his testimony, then informed Lynch of this. Two days later, Lynch called Biener and said, "They are going to try to stop the acceptance letter." Biener also testified that Lynch called one more time to notify him that the letter could not be stopped and that he, Biener, should stay away from Dr. Goldenberg.

Lynch is now seeking to challenge the bindover decision by petitioning for state habeas corpus relief. What result? Would the above evidence be sufficient to arrest Lynch? To convict him of bribery? Should these questions have any bearing on the validity of the bindover decision?

B.   EVIDENTIARY AND PROCEDURAL ISSUES; HARMLESS ERROR

(2) At defendant's preliminary hearing on charges of conspiracy to deliver and delivery of cocaine, the prosecutor called two police officers. Over defense counsel's objection, the officers testified about statements implicating the defendant that two alleged co-conspirators had given them. After the defendant's bindover, the two co-conspirators pleaded guilty pursuant to plea bargains and then testified at the defendant's trial. The defendant was convicted as charged.

What result when the defendant appeals his conviction?

(3) At the defendant's preliminary hearing on a charge of murdering his wife, a police officer testified that she received a radio report to investigate an incident at the defendant's house. The officer further testified, over objection, that when she arrived, the defendant appeared at the front door and said, "Hurry, I think I shot my wife."

The officer followed the defendant upstairs and discovered the wife's body, with one bullet wound, slouched against the tub and a bathroom wall. The officer also found a .32 caliber revolver with one spent cartridge on a hassock near the bathroom door. Returning downstairs, the officer found a woman's purse, hairpiece, and shoes scattered on the living room floor. The prosecution did not offer evidence about the ownership of these items, about the position of the body with respect to the hassock, or about whether the hassock was inside or outside the bathroom.

The prosecution's next witness was a medical examiner, who described the bullet wound as the cause of death. On cross-examination, he admitted that the wound could have been self-inflicted. The state then rested, and the court held the defendant for trial on an open charge of murder.

The defendant now seeks a pretrial writ of habeas corpus. What result? Is the evidentiary issue more significant in this problem than it was in the last problem? What result on appeal if the court denies the writ and a jury subsequently convicts the defendant on evidence sufficient to sustain its verdict?

(4) Officer Austin testified at defendant's preliminary hearing that he was assigned to monitor narcotics activity in the 1300 block of West 39th Street, a location from which he had made more than fifty arrests. On June 15, after observing what appeared to be a sale of narcotics at that

location, Austin called in other officers to arrest the alleged sellers, defendant and another man. Drugs were found on both men. •

Responding to cross-examination, Austin said that he had been watching the location for about ten minutes before he observed the defendant. Asked about the place from which he made the observation, Austin refused to answer, saying that the police were engaged in an ongoing investigation and that an answer could jeopardize that investigation as well as other people and property. The prosecutor then objected to the question.

After a short discussion, the prosecutor offered to provide defense counsel with the address in writing, but not in open court. Defense counsel complained that the address would only be useful for cross-examination if she could share it with her client. When the magistrate expressed doubt that disclosure of the address would endanger anyone, the following ensued:

> Austin: In the past at the same location, people who cooperated with me have had their property damaged and have received threats.
>
> Court: But if anyone was with you, that person would be a witness. Was anyone with you?
>
> Austin: No, Your Honor.
>
> Court: And you are saying that if you disclose the property where you maintained your post, the people and property would be subjected to vengeful acts.
>
> Austin: Most definitely, Your Honor.
>
> Court: O.K. Objection sustained.

Further cross-examination revealed that Austin was in the downstairs of a house some fifty feet from the defendant, that he had an unobstructed view, that he used binoculars, and that he was elevated about five feet over the defendant's head.

Defense counsel then moved to strike all of Austin's testimony because Austin would not disclose his location. The magistrate denied the motion and bound the defendant over for trial on a charge of selling narcotics. What result when the defendant moves to reopen the hearing? Would a similar ruling by the trial judge be sustainable? If Austin becomes unavailable at trial, would a transcript of his preliminary hearing testimony be admissible?

(5) At his federal preliminary hearing on a charge of rape in the District of Columbia, the defendant objected to the complainant's absence. In response, the court granted a continuance and issued a subpoena for the complainant. Despite her presence when the hearing convened, the prosecution, over defense counsel's objection, relied exclusively on the hearsay testimony of a police officer. After the prosecution rested, the defendant tried to call the complainant to the stand, but the judge would not permit this.

Bound over and subsequently indicted for rape, the defendant has moved to reopen his preliminary examination. What result?

(6) The prosecutor charged the defendants, two members of the police department, with conspiring to commit a lawful act in an unlawful manner. Several police officers, including the defendants, converged on a local motel in response to a report concerning a sniper. In seeking information, the defendants allegedly herded motel occupants from their rooms into a lineup facing a wall. Several of the occupants claimed that the defendants beat and otherwise mistreated them.

At the preliminary hearing, several of the motel occupants testified and described police misconduct. Finding the witnesses to lack credibility, the judge refused to bind the defendants over for trial:

> Despite evident rehearsing, the witnesses gave different accounts of some of the same incidents. In spite of their eagerness, their incredible testimony could not possibly convince a disinterested arbiter of facts of their good faith or their truthfulness. Their calculated prevarication to the point of perjury was so blatant as to defeat its object. After careful review, the court is unable to find any credible testimony supporting the theory of conspiracy.

What result on the prosecutor's appeal? Is it relevant to the issue in this problem that state law grants defendants a right of cross-examination at preliminary hearings?

C. THE RIGHT TO COUNSEL

(7) At a preliminary hearing on a rape charge, the 74–year–old prosecutrix identified the defendant and described how he entered her house, chased her outside, and forced her to walk to a vacant lot. She continued,

> He told me to lie down and so I did and he unzipped his pants. He asked me to help and I said that I wouldn't and I got up and started to struggle and I got away. I was sitting on the church steps and this fellow came along and he walked me home and helped me back into the house.

After appointed defense counsel's cross-examination, which focused exclusively on the woman's ability to identify her assailant in the dark, the judge bound the defendant over for trial.

At trial, with the defendant represented by a different lawyer, the woman testified that penetration had occurred. Defense counsel cross-examined her with the preliminary hearing transcript, but the woman insisted that the transcript did not accurately reflect her earlier testimony. After further defense efforts to discredit the woman's story, the jury convicted the defendant and the judge sentenced him to twenty years' imprisonment.

The defendant has recently learned that the man who represented him at the preliminary hearing was neither qualified nor licensed to practice law, but had been masquerading as a lawyer in the local courts. The defendant is now seeking habeas corpus relief. What result?

Chapter 11

THE GRAND JURY'S SCREENING FUNCTION

A minority of states requires the prosecution, in the absence of a defense waiver, to obtain a grand jury indictment to bring a serious or infamous criminal charge to trial. The Fifth Amendment indictment clause, of course, imposes this requirement on the federal government, but the states have had a choice in the matter because the Supreme Court has never "incorporated" this part of the Fifth Amendment into Fourteenth Amendment due process.

Whether the grand jury serves any useful screening function is still a subject of debate. Obviously, as with preliminary hearings, the fewer evidentiary and procedural challenges that the law allows, the weaker the screening function will be. This may be the appropriate cost, however, of seeking to avoid the delay that would result if challenges to the competency and adequacy of grand jury evidence were permitted. A necessary tension exists, therefore, between the desire for effective screening and the desire for pretrial efficiency. Further tilting the scales against allowing challenges is the traditional view of the grand jury as an independent and "inquisitorial" institution.

The problems in Section A explore the scope of the grand jury indictment requirement. Those in Section B explore various challenges to indictments based on alleged evidentiary and procedural irregularities. Because of the lack of uniformity among indictment states with regard to these issues, the problems usually focus on federal law. Students in indictment states should always be alert for local variances.

A. THE INDICTMENT REQUIREMENT

(1) After impaneling and swearing in a federal grand jury on August 25, 1994, the judge excused the jurors, telling them that the United States Attorney would notify them when to return. On October 17, 1994, the grand jury started to hear evidence on cases, and on March 27, 1996, it returned indictments against the defendant corporation and two of its officers for alleged felony violations of Section 1 of the Sherman Antitrust Act. Under the Sherman Act, individuals are subject to a maximum term of three years' imprisonment and/or a maximum fine of one hundred thousand dollars. Corporations are subject to a maximum fine of one million dollars.

Alleging violations of Federal Rule 6(g), all three defendants have moved to dismiss the indictments. In addition to contending that Rule 6(g) was not violated, the government is maintaining, over defense objection, that the indictment should be treated as an information with regards to the corporation. What result?

(2) A United States Attorney filed informations alleging that Yellow Freight System, Inc., knowingly and unlawfully gave, and that Duncan Ceramics, Inc., knowingly and unlawfully received, rate concessions on interstate shipments of goods. The maximum term of imprisonment for individuals who violate this law is two years in prison.

Yellow and Duncan have filed pretrial motions to dismiss the informations. (a) What result? (b) What result if the defendants lose their motion in the district court and seek to bring a pretrial appeal? (c) What result with regard to the defendants' alternative argument that if the government may proceed by information, they should have a right to a preliminary hearing?

B.   EVIDENTIARY AND PROCEDURAL CHALLENGES TO AN INDICTMENT

(3) A grand jury indicted the defendant for violating 18 U.S.C. § 656 (embezzlement by a bank officer). Shortly after the defendant filed a successful motion to quash this indictment, a new grand jury indicted him under the same statute. The new indictment alleged that defendant converted to his own use a promissory note, payable in the sum of $5,000, which should have been credited to the bank. More specifically, the indictment charged that the defendant obtained the note in exchange for bank property, sold the note to a brokerage agency, and kept the money.

Because embezzlement is a felony under the statute only when the value of the embezzled property exceeds $100, the defendant moved to quash the second indictment. Citing authority, he argued in a supporting brief that the indictment had to specify the note's actual *value*, not just it's face amount, because its actual value determined the grade of the offense and the possible punishment. Choosing not to file a reply brief, the government returned to the grand jury and obtained a superseding indictment that specifically described the note's value as exceeding $100.

The defendant has now moved to quash this third indictment. During argument, the government indicated that the second and third indictments were returned by the same grand jury two months apart. In obtaining the second indictment, the government acknowledged that it relied exclusively on the testimony of a government agent, who summarized statements given by prospective trial witnesses. In obtaining the third indictment, the government merely presented the newly worded indictment for the grand jury's approval.

What result? What if the third indictment was returned only two days after the second? What if a different grand jury had returned each of the indictments?

(4) A federal indictment charged Randy Yost with arson in connection with a fire that destroyed his auto repair shop. The indictment also charged Randy and Katherine Yost with mail fraud in connection with insurance claims that the Yosts submitted after the fire. Federal Agent Eberhardt testified before the grand jury that Tom West had told him that he had seen Mr. Yost's pickup truck outside the burned building just before the fire started. At a pretrial hearing on a motion to dismiss the indictment, however, Eberhardt admitted that West, when pressed on his identification of the vehicle, had said "he could not swear to it." Eberhardt did not mention West's uncertainty when he testified before the grand jury.

(a) What result on the defendants' pretrial motion to dismiss? (b) What result if the grand jury also received some or all of the following evidence: that West had informed a second person that he had seen Yost's pickup before the fire; that the Yosts had financial difficulties; that Mr. Yost had just renewed his previously lapsed business insurance; that Mr. Yost had called to check on the policy a week before the fire; that Mr. Yost, three weeks before the fire, had purchased a large quantity of DTL–10 paint thinner, the agent used to start the fire; that much heavy equipment had been removed before the fire, equipment that would have taken two strong people about five hours to remove; that the Yosts claimed a burglary had occurred in connection with the fire; and that Mr. Yost had been seen with a large van at the shop a few days before the fire? (c) What result on appeal after conviction? (You can assume that, unlike the grand jury, the trial jury was apprised of West's uncertainty regarding the truck.) (d) What would the answers to these questions be under state law in your state? (e) What should the answers be?

(5) The United States Attorney compelled defendant through a grant of use immunity to testify before a grand jury about her role in her employer's scheme to defraud the government. Sometime after her testimony, the government claimed that it independently discovered evidence of the defendant's involvement in the scheme, and on the basis of this evidence, the same grand jury indicted the defendant for obtaining payments from the government by making false claims.

Claiming that the government's evidence was not independently produced, the defendant has filed a pretrial motion to dismiss the indictment. Is she entitled to a hearing? If so, who has the burden of proof? Would the analysis be any different if the government obtained the indictment from a second grand jury?

(6) As part of a grand jury investigation into whether the state paid excessive prices for purchasing voting machines, the grand jury subpoenaed Dylan Raymond, an official with Voting Equipment, Inc. As a material witness to the investigation. After Raymond indicated his intention to invoke his privilege against self-incrimination, the prosecutor petitioned the court for an order compelling Raymond to testify, granting him use plus derivative use immunity. Raymond testified in compliance with the court order, and was questioned about his knowledge of business and financial arrangements between state officials and the president of Voting Equipment, Inc. After three months of testimony, the grand jury returned an indictment against the persons about whom Raymond testified in connection with a voting machine kickback scheme. Sixteen months later, the grand jury indicted Raymond as an accomplice in the same scheme about which he had been questioned. Raymond immediately moved to quash the indictment, charging that the indictment was based on his grand jury testimony. The trial court held a hearing, at which the state presented no witnesses about whether the state did or did not make direct or indirect use of Raymond's testimony. How should the trial court rule?

(7) Charged in a federal indictment with various counts of bank fraud, the defendant moved to dismiss the indictment because of alleged violations of Federal Rules 6(c) and (e). Regarding the 6(c) claim, the defendant acknowledged that the grand jury foreperson properly had recused himself because he knew the defendant. The problem arose, the defendant alleged, because on several days the deputy foreperson was also absent. As a result, the secretary of the grand jury, who was not appointed by the court, served as acting foreperson, swore in the witnesses, and signed the indictment. The defendant argued that the prosecutor may have picked the secretary to act as foreperson to assure that the defendant would be indicted.

Requesting an evidentiary hearing on his Rule 6(e) claim, the defendant alleged that three articles in local newspapers included one or more of the following while the grand jury was in session: details about the loans under investigation, mention that witnesses had appeared before the grand jury, and a prediction of when the indictment would issue. The articles attributed their information to "credible sources."

Should the court hold an evidentiary hearing on either claim? If the defendant's factual allegations are accurate, should he automatically win his Rule 6(c) claim? If not, what more would he have to show? What result if the court holds a hearing and the defendant proves that a person obligated to secrecy by Rule 6(e) was the leak?

Chapter 12

JOINDER AND SEVERANCE

Joinder and severance problems raise two issues that should be analyzed somewhat differently: first, whether joinder is permissible under the applicable rules—that is, whether *misjoinder* would occur by joining the offenses or defendants; second, whether, because of the risk of undue prejudice on the facts of a particular case, a severance should be granted even if the rules permit joinder. These issues arise when the prosecutor seeks to join offenses against a single defendant (Section A) and to join more than one defendant in a single trial (Section C). At least on appeal after conviction, it may sometimes matter whether the issue is misjoinder or prejudicial joinder.

The problems in Section B explore the double jeopardy ramifications of the failure to join offenses. A single course of conduct may violate more than one statute, as when a defendant both robs and murders a victim. In some rare instances, the prosecutor's failure to join offenses in a single trial will preclude a subsequent trial of the uncharged offenses. That is, even though double jeopardy doctrine may permit multiple convictions and multiple punishments, it may not permit multiple prosecutions. The Supreme Court has pursued a wavering course in this area, and a sufficient number of problems is presented to explore the complexity of the doctrine.

While double jeopardy doctrine does not really mandate joinder in these instances, it obviously creates a strong inducement for joinder by prohibiting subsequent prosecution of unjoined offenses. This aspect of double jeopardy doctrine is, therefore, appropriate for study in this chapter. Of course, any doctrine that may limit subsequent prosecutions of unjoined offenses will have the same effect. Problem 8 illustrates this by raising issues of double jeopardy and vindictive prosecution. (Hence, a chance to review.)

A. PERMISSIBLE JOINDER: OFFENSES

(1) An information charged the defendant with two counts of selling heroin to an undercover police officer, the two sales occurring twelve days apart and involving the same officer. According to preliminary hearing testimony, the officer waited ten days after the first sale before contacting the defendant to arrange a second sale, which occurred two days later.

Prior to trial, the defendant moved for severance of the offenses. What result? Consider the answer under the Federal Rules, the ABA

Standards, and the law in your state. Which approach is most desirable? If the judge improperly denies severance, will the defendant need to show a likelihood of prejudice to prevail on appeal after conviction?

(2) An information charged the defendant with armed robbery, possession of a firearm during a felony, and receiving and concealing stolen property over the value of $100, the last charge referring to the stolen car the defendant was driving at the time of the robbery. The prosecutor has conceded that the stolen property charge had nothing to do with the armed robbery. (Was this a necessary or wise concession?)

Prior to trial, the defendant moved for severance of the stolen property offense. What result? Consider the answer under the Federal Rules, the ABA Standards, and the law in your state. Which approach is most desirable? If the judge improperly denies severance, will the defendant need to show a likelihood of prejudice to prevail on appeal after conviction? If the defendant failed to object to the joinder at trial, should the objection be treated as waived, or at least forfeited, on appeal?

(3) A three-count indictment, charging murder, attempted murder, and concealment of a deadly weapon, alleged that the defendant walked into a bar, took a gun from his pocket, and began shooting, killing one person and wounding another. Under state law, the penalty for concealing a weapon depends upon the defendant's prior record: if the defendant has a prior felony conviction, the weapons offense is treated as a felony rather than a serious misdemeanor. The state, however, must both plead and prove the prior conviction. Because of this requirement, the defendant's indictment contained an allegation that he had previously been convicted of armed robbery.

The defendant has moved to sever the weapons count from the other two counts. What should the trial judge do? What result on appeal if the trial judge refuses to sever and the defendant is subsequently convicted on all counts? Should the result on appeal turn on whether the trial judge gave careful limiting instructions about the use that could be made of the previous robbery conviction? If reversible error occurred, should reversal be limited to the homicide charges?

(4) During the afternoon of May 30, a man in an orange car offered candy to a six-year-old girl riding a bicycle near her home in Shreveport, Louisiana. When the girl refused, the man grabbed her, drove to a nearby lake at the end of a dead-end street, and sexually assaulted her. The man then drove to a location near the girl's home and released her.

About a month later, a man in a car of unknown color approached a five-year-old girl riding a bicycle near her Shreveport home. The man ordered the girl into his car, drove to the local power plant, and sexually molested her. After the assault, the man drove to a location near the girl's home and released her.

On July 30, a man in an orange car approached a six-year-old girl playing near the front yard of her Shreveport home and asked her to get into his car and to direct him to a store. When the girl refused, the man grabbed her, drove to a vacant house near a lake, and sexually assaulted her. He then drove to a location close to the girl's home and released her.

On September 3, a man riding a bicycle approached a six-year-old girl playing in her front yard in Shreveport and asked her to go to the store with him. After receiving her mother's permission, the girl got on the bicycle. The man then took her to an abandoned house, where he sexually assaulted her. After the assault, the man released the girl at a location near her home.

An indictment has charged the defendant with four counts of attempted aggravated rape in connection with the above incidents. Claiming, among other things, that he wants to testify only with regard to the September charge, the defendant has moved to sever each of the offenses. What result, assuming the jurisdiction's rules on joinder and severance track Federal Rules 8 and 14? (Also consider the problem under the ABA Standards and under your state's law.)

B. MANDATORY JOINDER: OFFENSES (DOUBLE JEOPARDY IMPLICATIONS)

(5) Charged in a federal indictment with robbery of a Wells Fargo depository, the defendant was detained for seventeen months without bail. Upon his release on bail when the trial was further delayed, the defendant immediately fled. Following his subsequent arrest, a federal grand jury indicted him pursuant to 18 U.S.C. § 3146(a) on two counts of failure to appear following release on bail. To convict under this statute, the government must prove that the defendant (1) was free on bail, (2) was required to appear in court, and (3) knowingly failed to appear. A jury convicted the defendant on both counts, and the judge sentenced him to 318 days imprisonment. Between the defendant's conviction and sentence, the government dismissed the original robbery charge.

Shortly thereafter, the government obtained an indictment charging the defendant with three counts of possessing a firearm as a fugitive from justice, in violation of 18 U.S.C. § 922(g)(2). The charges stemmed from the defendant's possession of a semi-automatic pistol, ammunition, and a hand grenade at the time of his arrest on the bail charge. To convict under this statute, the government must prove that the defendant (1) possessed a firearm or ammunition while (2) being a fugitive from justice. (There is also a commerce clause element that you can ignore in this problem.)

The defendant has moved to dismiss the new indictment on double jeopardy grounds. What result? What *should* the answer be?

(6) The defendant was convicted of bank fraud in violation of 18 U.S.C. § 1344. To prevail, the government had to prove that the defendant, an officer of the victim bank, knowingly had executed a "scheme or artifice" to obtain funds from a federally insured bank. The government did this by proving that the defendant helped to prepare and submit fraudulent loan applications.

Thereafter, the government obtained an indictment charging the defendant with making false statements to a bank in violation of 18 U.S.C. § 1014. The second indictment referred to the same conduct as that involved in the first. To prevail on the second indictment, the government must prove that the defendant made a false statement for the purpose of influencing "in any way the action of ... any [federally insured] bank."

The defendant has moved to dismiss the second indictment. To demonstrate the differences in the two offenses, the government has suggested in its reply brief that a person having second thoughts about a home purchase contract would violate § 1014 but not § 1344 by understating his finances to induce a bank to *deny* his mortgage application. What result? Which way does it cut that Congress passed § 1344 to cover check-kiting after the Supreme Court ruled that a check was not a "statement" under § 1014? (If the charges were joined in one indictment, could the defendant be punished under both statutes?)

(7) After a jury convicted the defendant of armed robbery, the prosecutor filed an information charging the defendant with possessing a firearm during the commission of a felony, the offense stemming from the same robbery. A state statute makes it a two-year felony to carry a firearm during the commission of certain other felonies. The statute explicitly mandates that the two-year sentence shall be in addition to the sentence imposed for the underlying felony.

The defendant has now moved to quash the information on double jeopardy grounds. What result? If the offenses were tried together in one trial, would double jeopardy preclude consecutive sentences?

(8) Count I of a multi-count federal indictment charged Michael Rodgers and others with conspiracy to possess crack cocaine with intent to distribute. The indictment listed 16 overt acts alleged to have been committed in furtherance of the conspiracy. (See 21 U.S.C. § 846.) Count II of the same indictment charged Rodgers with possession of crack with intent to distribute.

After a trial, a jury acquitted Rodgers on the second count but could not reach a verdict on the first. The judge then declared a mistrial as to the first count. Subsequently, a grand jury returned a superseding indictment recharging Rodgers with the conspiracy count and adding two new counts, one for using a firearm in connection with a drug trafficking crime, 18 U.S.C. § 924(c), and one for aiding and abetting Theresa Slade to possess crack cocaine with intent to distribute.

What result when, alleging double jeopardy and vindictive prosecution, Rodgers moves to dismiss the superseding indictment? What if the conspiracy count involves the same conduct and evidence that produced an acquittal of the possession charge at the first trial? Does the acquittal add a consideration that was not present in the previous two problems?

What if in support of the conspiracy charge, the government intends to prove possession with intent to distribute on a different date than that involved in the acquittal? Is this an appropriate case for a presumption of vindictiveness? Reconsider the problems in Chapter 9.

(9) A two-count indictment charged the defendant with obstructing the mail in violation of 18 U.S.C. § 1708 and with uttering a forged United State Treasury check in violation of 18 U.S.C. § 495. According to the government, the defendant removed the check from the payee's mailbox, forged the payee's endorsement, and cashed the check at a drive-in bank window.

At trial, the payee testified that he had neither received the check nor authorized anyone to endorse it. A bank teller testified that the defendant's automobile license number corresponded to that of the person who cashed the check, but the teller was unable to identify the person. A fingerprint expert identified the defendant's latent fingerprint on the check, and a handwriting expert thought it "highly probable" that the defendant endorsed the payee's name.

After the government rested, the defendant testified and denied endorsing or cashing the check. The defendant said that he first saw the check when his wife's children brought it to him in a torn envelope, and he claimed that he instructed them to return it to the proper mailbox. The defendant also testified that he normally worked during the hour the check was cashed. While he worked, he added, his wife and brother-in-law sometimes used his car. In closing argument, defense counsel emphasized the teller's inability to identify the person who cashed the check.

The jury convicted the defendant on the first count but acquitted him on the second. The court then granted defense counsel's motion for a new trial on the first count. Before the second trial, the government obtained a superseding two-count indictment. The first count again charged obstruction of the mail. The second count charged the defendant with forging the endorsement of the check in violation of a different paragraph of 18 U.S.C. § 495.

The defendant has moved to dismiss the second count under the double jeopardy clause. What result?

(10) An information charged the defendant with driving while intoxicated, the charge stemming from an accident in which the defendant's passenger was killed. After suppressing a blood test report, the trial judge heard conflicting testimony from the state regarding whether the defendant appeared intoxicated after the accident. At the conclusion of the state's case-in-chief, the trial judge granted a defense motion to dismiss the charge for insufficiency of the evidence.

Shortly thereafter, the prosecutor filed an information charging the defendant with involuntary manslaughter in connection with the same accident. According to the state, the defendant drove at an excessive speed, failed to negotiate a curve, and crashed into some trees. Over defense objection, the prosecutor introduced the blood test report and other evidence of the defendant's intoxication. Also over defense objection, the prosecutor in closing argument stressed the defendant's intoxicated condition at the time of the accident.

What result on appeal? Did the double jeopardy clause's collateral estoppel doctrine prevent the state from relitigating the admissibility of the blood test report or from introducing any evidence of the defendant's intoxication at the second trial? Did collateral estoppel prohibit the state from introducing evidence that the defendant had been drinking?

(11) After escaping from a state prison in Jackson County, Michigan, the defendant and another individual immediately drove to nearby Livingston County, where they encountered a woman in a service station and forced her at knife point to accompany them to Detroit, about 100 miles from the prison. During the ride, the woman dropped a note from the car, which led to the arrest of the men on the same day.

A few months after his arrest, the defendant pleaded guilty in Jackson Count Circuit Court to prison escape. Five months later, the defendant pleaded guilty in Livingston County to assault with intent to commit a felony, the charge stemming from the kidnapping incident at the service station.

The defendant has now filed a motion to set aside his second plea under the double jeopardy clause. Assuming that the jurisdiction in question has adopted the "same transaction" test and that both charges could have been brought in one of the involved counties, what result? For double jeopardy purposes, do you want to know whether the defendant kidnapped the woman to help him escape or instead to rape her once he was safe in Detroit? What if the defendant and his companion had different purposes in mind? Did the defendant waive any possible double jeopardy defense by pleading guilty to the second charge?

C. PERMISSIBLE JOINDER: DEFENDANTS

(12) Count I of an indictment charged Cupo, Decker, Pelletreau, Palmer, and Carbonaro with conspiring to violate the false pretenses statute of the District of Columbia. Count II of the same indictment charged Cupo and Decker with obtaining merchandise from Bruce Hunt, Inc., by false pretenses. Count III charged Carbonaro, Palmer, and Pelletreau with obtaining automobiles by false pretenses. In essence, the government alleged that the defendants obtained merchandise on credit by making false statements about their employment and subsequently returned much of the merchandise for cash. The government did not allege that the automobile frauds were overt acts in, or connected in some way to, the conspiracy involving the other merchandise.

Contending that Federal Rule 8(b) does not permit the joinder of Count III in the indictment, Carbonaro, Palmer, and Pelletreau have now filed for severance. What result? If Count III must be severed, must Count II? Why (not)? What if the indictment charged each of the five defendants in each count but still failed to connect Count III to the other two counts? Does a defendant suffer cumulative prejudice when an indictment charges several defendants with similar but unrelated charges? If Carbonaro, Palmer, and Pelletreau lose their motion, must they show prejudice to win reversal on appeal? If they win their motion, what are the government's joinder alternatives? (Also consider this problem under the ABA Standards and the joinder rules in your state.)

(13) Two men, later identified as Hunter and Thomas, committed an armed robbery at a jewelry store. Two days later, uniformed officers approached Hunter and Thomas while they were standing beside an automobile in front of Hunter's home. As the officers approached, both men discarded objects that turned out to be jewelry taken in the robbery. The officers then arrested both men. They also arrested another individual, Slate, who was leaning into the car's trunk, which also contained jewelry taken in the robbery.

Count I of an information subsequently charged Thomas and Hunter with armed robbery. Count II charged Thomas, Hunter, and Slate with receiving and concealing stolen goods, the goods being the jewelry taken in the robbery. Slate has now moved for severance of the charge against him. What result under the Federal Rules, the ABA Standards, and your local rules? (Assume that no Fourth Amendment violations occurred.)

(14) An indictment charged Shuford, a personal injury lawyer, and Jordan, Shuford's investigator, with conspiracy to defraud insurance companies. According to the government, Shuford and Long, an unindicted physical therapist, established a physical therapy laboratory to provide treatment for Shuford's clients. Shuford allegedly instructed Long to bill clients and their insurance companies for both kept and unkept appointments.

Stating that he wanted to call Jordan as a defense witness, Shuford unsuccessfully moved before trial for a severance. Jordan joined in this motion. The government then presented its case, including testimony from Long that Shuford had instructed him to bill for unkept appointments in order to build stronger cases against the insurance companies.

After the government completed its case-in-chief, both Shuford and Jordan renewed their motion for a severance. Jordan said that he would not testify for Shuford in a joint trial because he wanted to avoid impeachment by prior convictions and because placing his credibility and demeanor before the jury would weaken his planned defense of insufficient evidence. When the judge offered to prohibit impeachment by prior convictions, Jordan said that he remained unwilling to testify for the second of his reasons. Shuford stated that if the trials were severed, Jordan would testify in Shuford's trial that no instructions to falsify records had been given to Long. Jordan did not say whether he would testify for Shuford after a severance.

After the judge again denied the motion, Shuford testified in his own behalf and admitted telling Long that it was legal to bill clients for unkept appointments. He also testified that he had instructed Long not to include such charges in the claims against insurance companies. Jordan did not testify. The jury convicted both Shuford and Jordan.

What result on appeal? Would reversal make it too easy for defendants to prevent joint trials? If Jordan opposed a severance after hearing the government's evidence, but the judge on Shuford's motion nevertheless severed Jordan's case and continued with Shuford's trial, would Jordan have a double jeopardy defense to a retrial?

(15) After a lawful search of their home, Blane and Tammy White were charged with possession of a controlled substance. Prior to trial, Blane and Tammy moved for a severance. Both expressed a desire to exercise their constitutional right to testify and to invoke a statutory right to prevent a spouse from testifying for or against a defendant without the defendant's consent. What result? Is it appropriate that one spouse's exercise of a constitutional right can cause the other spouse to lose a statutory right? Is there any way of insuring that the defendants will testify for themselves in separate trials?

(16) An information charged Norwood Hurst and Carolyn Kelker with manslaughter in connection with the death of their eighteen-month-old daughter. An autopsy revealed that the baby died of collapsed lungs, which in the pathologist's view resulted from blows to the upper part of her body with a flat instrument, such as a belt. After the baby's death, both Hurst and Kelker claimed that the baby had fallen down the stairs. Kelker also told the police that Hurst over a period of time had repeatedly whipped the baby with a belt. While denying that she had ever used a belt on the baby, Kelker admitted that she had spanked the baby on the day in question with a soft shoe.

What result when the defendants move for separate trials? Assuming the motion is denied, what result on Hurst's appeal after conviction if Kelker testified on her own behalf and put the blame directly and exclusively on Hurst?

(17) Ben Logan was indicted for several firearms violations. The prosecution wants to introduce the pretrial confession of Logan's codefendant, Zach Roan, through the testimony of a detective. He would testify that Roan told him that Roan planned and committed the crimes with "another individual." (Actually, Roan named Logan as his accomplice in his statement to the detective, but pursuant to Supreme Court precedent the prosecution intends to have the detective substitute the phrase "another individual" when Roan's statement is introduced.) The prosecution also wants the trial judge to instruct the jury that it is not to use Roan's statement as evidence of Logan's involvement.

Logan objects to the prosecution's introduction of Roan's statement, because its use would violate his Sixth Amendment right of confrontation. First, substituting his name with "another individual" would lead the jury to infer that he, Logan, is the person whose name was redacted. Second, he argues that, because he intends to testify that he was present at the time some of the crimes were committed but that he was coerced into committing them, admission of the redacted confession assumes added significance. How should the trial judge rule?

Chapter 13

THE RIGHT TO A SPEEDY TRIAL

The right to a speedy trial has both constitutional and statutory dimensions. The problems in Sections A and B explore the scope of the Sixth Amendment right to a speedy trial, with the two problems in Section A being more introductory in nature and the two problems in Section B being complicated by such issues as how to compute time. The problems in Section D explore the limited, supplementary role that due process plays in this area.

The problems in Section C provide an opportunity both to explore statutory efforts to deal with speedy trial issues and to engage in statutory analysis—a too-often neglected exercise in law school. Problems 5–7 require access to the federal speedy trial statute; problem 8 requires access to the Interstate Agreement on Detainers.

A. THE SIXTH AMENDMENT RIGHT—IN GENERAL

(1) Following a murder on January 12, 1990, the police focused their attention on Harvey Arrant, Mary Peak, Donald Edwards, and Joe Padget. Edwards died within a month, and shortly thereafter, Peak gave the grand jury a statement implicating Arrant and Edwards in the killing. On March 30, the grand jury indicted Arrant for murder. In April, Peak gave Arrant's appointed lawyer a sworn statement exonerating Arrant, and on May 1, she again exonerated Arrant at a court hearing. The court then released Arrant on $2,500 bail. On May 3, just five days before Arrant's trial was scheduled to begin, the prosecutor asked for and obtained a continuance because of Peak's inconsistent statements. In June the prosecutor obtained a second continuance, and in October she obtained an indefinite continuance. Explaining her actions, the prosecutor later said that she did not want to see Arrant acquitted of a killing he committed.

Between January and October, 1991, Arrant's lawyer filed four petitions demanding to have Arrant brought to trial. When the prosecutor failed to take any action, the lawyer filed a motion for release and payment. Noting the prosecutor's belief that the case could not be tried in the foreseeable future, the court discharged the appointed lawyer. The court never ruled on Arrant's speedy trial claim.

In January, 1992, a newly elected prosecutor rescheduled Arrant's trial. In February, the police arrested Peak for perjury, and the prosecutor informed her that he would seek $50,000 bail. When Peak responded by vouching for the reliability of her earlier grand jury statement, the prosecutor said that he would drop the perjury charge.

At Arrant's trial in March, 1992, Peak invoked the Fifth Amendment on the advice of counsel. After the prosecutor's case-in-chief, Arrant called Joe Padget as a defense witness. Padget at first claimed a memory loss, but after being declared a hostile witness, he also refused to testify on Fifth Amendment grounds. The jury convicted Arrant of first degree murder.

What result on Arrant's petition for a federal writ of habeas corpus after he exhausted available state remedies?

(2) On April 13, an FBI agent arrested the defendant for transporting a stolen car in interstate commerce four months earlier. The same day, the preliminary arraignment court appointed counsel and released the defendant on his own recognizance. Subsequently, federal agents offered not to prosecute the defendant in exchange for his cooperation in an unrelated prosecution. The defendant cooperated, meeting with the agents on numerous occasions during the ensuing months. In December, the defendant was prepared to testify as a government witness, but the person on trial jumped bail. The FBI agents then agreed to contact the defendant after the person's capture.

The following March, an FBI agent arrested the defendant for illegally transporting a second stolen car. On March 20, a grand jury indicted the defendant for both offenses. The defendant, alleging a denial of his constitutional right to a speedy trial, immediately moved to dismiss the count relating to the first offense. What result?

B. THE SIXTH AMENDMENT RIGHT—ISSUES RELATING TO STARTING POINT, EXCLUDED TIME, ETC.

(3) In April, 1990, officials in Otero County obtained an arrest warrant against the defendant for participating in a confidence game. Immediately thereafter, they filed a detainer in Montrose County, where the defendant was being held in custody on other state charges. After his conviction in Montrose County in October, the defendant began to serve a five year sentence in the Colorado State Penitentiary. The Montrose officials then forwarded the detainer to the warden of the prison, who acknowledged its receipt.

In August, 1991, the defendant filed a motion in the Otero County district court to dismiss the Otero charge: Because the court's administrative office returned the motion to the defendant with advice that no charges were pending against him, the contents of the motion remain unclear. This advice was true, as the Otero officials had not yet filed charges against the defendant. In September, the defendant wrote to the Otero sheriff requesting that the detainer be dropped, but the sheriff never responded.

In January, 1992, an appellate court overturned the Montrose County conviction. Otero County officials then went to the penitentiary and took custody of the defendant. At his initial appearance, the Otero officials filed a formal complaint, and the magistrate released the defendant on bail. Thereafter, the Otero officials took no further action until October, when they filed an information against the defendant. In January, 1993, a court convicted the defendant of the Otero charge and sentenced him to prison.

On appeal, what result? When did the Sixth Amendment speedy trial rights begin to run?

(4) On January 17, the defendant, a division chief of the District of Columbia Sewer Operations Division, allegedly asked Glen Carrico, an employee of the Division, to pay him $400 for approving a desired promotion. Carrico refused but nevertheless received the promotion. When the defendant continued to make demands and threats for payment, Carrico reported the incident to the FBI. On April 24, FBI agents arrested the defendant after Carrico paid him $100 in marked bills. Upon arrest, the defendant stated, "This is gratitude for you. I paid $400 out of my own pocket to get Glen this promotion."

The government's information charged the defendant with a misdemeanor under a D.C. Code section that prohibits the receipt of money for procuring a person's promotion in any office under "the Commissioners of the District of Columbia." On July 26, the scheduled trial date, the court reluctantly dismissed the information for failure to charge a crime. The District Reorganization Act had replaced the District's three-member Board of Commissioners with a single Commissioner and a City Council, but the Criminal Code had not been amended to reflect the District's new political structure. Arguing that this was a technical flaw that was not fatal, the government appealed to the Court of Appeals, which affirmed the dismissal the following April.

On July 22, just about a year after the scheduled date of the misdemeanor trial, the government obtained an indictment charging the defendant with bribery by a public official in violation of 18 U.S.C. § 201(g). The indictment was based on the same conduct that had led to the previous information. On September 15 and again before trial in the first week of January, the defendant unsuccessfully moved to dismiss the indictment for lack of a speedy trial.

What result on appeal after conviction? When did time begin to run for constitutional speedy trial purposes? Should the time resulting from the government's appeal be included in calculating the length of delay? What if the government appealed in bad faith, or with knowledge that its position was weak? What result under the federal Speedy Trial Act?

C. STATUTORY SPEEDY TRIAL RIGHTS

(5) On May 22, the defendant escaped from a federal correctional institution in Petersburg, Virginia. Later that day, federal officers apprehended him after he got off a plane in Louisiana. On December 16, a federal grand jury indicted the defendant for escaping from a federal institution in violation of 18 U.S.C. § 751. The defendant then filed a motion to dismiss under the federal speedy trial statute. After argument, the district court granted the motion, finding that the indictment was not returned within the statute's 30–day limitation period, 18 U.S.C. § 3161(b).

What result on the government's appeal?

(6) On November 28, a federal grand jury indicted the defendant on narcotics offenses, but federal officials did not locate and arrest him until November 20 of the following year. On December 17, the defendant waived his right to appear at his arraignment. Trial was scheduled to occur on April 6, sixty-nine days after the December 17 waiver. Just before trial, the defendant filed a motion to dismiss the indictment under the federal Speedy Trial Act's 70–day limitation period, 18 U.S.C. § 3161(c). The court denied the motion.

The government then moved for a one-week continuance because an essential witness was unavailable. At a hearing on the motion, a federal officer testified that the witness had informed him that she had been receiving threats and that her house had been "shot up." The weekend before trial, the witness failed to come to a scheduled meeting, and the official stated that the government had not been able to determine her whereabouts. Finding the witness to be "essential," the judge granted the government's motion. Trail began on April 13, and the defendant was convicted as charged.

What result on appeal under both the Sixth Amendment and the federal statute? How long was the delay for constitutional purposes? For statutory purposes?

(7) On July 7, a federal grand jury indicted Eric Thompson and Tammy Leavoy for an armed bank robbery that occurred the previous month on June 8. Both defendants, who were arrested on the day of the robbery, were held without bail. Largely because of pretrial motions made by Thompson contemplating the use of expert testimony on the issue of his mental condition, and also because the government filed a successful motion to have a mental examination of Thompson, the joint trial of the defendants did not begin until November 12, 128 days after they were indicted. A jury convicted both defendants as charged.

What result on Leavoy's appeal under the federal Speedy Trial Act's 70–day limitation period, 18 U.S.C. § 3161(c)? Should the 21 days it took the trial judge to rule on Leavoy's dismissal motion be counted?

(8) On November 10, 1994, police in Baltimore, Maryland, arrested the defendant for a robbery committed four days earlier in Wilmington,

Delaware. After refusing to waive extradition, the defendant remained incarcerated in Maryland on other Maryland charges. Near the end of the month, the defendant incorrectly heard that Delaware had dropped the robbery charge.

On May 4, 1995, after discovering Delaware's detainer against him, the defendant requested a Maryland prison official to notify the appropriate Delaware authorities of his desire to return for a speedy trial. The official mistakenly replied that Delaware had not become a party to the Interstate Agreement on Detainers, and he advised the defendant to write directly to the Delaware prosecutor. On July 2, the defendant wrote to the Delaware Attorney General's office requesting "to answer the detainer immediately." The Attorney General's office failed to respond to the letter. In August, the defendant wrote to the Delaware Supreme Court expressing his desire to return to Delaware for trial. The Court's staff forwarded the letter to the Attorney General's office, which again failed to respond.

On November 17, 1995, a Delaware I.A.D. official requested the Maryland Attorney General to surrender the defendant for trial, then scheduled for December 16. The Maryland Attorney General failed to respond. On February 25, 1996, the defendant again refused to waive extradition. In May, 1996, pursuant to a written request under the Interstate Agreement, Delaware finally obtained custody of the defendant. Two months later, a Delaware jury convicted the defendant of robbery.

On appeal, what result under the Interstate Agreement? When did the statutory 180–day time period begin to run? Does it matter that the defendant's speedy trial requests failed to comply with the Interstate Agreement's procedural requirements? Did Delaware's letter of November 17 give the state an additional 120 days, after extradition, to try the defendant? Can the defendant successfully maintain a constitutional argument on these facts?

D. DUE PROCESS LIMITATIONS

(9) In July, 1989, Betty Tucker gave the Earlimart, California, District Attorney's Office a statement implicating Moss, who was Tucker's husband, and Penney in a liquor store robbery-murder, which she claimed to have watched from her apartment window. She also claimed that Moss, wounded in his right leg, had returned to the apartment with $200 and the decedent's gun. Tucker gave similar statements to the sheriff's office in August, 1989, and again in November, 1990. Shortly thereafter, local officials recovered the decedent's gun in rusted condition and photographed recent gun shot scars on Moss's right leg.

Early in 1991, Louisiana police notified the sheriff that a Donna Potter had accused two other men of the robbery-murder: one of these men was in custody in Louisiana for beating Potter, and the other was in custody in California. The sheriff, who had previously interviewed Potter about the crime, spoke to her by telephone, as did an FBI agent, and both concluded that her charges were fabricated. Potter's story was not further investigated.

In January, 1995, a grand jury indicted Moss and Penney after receiving Tucker's testimony and the photograph of Moss's leg. Responding to a subsequent motion to dismiss because of preindictment delay, the prosecutor argued that Tucker's testimony was inadmissible against Moss until their divorce in September, 1992. (State law, however, permits one spouse to testify against another. Confidential marital communications are privileged, except those made to assist a spouse in committing a crime.) The prosecutor also argued that Tucker's statements suggested that she may have been an accomplice; if so, state law would have required her testimony to be corroborated. Finally, the prosecutor said that her office had viewed Tucker's credibility as uncertain because the sheriff had promised her immunity. The judge denied the motion.

At trial, Moss testified that during the robbery, he and his brother were in Tucker's apartment preparing to leave for work. Moss's brother died in 1994. Penney testified that he was in a bar talking to the owner and a bartender. The owner died in 1994, and the bartender died shortly after the robbery. Penney could not recall the other people in the bar. The prosecutor acknowledged not knowing the whereabouts of the two men whom Potter had implicated in the crime. The prosecutor further informed the court that the investigator who first interviewed Tucker had died in September, 1994.

What result when Moss and Penney appeal after conviction?

(10) On August 8, Officer Smith and an informant purchased narcotics from a man whom Smith did not then know. The sale, which occurred on a dimly lit street, took less than two minutes. When Smith returned home, he made notes about the sale, including a description of the seller's height, weight, race, and facial hair. A week later, Smith identified the defendant while examining police photographs of individuals with narcotics convictions. Early in February, Smith ceased his undercover operations. He then arrested the defendant for the August 8 sale. Between August and February, Smith had purchased narcotics from over sixty individuals.

Prior to trial, the defendant filed a motion to dismiss the charge because of prearrest delay. At a hearing on the motion, Officer Smith testified that he needed to examine his notes to refresh his recollection about the event. He claimed, however, that he could identify every person, including the defendant, from whom he had purchased narcotics. The defendant testified that on the evening of the sale, he was home with a woman who had lived with him "off and on" and who had died unexpectedly of a heart attack on January 15. The informant's whereabouts are unknown.

What result on the motion to dismiss?

Chapter 14

DISCOVERY

Because the law varies so much from one jurisdiction to another, discovery is not an easy area to study if one's goal is to master a body of black letter law. The study of discovery, however, is much more rewarding if approached from the standpoint of understanding the underlying policy issues. The contrast between the Federal Rules of Criminal Procedure and the ABA Standards for Criminal Justice provides an opportunity to explore the competing policy arguments, and the one problem in Section A is good for this purpose.

The problems in Section B provide students an opportunity to grapple with some of the difficult interpretational issues that have arisen with regard to particular rules. While most of the problems in this section focus on the meaning of the federal rules, which are relatively narrow in scope, the problems may also be used to explore the underlying policy issues. Students should also use these problems to become familiar with the drafting difficulties that rule makers confront.

The problems in Section C explore the issue of reciprocal discovery. Students should use the problems, first, to focus on the policy arguments for and against broad discovery for the prosecutor. That is, what would an ideal system look like if we did not have constitutional limitations to worry about? Second, the problems require the students to consider the constitutional and even nonconstitutional (e.g., work product) limitations on broad reciprocal discovery.

The problems in Section D explore the limited constitutional obligation that the prosecutor has to make certain disclosures.

A. DISCOVERY FOR THE DEFENSE—
IN GENERAL

(1) A ten-count federal indictment charged the defendants, members of a local militia, with conspiracy to destroy government records and property and with nine substantive offenses related to the conspiracy. In particular, the indictment alleged that the defendants planned to enter federal office buildings throughout the country to destroy government files. It also alleged that they planned to bomb the heating pipes in Washington's underground tunnels to disable the heating systems in government office buildings.

Prior to trial, the defendants filed a motion seeking the following discovery from the prosecution:

1. All written or recorded statements and all oral statements, whether reduced to writing or summarized in government reports, made or adopted by any defendant, including statements made to persons who were not government agents.

2. All results or reports of physical or mental examinations and of tests and experiments arguably relevant to this case, including examinations of potential government witnesses, handwriting analyses, and fingerprint comparisons.

3. The recorded testimony of any named or unnamed coconspirator before the grand jury.

4. The inspection, and copying when feasible, of all tangible objects that arguably relate to this case, including (a) the underground tunnels the defendants allegedly were planning to bomb, (b) maps, diagrams, or photographs of these tunnels, and (c) letters, notes, or other written communications made by the defendants.

5. The names and addresses of all persons who have been interviewed by government agents in connection with this case or who have knowledge pertaining to it.

6. The written, recorded, or summarized statements of all persons in paragraph 5, whether or not the government plans to call such persons to testify at trial.

7. All penal records of the defendants and of all witnesses the government plans to call at trial.

What result under Federal Rule 16? Under the ABA Standards (the first edition)? What parts of this motion *should* the rules be designed to grant or deny? Can you draft rules that would make your desired distinctions?

B. DISCOVERY BY THE DEFENSE— PARTICULAR ISSUES

(2) Defendant, charged with robbery, filed a motion seeking discovery of "any and all purported confessions, admissions, or statements made by the defendant within the possession, custody, or control of the state." During argument on the motion, the prosecutor revealed that the defendant had made statements to a witness who was not a state employee, that police had interviewed this witness, and that a police memorandum of this interview, which was in the prosecutor's file, included the witness's version of the defendant's remarks.

After argument, the trial judge ordered the prosecutor to turn over that portion of the witness's statement that referred to the defendant's remarks. When the prosecutor refused, the judge dismissed the robbery indictment. What result on the state's appeal, assuming that the jurisdiction in question has discovery rules patterned after the Federal Rules of Criminal Procedure? What are the policy arguments for and against this discovery request?

(3) A federal indictment charged Clarence Roberts and Linwood Lloyd with conspiracy to obstruct justice by participating in sham real estate transactions with Douglas Ross, who was attempting to conceal illicit drug proceeds. The indictment also charged Roberts and Lloyd with making false statements to a grand jury that was investigating the real estate transactions.

Prior to trial, Roberts and Lloyd moved under Federal Rule 16(a)(1)(A) for the disclosure of any statement by any codefendant, including Douglas Ross, that might be imputed to Roberts under the government's conspiracy theory. The district court granted the request, and when the government refused to comply, the court issued an order barring the government from using at trial any statement by Ross that would be admissible under FRE 801(d)(2)(E) (coconspirator hearsay declarations admissible against defendant as admissions).

What result on the government's appeal? Do Federal Rules 16(a)(2) and 26.2 have any bearing on the correct outcome? What interest might the government have in not granting the desired discovery?

(4) A federal grand jury indicted the Professional Foundation for Health Care, Inc., for conspiracy to defraud the government's Health and Human Services Department. Before trial, the Foundation moved to compel the government to produce grand jury, written, and oral statements of all its employees. The government's response requested the court to narrow the request for grand jury testimony and to deny the rest of the motion.

What result under Federal Rule 16? What are the government's interpretational arguments? What are the concerns in this area? What special concerns, if any, are posed when the defendant is a corporation?

(5) The defendant was charged with possession and sale of marijuana and possession of LSD. According to the state, an undercover agent purchased marijuana from the defendant, arrested him, and found one LSD tablet in a subsequent search.

Prior to trial, the defense moved for a sample of the "alleged" LSD so that it could conduct its own test. A state rule provides that "[u]pon motion of a defendant, the court may order the prosecuting attorney to permit the defendant to examine and copy or photograph any relevant tangible objects belonging to or seized from the defendant." The state opposed the motion, arguing that its own test consumed 3/4 of the tablet and that it was planning to introduce the remaining 1/4 into evidence at trial.

Should the motion be granted?

(6) Defendant was charged with assaulting a park ranger in a national park. The government claimed that the defendant hit the ranger several times, banged his head against the ground, and tried to strangle him. The defendant claimed that the ranger's injuries were caused when the ranger tripped over the defendant's ice cooler.

Prior to trial, the government indicated that, if necessary, it would call in rebuttal a forensic pathologist who had examined photographs of the ranger taken after the incident. Speculating that the pathologist would attempt to impeach the defendant's credibility by testifying that the ranger's injuries were inconsistent with a trip and fall, defense counsel moved the court under Federal Rule 16 to order the government to disclose the results of any examinations or tests conducted by the pathologist. In its response, the government denied that it had anything to disclose because the pathologist had not prepared a written report. The government also contended that the pathologist had not conducted any "examination" or "test."

What result? As a policy matter, are there good reasons to deny this type of discovery?

(7) An indictment charged the defendants with robbing James Gibbs. Seventeen days after the robbery, Gibbs, who had been unable to identify anyone from police photographs, saw two men whom he believed to be the robbers. Gibbs called the police, who arrested the defendants. Subsequent investigation failed to uncover the robbery proceeds or other physical evidence linking the defendants to the crime.

At trial, Gibbs identified the defendants. Before beginning cross-examination, counsel for both defendants asked the prosecutor to produce any statements that the prosecution had obtained from Gibbs. The prosecutor responded that a police officer who interviewed Gibbs after the robbery only made rough notes of the interview. The officer's notes included some reference to Gibbs's initial description of the robbers.

What result under a discovery rule patterned after the Jencks Act?

(8) An investigative grand jury indicted the defendant, a lawyer, for perjury in connection with the following facts. On July 18, Ann Decker, represented by the defendant, appeared before a grand jury. She again appeared on August 4, this time without counsel. When asked on August 4 how she had acquired the defendant as her lawyer, Decker responded, "I didn't acquire him; he acquired me." The defendant appeared before the grand jury on August 10 and, in response to a question, denied soliciting Decker. His denial constituted the basis of the perjury charge.

Before the preliminary examination, the defendant moved for a complete transcript of Decker's and his own testimony before the grand jury. The court denied the motion as to Decker's testimony.

What result on appeal? Would Federal Rule 26.2 preclude a federal defendant from obtaining the transcript of Decker's testimony?

(9) An indictment charged the defendant with five counts of aggravated incest, the charges stemming from conduct that allegedly occurred when his six-year-old daughter, who lived with her mother and stepfather in another state, stayed with him one summer. When the child returned home, she complained of pain, and the mother noticed apparent injuries around the child's vaginal area. Several months later, after consulting a lawyer, the mother took the child to a pediatrician, who concluded that the child had been subjected to penile penetration of the vagina and anus over an extended period of time. The pediatrician then referred the child to a therapist, who interviewed the child and concluded that she had been sexually abused. The defendant was indicted shortly thereafter.

After his indictment, the defendant moved to compel his daughter to undergo a second physical and psychological examination. He argued that a second physical examination could indicate whether the abuse was continuing, which would suggest that the stepfather, not he, was the guilty party. In support of a second psychological examination, the defendant argued that custody battles can undermine the reliability of sex abuse claims, that the child may have been unduly influenced by the mother and stepfather, and that the child had been exposed at home to material of a sexual nature. Opposing the motion, the prosecutor argued that the requested examinations would be traumatic and painful to the child.

How should you rule on the motion as trial judge? Do you have any discretion in the matter if no discovery rule speaks to the issue? If you do, what standard should you apply in deciding whether to grant the motion? Can the defendant make a constitutional argument to support his motion? What kind of rule would you propose as a rule maker to govern requests for physical and mental examinations of complainants and witnesses?

C. DISCOVERY BY THE PROSECUTOR

(10) An indictment charged the defendant with embezzlement and murder. According to the state, the defendant stabbed to death a co-worker who discovered his thefts. Prior to trial, both sides filed discovery motions. The prosecutor requested, among other things:

1. Production of all exculpatory evidence in the defendant's or his counsel's possession.

2. Production of a letter the defendant had written to his wife while in jail after arrest.

3. Production of the names of all witnesses the defendant, his counsel, or counsel's investigators had interviewed in connection with this case.

4. Production of the names of all witnesses the defense planned to call at trial, the nature of the testimony the witnesses would give, and the written or recorded statements, if any, said witnesses had given to the defendant, his counsel, or counsel's investigator.

The jurisdiction in question is a common law jurisdiction with respect to discovery, with the relevant case law basically holding that discovery orders are within the sound discretion of the trial judge.

How should the trial judge respond to the prosecutor's motion? Are some of the requested items simply outside the scope of the defendant's Fifth Amendment protection? Is "exculpatory" evidence protected by the

Fifth Amendment? Assuming that some of the evidence is otherwise protected by the Fifth, would the defendant lose this protection by planning to introduce the evidence at trial? On the same assumption, could the trial judge condition discovery to the defendant upon the defendant's compliance with the prosecutor's request? Assuming no constitutional impediments, should the rules of criminal procedure provide for broad discovery for the prosecutor?

(11) An information charged the defendant with two counts of first degree murder. At defense counsel's request, two psychiatrists, Dr. Harris and Dr. Tanay, examined the defendant. Thereafter, complying with state law, the defense gave notice that it would rely on an insanity defense and that it would call Dr. Tanay to support this defense. The prosecution immediately moved to discover Dr. Tanay's written report of his examination of the defendant. When the prosecution learned that Dr. Harris had also examined the defendant, it moved to discover his written report as well. The defense opposed the motion, arguing, among other things, that it did not intend to call Dr. Harris as a witness.

A discovery rule provides that the defense must disclose the names and addresses of witnesses that the defense intends to call at trial together with the written or recorded statements of such witnesses and the substance of their oral statements. Another rule authorizes the court to allow discovery of reports and results of physical and mental examinations, tests, and experiments that the defense intends to introduce at trial. Yet another rule authorizes the court to permit discovery of "physical or documentary evidence in [the defense's] possession."

What result on the prosecution's motion? (You should assume the rules provide for reciprocal discovery.) Do the rules authorize the requested discovery? Do any defenses, constitutional or otherwise, shield the defendant from being required to provide such disclosures? What defenses should the defendant try to assert? Is it relevant that a statute entitles the prosecution to have a state-selected psychiatrist examine the defendant?

(12) An indictment charged the defendant with robbing Lonnie Richardson. At trial, William Holloway testified for the defense that he, Teresa Fleming, and the defendant were riding in a car far from the robbery location at the time of the crime. The defense also called Teresa Fleming, but the trial judge dismissed her when she said that she could not recall the morning in question. The defense finally called a defense investigator who, without referring to notes, described an interview with the victim Richardson five months after the robbery and just one month before trial. With only minor exceptions, the described interview was consistent with Richardson's testimony.

Before cross-examining the investigator, the prosecutor requested disclosure of the investigator's written report. Over vehement defense objection, the trial judge ordered the investigator to reveal his full report to the prosecutor. The prosecutor then used the report in cross-examining the investigator about the minor inconsistencies that existed between Richardson's trial testimony and his pretrial interview statement.

When the defense rested, the prosecutor called the investigator back to the stand as a rebuttal witness. Responding to direct examination, the investigator then revealed that Fleming had emphatically denied in an interview with him that she had been with the defendant on the morning in question. Fleming, moreover, had said in the same interview that the defendant was a liar if he claimed otherwise. This interview, and interviews with other possible witnesses, were fully described in the investigator's report.

What result on appeal?

(13) A federal indictment charged the defendant with bank robbery. At a pretrial hearing, a codefendant, who had earlier agreed to cooperate, refused to testify against the defendant. The codefendant, who had already been convicted and who was granted immunity, stated that he feared for his and his family's safety. Claiming that it could not convict the defendant without the codefendant's testimony, the government then moved to take the codefendant's deposition under Federal Rule 15, and the court granted the motion. When the codefendant still refused to testify at the appointed time for the deposition, the court held him in contempt under the Recalcitrant Witness Act, 28 U.S.C. § 1826.

(a) What result on the codefendant's appeal? (b) What result if the codefendant cooperated at the deposition but refused to cooperate at the defendant's trial, and the prosecutor then moved to have the deposition transcript introduced into evidence?

(14) After a search of his home uncovered a large quantity of cocaine, defendant Chappee was charged with trafficking in cocaine. Pursuant to the state's rules providing for reciprocal discovery, Chappee's lawyer agreed to provide the prosecutor with the names and addresses of witnesses the defense intended to call at trial. When the trial began, the prosecutor had not received the names of any defense witnesses.

In its case-in-chief, the prosecution called a chemist who identified the substance seized from Chappee's home as cocaine and as a controlled substance under state law. On cross-examination, defense counsel sought to establish that the chemist's testing could not distinguish "cocaine L" from "cocaine D," a synthetic substance that the defense maintained does not qualify as a controlled substance under state law. The chemist insisted, however, that the tests he employed were generally accepted in the scientific community.

The defense then sought the court's permission to call three out-of-state chemists, who were sitting in the courtroom. Counsel indicated that the chemists would testify that cocaine D is not equivalent to cocaine L, that the former is not a controlled substance under state law, and that the tests employed by the state's chemists could not distinguish the two. Claiming surprise, the prosecutor moved to bar the chemists from testifying, and the court granted the motion. The jury subsequently convicted the defendant as charged.

The defendant, who has exhausted his state appellate rights, now seeks federal habeas corpus relief. What result? Apart from his other arguments, can the defendant get relief on ineffective assistance of counsel grounds? Of what relevance is the fact that the attempted defense distinguishing cocaine D and cocaine L has not prevailed in other courts?

D.   THE PROSECUTOR'S CONSTITUTIONAL DUTY TO DISCLOSE

(15) At Smith's trial for possession of an unregistered M–16 gun, which had been stolen from the military, government witness Moran testified that Smith had shown him the gun and evidence indicating that the gun was United States property. On cross-examination, Moran admitted that he had pleaded guilty in an unrelated case to making a false statement on a firearms transaction record, but he indicated that the government had promised only that it would not make any recommendation as to sentence if he cooperated in other cases. At Moran's sentencing, however, which occurred after Smith's trial, the prosecutor, to Moran's apparent surprise, recommended that Moran be given probation because of his cooperation. The prosecutor informed the sentencing court that her recommendation went beyond the terms of Moran's plea bargain.

What result on Smith's appeal? Assume that Moran was an essential witness in Smith's trial.

(16) At defendant's trial for first degree murder, one witness testified that defendant had come up to him and indicated that he was going to get the pocketbooks of two approaching women. Within five minutes of that declaration, two women were assaulted and robbed of their purses. One of the women died from a resultant brain hemorrhage. Although the other woman could not identify the defendant, she gave a description of the assailant that matched his. A third witness testified that she heard screams from below her apartment and, looking down from the window, saw a single male fleeing from two women whom she identified as the victims. Neither party asked this witness to identify the assailant.

Defendant did not seek pretrial discovery. During post-trial motions after conviction, defendant contended for the first time that the prosecutor had suppressed favorable evidence. In an affidavit, the third witness now stated that she told the prosecutor before trial that she could not identify the person she had seen fleeing the crime, but the prosecutor had said not to worry about that.

If the court believes this witness, must it under the constitution grant defendant's petition for post-conviction relief? What if the witness had told the prosecutor that the defendant was definitely not the person fleeing from the women and the prosecutor had told her to forget about it?

(17) Defendant was charged with second degree murder in connection with the death of his four-year-old son. The defendant contended that the boy sustained his fatal injuries by falling down the stairs, but the prosecution maintained that the defendant inflicted the fatal injuries before the boy's fall. During the trial, the prosecutor introduced substantial evidence that the defendant physically abused the boy and his other children. Indeed, while denying that he hit the boy on the night in question, the defendant acknowledged the pattern of abuse.

During trial, the defense learned of a videotape in the prosecution's file of an interview with the defendant's six-year-old son conducted by a police officer and a psychologist. In the interview, the boy made fundamentally inconsistent statements about whether his father had physically abused the children. The boy also denied that his father had hit the younger son on the night in question. The defense moved for disclosure of the tape, but the trial judge, after examining it, denied the motion at the end of the trial. Neither side called the boy as a witness.

What result when the defendant appeals after conviction? Did the prosecution have a constitutional obligation to disclose the tape? What result under a discovery rule such as Federal Rule 16(a)(1)(C)?

(18) On March 11, a man kidnapped a six-year-old girl and took her to a house, where he performed sexual acts on her. After the attack, the girl was taken to a hospital, where an examination revealed extreme swelling of the vaginal area and fresh bleeding of the hymen.

After the incident, the girl identified defendant at a photo and a corporeal lineup. Her four-year-old brother identified defendant from photographs as the man who had taken his sister away. Both the girl and her brother selected a photograph of defendant's father's yellow Mazda station wagon, which defendant sometimes drove. The girl also selected a picture of the house of defendant's grandparents as the place where the sexual acts took place. A subsequent search of the house showed that the girl had given an extremely accurate description of its interior and contents. On the other hand, the defendant and his father claimed that the defendant was watching television at the time of the crime.

After conviction, the defendant filed a motion for a new trial, claiming that a test performed by a DNA expert had eliminated him as the source of sperm on the girl's panties. Because of the small size of the sample, the expert did not rely on Restriction Fragment Length Polymorphism analysis, which had been accepted by the state's courts, but instead used the newer Polymerase Chain Reaction analysis, which had not yet gained judicial approval. The state's experts countered both by criticizing the expert's omissions in conducting the test and by indicating that contamination of the samples, which was quite evident in this case, was of special concern in PCR analysis.

What result (a) assuming that the expert's report was newly discovered evidence, and (b) assuming instead that the prosecutor had the expert's report in the file during trial? What result if, making the same assumptions about the original PCR test, new DNA tests, conceded to be reliable by the state, confirm that the defendant was not the source of the semen on the panties?

(19) Approaching a convenience store late one rainy night, a thirty-seven-year old woman noticed a man, whom she later identified as the defendant, standing near a pay phone. The woman continued walking until the man suddenly grabbed her from behind and stabbed her in the side. The man then took the woman, who lost but regained consciousness, into some bushes, where he forced her to engage in various sexual acts. When the assailant left, the woman reported the incident to the police. A rape kit used on the woman confirmed that she had been raped.

The woman told the police that she had seen her assailant in the neighborhood before the attack but did not know his name. When the woman reported again seeing her attacker several days after the incident, she called the police. The police came to the scene and arrested the defendant.

Claiming that the woman had identified the wrong man, the defendant insisted that he was watching television with his mother the night of the crime. He moved to have DNA testing done on vaginal swabs taken from the victim when the rape kit was used, but the prosecutor objected and the court denied the motion.

What result on appeal after conviction? Does it matter whether the state allows DNA test results to be used as evidence? What if the police no longer have any samples that could be used for DNA testing?

Chapter 15

PLEAS

A. THE VALIDITY OF PLEAS INDUCED BY PLEA BARGAINING

Although plea bargaining is now an accepted part of the criminal justice system in virtually all jurisdictions, constitutional, policy, and ethical issues still remain. For example, certain bargains may render a plea involuntary in a constitutional sense, and a sentence imposed on a defendant who refuses to plead may in an occasional case constitute an unconstitutional penalty on the exercise of the right to go to trial. Even when constitutional arguments are not available, policy and ethical issues remain concerning plea bargaining in general and the facts of specific cases. In the problems in this section, students should consider both constitutional and non-constitutional policy and ethical issues.

(1) A ten-year-old girl accused a middle-aged man from the neighborhood of raping her. After interviewing the girl, the prosecutor with charging responsibility charged the man with rape, a felony carrying a four-year minimum, a discretionary maximum, and no possibility of probation. The prosecutor rejected a charge of indecent liberties with a child, a felony carrying the same penalty as rape except that probation is permitted. This offense includes having sexual intercourse with a child under sixteen. The prosecutor did not even consider a charge of contributing to the sexual delinquency of a child, a misdemeanor with a one-year maximum and a possibility of probation. This offense includes sexual intercourse with a child under eighteen. Consider the following fact situations:

(a) For unspecified reasons, the trial prosecutor (not the same person as the charging prosecutor) offered to reduce the charge to the above-described misdemeanor in exchange for a guilty plea. Although maintaining his innocence, the defendant accepted the offer after concluding, with counsel's advice, that testifying at trial would be unwise given the likelihood of impeachment with a prior rape conviction. What result when the defendant moves to challenge the voluntariness of this plea?

(b) To spare the victim the ordeal of trial, the prosecutor offered to recommend a four-to-six-year sentence if the defendant pleaded guilty to rape. Asked by defense counsel what she would do if the defendant rejected the offer, the prosecutor replied, "I'll go for the maximum." The defendant accepted, and the judge, commending the defendant for saving the victim from an emotionally traumatic trial, followed the prosecutor's recommendation. What result when the defendant seeks to vacate the plea?

(c) Same facts as (b) except that the defendant rejects the offer, is convicted by a jury, and receives a sentence of 20 years to life in accordance with the prosecutor's recommendation. What result on appeal? What if the prosecutor had not informed the defendant during pleas negotiations what she would do if he rejected her offer?

(d) After the girl's parents indicated that they would not permit her to testify under any circumstances, the prosecutor offered to reduce the charge from rape to the indecent liberties felony offense. The prosecutor did not inform the defendant of the parents' decision. What result when the defendant appeals his guilty plea?

(e) After the girl admitted to the prosecutor that she had consented to the defendant's actions, the prosecutor offered the same deal as in (d) without informing the defendant of the girl's admission. What result when the defendant appeals?

(2) Each of the following four fact situations raises a common issue. Does the context affect your analysis?

(a) The defendant was charged with third degree burglary in connection with his unlawful entry into a bank. He pleaded guilty to attempted third-degree burglary pursuant to a plea bargain in which he agreed both to pay restitution for damage to the bank and to waive his right to appeal. At sentencing, the court added a 5% surcharge to the Probation Department's recommendation of $1,564 for restitution. What result on the defendant's appeal alleging that the sentence of restitution was illegal because the court relied on the Probation Department's recommendation without conducting an independent inquiry? What if the claim on appeal is that the court lacked authority to include restitution in the defendant's sentence?

(b) After losing a motion to dismiss based on constitutional and statutory speedy trial arguments, defendant pleaded guilty to reduced drug charges pursuant to a bargain in which he agreed to waive "any and all rights to appeal." What result on defendant's subsequent appeal alleging a denial of his speedy trial rights? What if the speedy trial claim lacks merit but the defendant wants to vacate his plea?

(c) Charged with several serious drug offenses, defendant pleaded guilty to one drug offense pursuant to a written bargain in which he agreed to waive all his rights to appeal. What result on defendant's appeal challenging the length of his sentence and alleging that the trial court failed to conduct an inquiry into whether his plea was knowingly and voluntarily made?

(d) Separate indictments charged the defendant with armed robbery and assault with intent to murder. The judge declared a mistrial in the robbery trial because of unspecified misconduct by the defense and prosecuting attorneys. The defendant then pleaded guilty to assault with intent to do great bodily harm less than murder, pursuant to a bargain in which the prosecutor promised to dismiss the robbery charge after the time to appeal from the guilty plea had expired.

When the judge sentenced the defendant to nine to ten years on the assault charge, the defendant immediately appealed. The prosecutor then reinstituted the robbery charge, but on the defendant's motion, the court dismissed this charge on double jeopardy grounds, finding no manifest necessity for the mistrial. Should the Court of Appeals hear or dismiss the defendant's appeal from his plea? Without regard to the merits of his appellate claims, should the appellate court vacate his plea?

(3) An indictment charged Smith with two counts of rape, the offenses involving different victims who were attacked nine months apart. Because the crimes had some similarities, the charges were joined for trial. Smith claimed consent in both instances. Before trial, Smith's lawyer, with Smith's approval, entered into an agreement with the prosecutor to separate the charges. The prosecutor promised to drop the second count if Smith was acquitted of the first; Smith in turn promised to plead guilty to the second count if convicted of the first. The prosecutor also agreed not to introduce evidence of the second incident at the trial of the first.

After a hung jury, Smith was tried again and convicted of the first count. When Smith said that he did not want to plead to the second count, his lawyer told him that he was bound by the agreement. Smith then entered a guilty plea to the second rape. What result when Smith seeks postconviction relief seeking to vacate his plea?

(4) An information charged defendant and his wife with child molestation and child abuse. In return for the defendant's plea to the child molestation charge, the prosecutor agreed to permit the defendant's wife to withdraw from a previous agreement and to enter a plea on more favorable terms. Under the new agreement, the wife was subject to a maximum sentence of ten years, instead of fourteen years under the original agreement, and she was eligible for probation. In addition, the prosecutor promised to refrain from opposing the defendant's efforts at sentencing to obtain conjugal visits from his wife.

What result when defendant moves to withdraw his plea?

(5) A six-count federal indictment charged the defendant with various narcotics offenses. In plea negotiations, the prosecutor offered to permit the defendant to plead guilty to one offense and to dismiss the others. The following colloquy occurred at a pretrial conference in open court:

Court: Mr. Prosecutor, I want you to outline your offer to defense counsel.

Prosecutor: [Outlines offer.]

Court: Based on the indictment, what is he looking at?

Prosecutor: A minimum of at least ten years; a maximum of life.

Court: Do you understand that?

Defendant: Yes.

Court: We are talking about a life sentence.

Defendant: I understand.

Court: Versus 42 months under the offer. I mention the life sentence because the new laws are so heavy, so very, very heavy. If you are found guilty on all these things, the law says I have to give you life. You have to think about that. Think carefully about it tonight. Will you leave the offer open tonight?

Prosecutor: At the court's request I will.

Court: Life in prison is a long time. It's really nothing to play with. Are you a parent?

Defendant: Yes.

Court: If I were a parent, I would think about it carefully. If it comes down to that, I have to give it.

The next day, the defendant accepted the offer and pleaded guilty? What result under Federal Rule 11 when the defendant now moves to withdraw his plea? What result under the Constitution?

(6) An information charged the defendant with drunk driving, carrying a loaded firearm, and possessing a firearm as an ex-felon. The prosecutor offered to recommend a 30–day suspended sentence, a $315 fine, and one year of informal probation if the defendant pleaded guilty on the driving charge and agreed to attend "drunk driving school." The defendant declined because the prosecutor refused to dismiss the weapons charges. A jury then convicted the defendant of the drunk driving charge and acquitted him of the weapons charges.

At sentencing, the Probation Department and the prosecutor recommended formal departmental probation. When defense counsel objected that informal probation was standard in drunk driving cases, the judge responded, "You mean whether or not there's a disposition after a jury trial?" The judge then imposed a 90–day suspended sentence, a $315 fine, and three years of formal departmental probation conditioned upon the defendant's spending 15 weekends in jail, attending "drunk driving school," submitting to alcohol and drug rehabilitation, and not possessing weapons. The judge then stated,

I think I want to emphasize that there's no reason in having the District Attorney attempt to negotiate matters if after the defendant refuses a negotiation he gets the same sentence as if he had accepted the negotiation. It is just a waste of everybody's time and what's he got to lose? And as far as I'm concerned, if a defendant wants a jury trial and he's convicted, he's not going to be penalized with that, but on the other hand he's not going to have the consideration he would have had if there was a plea.

Defendant now seeks post-conviction relief from the judge's sentence. What result? What result under the A.B.A. Standards Relating to Pleas of Guilt (2d ed. 1979)?

B. BROKEN PROMISES, MISTAKEN BELIEFS, AND UNREALIZED EXPECTATIONS

To be valid constitutionally, guilty pleas must be voluntarily and knowingly made. When made in response to a promise that the prosecutor breaks, the plea is made in ignorance of the actual consequences and hence is unknowingly made. (Although some courts prefer to view this as an issue of voluntariness, the voluntariness of a plea should not depend on what happens *after* the plea is taken.) In any event, the law is clear that a prosecutor or judge violates due process by breaking a promise that induces the defendant to plead guilty. Why is this so? Still, difficult issues arise concerning whether a promise was in fact broken and, if so, the appropriate remedy. Problems 7–9 deal with the issues of broken promises.

More difficult are the cases in which the defendant erroneously believes that a promise was made in return for his plea. The defendant's erroneous belief can stem from his misunderstanding of remarks that were actually made or from misrepresentations by his defense lawyer. Should the outcome differ in these two instances? By far the easiest cases are those in which the defendant knows that no promises were made in exchange for his plea but nevertheless expected, perhaps reasonably, a lighter sentence. Is there any argument for granting relief in this category of cases? Problems 10–11 deal with these issues.

(7) An indictment charged the defendant with embezzlement and bankruptcy fraud. In return for the prosecutor's promise to recommend a one-year sentence, the defendant agreed to plead guilty and "to cooperate fully" with government investigators and grand jury proceedings "regarding all matters which are of interest to the Government." The defendant also agreed "to take any polygraph examinations that the Government shall, from time to time, reasonably require." The prosecutor promised to notify the sentencing court if the defendant "cooperated fully." The prosecutor retained "sole discretion to determine whether or not the defendant's disclosures and testimony amount[ed] to full cooperation within the terms of this agreement."

Pursuant to the agreement, the court deferred sentencing on the defendant's plea to allow him to cooperate. After the defendant responded to questions from investigators on several occasions, the government subjected him to a polygraph test, which indicated that many of his answers were not truthful. The prosecutor then informed the defendant that he had not cooperated fully under the terms of the agreement. Subsequently, after denying the defendant's motion to withdraw his plea, and after reading the pre-sentence report, the judge sentenced the defendant to three years' imprisonment. The prosecutor did not recommend a one-year sentence.

What result on appeal? If the defendant wins the appeal, what relief is he entitled to? Are the issues presented of constitutional dimension?

(8) A federal indictment charged the defendant with three counts of wire fraud in connection with a scheme to defraud merchants. Thereafter, defendant pleaded guilty pursuant to a bargain in which he promised to make restitution and the prosecutor promised to recommend that the defendant be sentenced under level 13 of the sentencing guidelines and that he receive 12 months' incarceration, the shortest sentence for that level. Because of the defendant's similar activities in other states, however, the Probation Department's pre-sentence report recommended a higher guidelines level, and at the first of three sentencing hearings, the prosecutor endorsed the pre-sentence report's recommendation.

At the second hearing, the defendant moved that sentencing be assigned to another judge and that the prosecutor be ordered to keep the agreement. After the judge refused to recuse himself, the prosecutor withdrew her initial recommendation and recommended a sentence in accordance with the bargain. When the defendant, in response, renewed his motion, the judge again denied it. The judge stated that he had not been influenced by the prosecutor's initial recommendation and that the prosecutor was now in compliance with the plea agreement. Nevertheless, the judge gave the defendant the option of withdrawing the plea. The defendant's lawyer responded by repeating that the defense wanted specific performance before another judge.

At the third hearing, the judge imposed a sentence of 36 months in accordance with the recommendation in the pre-sentence report. What result on appeal? If the defendant is entitled to a remedy, is he entitled to specific performance? Did the defendant relinquish any claim when he refused to withdraw his plea?

(9) Charged with breaking and entering, forgery, and possession of a stolen automobile, the defendant, pursuant to a plea bargain, pleaded guilty to the stolen vehicle charge and received a seven-to-ten-year-sentence. As agreed, the prosecutor then dismissed the other charges. Four days later, in an unrelated case, the state Supreme Court ruled that the motor vehicle statute only applied if the possessor had the intent to transfer title fraudulently. Citing the new case, the defendant immediately appealed and the state conceded error. In the meantime, the prosecutor reinstituted the breaking and entering and forgery charges.

The defendant has now moved to dismiss these charges. What result? Can this case be distinguished from one in which the prosecutor agrees to dismiss other charges provided the defendant does not appeal his guilty plea conviction? Reconsider Problem 2.

(10) Charged in state court with conspiring to place explosives with the intent to destroy property, the defendant pleaded guilty and received a ten-to-fifteen-year sentence. Thereafter, with the aid of a newly retained attorney, the defendant moved to withdraw the plea, claiming an unfulfilled promise of leniency. At an evidentiary hearing, the defendant testified that he was present when defense counsel and the prosecuting attorney received a phone call from the judge. From what he could overhear, the defendant gained the impression that the judge offered a one-to-ten-year sentence in an effort to get a quick disposition of the case. When the prosecutor objected, the judge offered a three- or five-year minimum and a twenty-five year-maximum, which the prosecutor accepted. Defense counsel, who also spoke with the judge on the phone, testified that although the judge did discuss three- and five-year minimums, he did not make any promises:

> The court indicated that it would be probably inclined to offer, or pardon me, the court would be inclined to sentence a minimum of three years and a maximum term and discussion then occurred at the other end of the line. . . . The court then continued and indicated that probably he would be inclined to go with a five-year minimum. At no time was a promise made however.

Defense counsel, according to his testimony, then told the defendant that the judge "would probably be inclined to go three- to twenty-five or five-to-twenty-five," but he also cautioned that no guarantees were being made. Defense counsel admitted that the defendant became extremely distraught at sentencing, saying, "I thought I was going to get five."

Is the defendant entitled to relief? What if the court rejects the "subjective approach" and finds that neither the judge nor defense counsel actually made any promises?

(11) An evidentiary hearing on a habeas corpus petition disclosed that the defendant was serving a forty-to-sixty-year sentence after pleading guilty to armed robbery. The hearing also disclosed that prior to the plea, the prosecutor, the defendant's lawyer, and the lawyer representing one of two co-defendants met with the trial judge in chambers. Only the defendant's lawyer and the judge testified at the habeas corpus hearing about the meeting. According to the defendant's lawyer, the judge urged the two defense attorneys to discuss guilty pleas with their clients and stated, "I don't think in maximums." The judge, however, denied saying anything to indicate that she would be lenient if the defendants pleaded guilty.

The other co-defendant's attorney, who was absent from the meeting with the judge, testified that based upon discussions with the defendant's lawyer after the meeting, she advised her client that he would receive a minimum sentence by pleading guilty. The defendant's lawyer also testified that he told the defendant that the judge would give him a sixty-year sentence after trial but would impose the minimum sentence of fifteen years if the defendant pleaded guilty. The two co-defendants testified that they heard the defendant's lawyer say this, and they both added that the defendant decided to plead guilty thinking that a deal had been made. The guilty plea transcript showed that the defendant had denied, when questioned by the judge, that any promises had been made to him.

Should the habeas corpus court grant relief? How, if at all, does this problem differ from the previous one?

C. THE CONSEQUENCES OF PLEADING GUILTY

A guilty plea precludes a defendant from raising many, but not all, legal issues that could otherwise be raised on appeal or collateral review of a conviction. The problems in this section explore the legal principles that govern this area. What rationale should determine what issues remain viable on appeal after a guilty plea?

(12) Charged with possession of heroin for sale, possession of heroin, and possession of a firearm, the defendant pleaded guilty to possession of heroin after his lawyer indicated that he had no viable defenses. Thereafter, alleging that a coerced confession and an illegal search induced his plea, the defendant filed a petition in federal court for a writ of habeas corpus. In their police report attached to the prosecutor's answer, the arresting officers claimed that the defendant tossed a brown bag with heroin from his car after they approached him during a traffic stop.

The defendant's petition alleged that after the traffic stop, several police officers escorted the defendant to the home of his estranged wife, who was recuperating from surgery. The petition further alleged that after pulling his wife from bed and conducting a warrantless search, the police found a gun, some cash, and equipment that could be used in narcotics traffic. Finally, the petition alleged that the defendant admitted at the police station that he possessed the brown bag of heroin, but only after the police threatened to arrest his wife and take his minor children into custody.

Is the defendant entitled to an evidentiary hearing? If so, what result if he proves his allegations? Is it an answer that the defendant could still have been found guilty even if he had successfully suppressed both his admission and the fruits of the search of his wife's home? What if the defendant alleges that he was still operating under the coercive pressure from the police station at the time he entered his guilty plea?

(13) A nine-count indictment charged Cedric Riles, a football player at the University of Utah, with conspiracy to distribute cocaine, with six acts of distributing cocaine at a public university (21 U.S.C. § 845a), and with two acts of distributing "crack" cocaine (21 U.S.C. 841(a)(1)). Pursuant to a plea bargain, Riles entered a guilty plea to one count under § 845a and to one count under § 841(a)(1). Relying on the sentencing guidelines, the judge imposed a sentence of 51 months in prison.

Riles then filed an appeal alleging that he distributed the crack cocaine only after repeated requests that amounted to entrapment from an undercover officer. Riles maintained that without the crack cocaine charge, he would have been entitled to a lighter sentence under the guidelines. What result?

(14) The defendant received a ten-year sentence after pleading guilty to obtaining marijuana without paying the transfer tax in violation of 26 U.S.C. § 4744(a)(1). Immediately thereafter, federal authorities returned the defendant to California, where he had originally been incarcerated awaiting trial on state charges. Following conviction on those charges, the defendant began to serve a term of imprisonment in the state penitentiary. Five years later, California paroled the defendant into federal custody to begin serving his federal sentence.

The defendant has now petitioned a federal court to vacate his guilty plea to the federal charges. In his petition, the defendant cited a recent Supreme Court holding that the Fifth Amendment constitutes a complete defense to charges under 26 U.S.C.A. § 4744(a)(1), as payment of the transfer tax can involve an appreciable risk of self-incrimination with respect to other criminal laws. What result on the prosecutor's motion to dismiss?

(15) A federal complaint charged the defendant with possession of narcotics with intent to distribute, a felony. Pursuant to plea bargaining, the government agreed to file an information charging the defendant with possession of a controlled substance, a misdemeanor that carries a one-year maximum. During the plea-taking colloquy, the defendant said that she understood the maximum sentence that could be imposed was one year. The judge then stated that because of her age, the defendant was also subject to the provisions of the Youth Corrections Act and could be confined for as long as six years. The defendant said that she understood. [The Youth Corrections Act, applicable in certain cases to offenders under age 26, permits "treatment and supervision" in the Attorney General's custody "in lieu of" imprisonment; custody is in a youth facility, but if the individual is a management problem, the government has authority to transfer him or her to a penitentiary.]

After accepting the defendant's guilty plea, the judge placed her on probation. Less than a year later, as a result of subsequent offenses, the judge revoked the defendant's probation and sentenced her to the custody of the Attorney General under the Youth Corrections Act for appropriate treatment and supervision.

Defendant now appeals from this sentence, claiming that because the sentence under the Youth Corrections Act exceeds one year, the government was required under the Fifth Amendment to proceed by way of indictment. She also claims that the six-year sentence under the Youth Corrections Act violates due process and equal protection because adults (i.e., those 26 or over) charged with the same misdemeanor offense may receive only a one-year sentence. Should the court reach these issues?

D. REQUIREMENTS FOR ENTERING A VALID PLEA; DISCRETIONARY PLEA WITHDRAWAL

To be valid, a guilty plea must be taken in accordance with constitutional requirements and with requirements set forth in local statutes or court rules. While the problems in this section focus on Federal Rule of Criminal Procedure 11, students may also find it helpful to analyze the problems under the rules that apply in their own jurisdiction. In analyzing the problems, consider not only whether legal error occurred entitling the defendant to relief (much legal error will be subject to harmless error analysis) but also whether the facts would warrant the judge in exercising discretionary authority to permit the defendant to withdraw the plea in the interest of fairness and justice under rules such as Federal Rule 32(e).

(16) State law defines "malice murder" as the killing of another person with express or implied malice aforethought. It further defines "express malice" as being present when one has the intention to kill and states that malice shall be implied when the killing occurs without provocation and "with an abandoned and malignant heart." Malice murder is punishable by death or life imprisonment.

Charged with malice murder in connection with a robbery and shooting in the victim's home, defendant Moore pleaded guilty and was later sentenced to death. Questioned by the judge at the time of his plea, Moore stated that he was pleading voluntarily to murder, that he had shot the victim when the latter resisted the robbery, that he had conferred with his lawyer concerning the charges, that he knew he could be sentenced to death, and that he understood the rights (as specified by the judge) that he was waiving. When the judge later imposed the death sentence, Moore unsuccessfully moved to withdraw his plea.

After being denied appellate relief, Moore sought a state writ of habeas corpus. He claimed, with support in the record, that the judge who took the plea never explained the terms "malice aforethought," "intention," "provocation," or "abandoned and malignant heart." Moore further claimed that he did not intend to kill the victim and did so only in self-defense when the latter shot at him first. At an evidentiary hearing, the defense lawyer who tendered the plea testified that he explained to Moore both the elements of the crime and the aggravating circumstances that could support the death penalty.

Denied relief, Moore has now filed a petition seeking a federal writ of habeas corpus. What result? Is Moore's level of intelligence relevant to your analysis? What result if the state habeas court had not held an evidentiary hearing? If the trial judge had permitted Moore to withdraw his plea in the interest of justice, would the prosecutor have had valid grounds to appeal?

(17) A two-count federal indictment charged Stead with receiving, concealing, and storing stolen jewelry. Each count of the indictment carried a maximum penalty of ten years' imprisonment and/or a $10,000 fine.

On the day of trial, the prosecutor and defense agreed that Stead would plead guilty to Count 2, that Stead would receive a ten year-term of imprisonment to run consecutively to a term he was already serving, and that the prosecutor would drop Count 1 and not prosecute Stead for an unrelated escape from jail. Before accepting the plea, the judge questioned Stead extensively about the voluntariness of his decision and about his understanding of the charges and the consequences of pleading guilty.

A few days after sentencing, Stead moved to withdraw his plea. When that motion was denied, Stead brought this appeal. He alleges, with support in the record, that the judge who took the plea had not informed him of his right to confront the prosecution's witnesses and his right not to be compelled to become a witness against himself. What result under the Constitution and under Federal Rule 11?

(18) Pursuant to a plea agreement, defendant DeCicco, who was college-educated, pleaded guilty to three counts of interstate transportation of stolen property. The written plea agreement, which was signed by DeCicco and submitted to the judge, provided that the government would recommend a sentence in the range of 21–27 months' imprisonment, in accordance with the parties' calculations under the Sentencing Guidelines. The agreement also stated that the judge was not bound by the government's recommendations and that DeCicco understood that he would not be entitled to withdraw the plea once it was entered. In accepting the plea, the judge did not inform Decicco that she was not required to follow the government's sentencing recommendation; nor did she mention that DeCicco would not be permitted to withdraw his plea once it was accepted.

Using a higher offense level and a higher criminal history level than the parties had used, the Probation Department thereafter filed a pre-sentence report that calculated the appropriate Guidelines range as 33–41 months' imprisonment. The judge accepted the calculations in the pre-sentence report and, over defense objection, sentenced DeCicco to 37 months' imprisonment. What result when DeCicco moves to withdraw his plea alleging that the trial judge did not comply with Federal Rule 11? Assuming that the judge denies the motion, what result on appeal or on collateral attack under 28 U.S.C. § 2255? (You may assume that the parties' calculations under the guidelines were reasonable.) Should the trial judge have permitted DeCicco to withdraw his plea in the interest of justice under Federal Rule 32(e)?

(19) Defendant DeFusco, an experienced businessman with two years of college education, signed a written agreement in which he agreed to plead guilty to federal charges of money laundering (18 U.S.C. § 1956(a)) and conspiracy to defraud a bankruptcy trustee (18 U.S.C. §§ 152, 372). DeFusco faced possible sentences of 0–20 years on the first charge and 0–5 years on the second.

In taking DeFusco's plea, the judge advised him of the potential maximum sentences for each offense. The judge did not advise DeFusco of the statutory minimums or of the low ends of the ranges of possible sentences permitted under the Sentencing Guidelines. At a later sentencing hearing, DeFusco unsuccessfully argued for a downward departure from the range of punishments calculated in the pre-sentence report. The judge then sentenced DeFusco within the Guidelines to 60 months in prison.

What result on appeal?

(20) Defendant pleaded guilty in Washington state to larceny pursuant to a written plea agreement specifying that the maximum sentence was 15 years and that the offense did not have a mandatory minimum. Before sentencing, the prosecutor filed a supplemental information seeking to have the defendant adjudged a habitual offender. The information alleged that the defendant had a nine-year-old felony conviction in Oklahoma and a six-year-old felony conviction in California. (The defendant had mentioned only one of these when questioned about prior convictions at his bail hearing.) If the prosecutor invokes Washington's habitual offender statute, punishment of a third felony carries a minimum sentence of 15 years and a maximum of life. At the time of his plea, neither the judge nor defense counsel had advised the defendant of the habitual offender law.

After the defendant unsuccessfully moved to withdraw his larceny plea, a jury found that the larceny conviction constituted his third felony conviction. The judge then sentenced the defendant to life imprisonment on the larceny charge. What result on appeal? Discuss under the Constitution and under a state rule patterned after Federal Rule 11. What should the trial judge have done under a rule patterned after Federal Rule 32(e)? Are there any due process problems in the Washington procedure?

(21) Humphries was charged with sexual contact with a minor child and initially entered a plea of not guilty. Two weeks after his arraignment, his attorney filed a request for discovery and inspection with the court and the prosecution. The request included a demand for all exculpatory evidence that would lead to further investigation. Two months later, and before the prosecution responded to his demand, Humphries pled guilty to sexual assault and was sentenced to thirty years. Shortly after sentencing, the prosecutor notified Humphries's attorney that just before she has accused Humphries the same minor child had alleged that her grandfather had sexually assaulted her in a similar manner. Humphries's attorney filed a motion to withdraw the guilty plea, claiming that her client would not have pled guilty if the evidence had been disclosed. Did the prosecutor fail to turn over potentially exculpatory evidence in violation of Humphries's constitutional rights? Should the court have required the prosecutor to provide the defendant with the evidence before accepting the plea? Should the court permit Humphries to withdraw his plea?

Chapter 16

THE RIGHT TO COUNSEL AND OTHER ASSISTANCE

A. SCOPE OF THE RIGHT TO COUNSEL

The Sixth Amendment right to counsel applies not only at trial but at all "critical stages" of the "criminal prosecution." The problems in this section explore the meanings of these terms. Even if Sixth Amendment rights do not apply, other sources, such as due process, may provide a right to counsel. Although due process may only infrequently provide a basis for recognizing a right to counsel when Sixth Amendment rights are inapplicable, students should remain alert for this possibility.

(1) Officers from the United States Coast Guard arrested defendant Greenberg for trafficking in marijuana. At his initial appearance, the magistrate judge read Greenberg the charges the government was filing against him, recited his *Miranda* rights, set a date for the preliminary examination, appointed counsel to represent him at subsequent proceedings, and set bail. Prior to and during the setting of bail, the magistrate judge warned Greenberg that he had the right to remain silent. Nevertheless, without prompting, Greenberg admitted his guilt.

What result when Greenberg seeks to suppress his admission on Sixth Amendment grounds? (Would Greenberg be entitled to relief under the Fifth Amendment?)

(2) Hicks pleaded guilty to one count of possessing cocaine with intent to distribute. After taking his plea, the judge told Hicks to cooperate with the probation officer, who would compile the presentence report and make recommendations as to what sentencing guidelines to apply. The judge did not offer to permit Hicks legal representation during the interview.

In arriving at an offense level of 32, the probation officer considered the quantity of both the cocaine and the cash that had been seized from Hicks. The probation officer added two levels to the offense level because Hicks told him he had paid his attorney $6,000 when in fact he had paid him $60,000. The Guidelines permit an upward departure for "material" falsehoods to a probation officer during a presentence interview. The probation officer also subtracted two levels because Hicks accepted responsibility by pleading guilty.

At sentencing, counsel for Hicks objected to the use of the cash to calculate an offense level and the falsehood to make an upward departure. The judge rejected the objections and sentenced Hicks to eleven years in prison and a $20,000 fine. What result on appeal? What was the relevance of the fee?

(3) The state of Arkansas charged defendant Smith with seven counts of terroristic threats and seven counts of false imprisonment after he held seven people at gunpoint at his place of employment. At Smith's arraignment, the trial judge appointed the sole public defender in the county to represent him. When Smith objected that the public defender had done a poor job in representing other defendants and that he had formerly been a municipal judge, the trial judge told Smith that he could either accept the public defender or proceed pro se. Smith responded that he would not accept the public defender. The judge then stated for the record that Smith had waived his right to counsel.

Two months later, the same judge, in accordance with the Arkansas Rules of Criminal Procedure, conducted an omnibus hearing, a pretrial hearing at which motions are made and ruled upon. Issues and defenses not raised at the omnibus hearing are generally treated as waived. Although the public defender was present, Smith appeared pro se. When Smith requested a lawyer, the judge gave him the same choice as before. After revealing that he was filing a class action suit in federal court against the judge and the public defender for violating the fundamental rights of criminal defendants, Smith continued with his pro se defense. He then filed several motions, including a motion to reduce bail and a motion to dismiss the charges on speedy trial grounds. The judge denied all the motions.

Shortly thereafter, the judge appointed a criminal defense lawyer from the private bar to represent Smith. A jury subsequently convicted Smith on all counts. What result on appeal?

(4) Ricardo Perez was arrested six months ago on several misdemeanors, including illegally entering the United States, and transporting illegal aliens in violation of federal law. The authorized penalty for both charges includes jail time and/or monetary fines. Appearing pro se, Perez entered a plea of guilty. You are the law clerk for the trial judge in *United States v. Perez*. The judge inadvertently forgot to appoint counsel for Perez. She asks you what her options are for sentencing Perez on the misdemeanor charges. Can she sentence him to serve time in jail? Fine him for the violations? Sentence him, suspend the sentence and place him on probation? Place him on probation without suspending the sentence?

(5) Charged with murder, the defendant entered a guilty plea to a charge of manslaughter and received a ten-year suspended sentence and eighteen months' probation. Twelve months later, the police arrested the defendant for obstruction of justice, disorderly conduct, open profanity, and public drunkenness, each a misdemeanor punishable by a possible fine and imprisonment not to exceed six months. Without informing the defendant, an indigent with a sixth grade education, of his right to appointed counsel, the judge found the defendant guilty of all four offenses. She then sentenced him to concurrent 10 day sentences on the first two charges and suspended sentences on the last two.

After serving the ten-day sentence, the defendant appeared in court for a probation revocation hearing on the manslaughter charge. Without informing the defendant of his right to appointed counsel, and relying solely on the misdemeanor convictions, the judge revoked the defendant's probation.

What result when the defendant challenges both his misdemeanor convictions and his probation revocation in a federal habeas corpus proceeding?

B.   WAIVER AND THE RIGHT OF SELF-REPRESENTATION

The Court's cases recognize not only a right to counsel but a correlative right to waive counsel and proceed pro se. The existence of these correlative rights can give rise to some thorny issues: for example, a judge who responds too quickly to a defendant's request to dismiss his lawyer may risk violating the right to counsel, while a judge who is overly protective of the right to counsel may risk violating the defendant's right to proceed pro se. Even the practice of appointing standby counsel entails risk, for standby counsel may do too much and thus violate the right to proceed pro se. In addition, several procedural issues have arisen, such as the stage at which the right to proceed pro se must be asserted or lost.

(6) Charged with first-degree murder, defendant moved to dismiss his appointed lawyer and to represent himself. After noting that defendant's speech impediment might cause him considerable difficulty, but after also concluding that defendant's waiver of counsel was knowing and intelligent, the judge reluctantly granted the motion. For the next two months, defendant attended hearings and filed and argued motions.

Thereafter, following a hearing in which the judge concluded that defendant's speech impediment was so severe that it would effectively preclude him from articulating his defense to the jury, the trial judge appointed attorney Fogelman to act as co-counsel. The judge ruled that defendant would not be permitted to question jurors or witnesses, make objections, or argue to the jury. On the other hand, defendant would retain full *in propria persona* privileges in jail, including access to the law library and private meetings with the court-appointed investigator. Defendant also retained the right to file motions.

Defendant subsequently objected to Fogelman's appointment:

I—it is my understanding that I have a constitutional right to—that I have a right to waive counsel and to—to proceed with—with—without the assistance—without the assistance of counsel, which I would—which I would—which I would—which I would request at—

at—which I would request at this time here. I would like to call to the court's a—to the court's a—attention that I have also filed similar motions—similar motions on—on July 29 and on September—on September—excuse me—Sep—Sep—September 26.

What result on appeal after conviction with Fogelman assuming the role envisioned by the court?

(7) After representing the defendant on a burglary charge at his preliminary hearing, arraignment, suppression hearing, and jury selection, privately retained counsel Kubiak filed two motions with the court. One advised the court that the defendant wanted Kubiak to withdraw his appearance for the defendant; the other requested a continuance. Kubiak indicated that he knew of no reasonable basis for his discharge. When the court informed the defendant that it viewed the motion for a continuance as a delay tactic intended to "thwart the ends of justice," the defendant, citing tactical differences, indicated he still wanted Kubiak to withdraw.

The court then explained to the defendant how the trial would proceed: that the prosecution would go first in presenting evidence; that he would then have a right to present his defense; that he could testify or not testify; and that he could object to any evidence. Saying it would not advise him about the law or decisions he should make, the court indicated it was appointing an assistant public defender as standby counsel who would perform these tasks. The defendant then confirmed that he wanted to discharge Kubiak and that he wanted to continue with a jury trial.

What result on appeal after conviction?

(8) Charged with mayhem and armed robbery, defendant Menefield dismissed two appointed lawyers before trial and elected to represent himself. (No error is alleged in the judge's allowing this.) After his conviction, Menefield asked the court to appoint counsel to assist him in preparing a motion for a new trial. His request cited the intricacies of state law governing new trials. The judge denied the request:

> If I appointed counsel at this point, we would have to get the entire transcript done. Counsel would have to read every word of it to make the motion. As a practical matter, we are only talking about a new trial motion. If I could see any significant impact in appointing counsel at this stage, I would do it. But I can't. So, denied.

What result when Menefield seeks federal habeas corpus relief after exhausting possible state remedies?

C. RIGHT TO COUNSEL OF ONE'S CHOICE

While it is frequently said that defendants with means have at least a qualified right to retain counsel of their choice but that indigents have no right to determine who will represent them, difficult issues can arise in both categories of cases. Often, in cases involving appointed lawyers, the issue of counsel of one's choice combines with issues concerning a defendant's right to proceed pro se. A judge may respond to a defendant's dissatisfaction with appointed counsel by dismissing the lawyer but by requiring the defendant to continue pro se. Although this sometimes may be an acceptable choice to impose upon a defendant, judges can be too hasty in dismissing counsel from the case.

(9) Attorney Occhetti, of New York's Legal Aid office, was appointed to represent defendant McKee on drug charges. On the morning of the second day of jury selection, McKee requested the court to appoint a different lawyer:

> McKee: Your Honor, the attorney here has been telling me I'm guilty before I even get to trial. If he says that to me, I don't need him.

> Court: Are you saying you want to represent yourself?

> McKee: No Ma'am, I want a new lawyer.

> Court: That application is denied.

> McKee: He is not representing me, and I won't let him speak on my case.

> Court: Your choices are (1) to continue with Mr. Occhetti, (2) to retain your own lawyer, or (3) to represent yourself.

> McKee: I am not going to let this man represent me when he says I am guilty and my chances are slim.

As to his other options, McKee said he did not want to represent himself and that he could not afford to hire an attorney. Finally, after some further colloquy, McKee agreed to represent himself with the help of a "legal advisor."

What result on appeal when McKee complains about the options imposed on him? Did the judge err procedurally in responding to McKee's motion?

(10) Defendant Durfee pleaded guilty to unauthorized use of a telephone credit card. Before sentencing before a different judge, the judge, on his own motion, removed the assistant public defender who was representing Durfee. The judge did this because the lawyer "has engaged in a course of unprofessional, insolent, and contemptuous behavior involving making numerous, unsubstantiated allegations of personal impropriety and lack of integrity on the part of the undersigned judge." The judge also said that continuing the lawyer as court-appointed counsel might cause Durfee "to be concerned that her interests would be lost sight of and may lead to the appearance of injustice." The lawyer's conduct that the judge referred to took place in other cases or outside the courtroom. When Durfee objected, the judge stated he could not trust the lawyer, who had frequently misrepresented the law. The judge then appointed another lawyer to represent Durfee at sentencing and postponed sentencing for three weeks to give the new lawyer time to prepare.

What result on appeal of the 32–to–48 month sentence imposed by the judge?

(11) On May 8, the defendant was arraigned in the Ohio Common Pleas Court on four counts of rape and one count of kidnapping. At the arraignment, the defendant's retained counsel requested that the judge reschedule the trial from May 18 to sometime in early June. She stated that other obligations prevented her from adequately preparing for trial on the 18th. When the judge refused to reschedule the trial, counsel withdrew from the case. The judge then instructed the defendant to hire another attorney for trial on May 18. When the defendant stated that he could not hire another lawyer, the judge appointed one for him.

Appointed counsel immediately moved for a continuance, which the judge denied. On the 18th, counsel again moved for a continuance so that defendant's original retained counsel could resume her representation of the defendant. While the judge denied the motion, she did move the trial to May 22 because of her own scheduling problems.

On May 22, with appointed counsel representing the defendant, trial commenced. On May 24, the jury returned a verdict of guilty on four of the five counts, and the judge ultimately sentenced the defendant to seven to twenty-five years imprisonment. What result on appeal? What role does prejudice to the defendant play in your analysis?

(12) Defendant, who was facing two other felony charges, was arrested on May 14 for the unlawful possession of a blackjack. Joseph Louisell, who represented the defendant in all three cases, obtained two continuances in the blackjack case in October. Complicating rescheduling, Louisell had made arrangements to enter the hospital on Sunday, November 10, for non-emergency diagnostic tests for a heart condition. In addition, Louisell was scheduled to appear as defense counsel in a big federal case with over two hundred witnesses in November.

After negotiations with the judge, Louisell agreed to try one of the defendant's cases in early November, to try the blackjack charge on November 14, to begin the federal trial on November 18, and to try the third charge against the defendant thereafter. On November 12, however, Louisell's partner requested a continuance in the blackjack case because Louisell's hospital tests were taking longer than anticipated. The partner, who was fully familiar with the blackjack case, could not say when Louisell would be ready for trial. Although the partner did not present a medical certificate or an affidavit, Louisell's doctor informed the judge in a phone conversation that Louisell's life was not in danger, but that she had recommended that he stay in the hospital to complete the tests.

Over the defendant's protests, the judge denied the motion for a continuance and ordered Louisell's partner to proceed with the trial. In a trial that lasted less than one day, the defendant was found guilty on the blackjack charge on November 14. What result on appeal?

D. THE EFFECTIVE ASSISTANCE OF COUNSEL

The right to counsel generally means the right to the effective assistance of counsel. Courts have had difficulty, however, in defining what effective assistance means. In particular, courts have struggled with the issue of when a defendant alleging ineffective assistance must prove prejudice and when prejudice will be presumed. The problems in this section explore the problem of ineffective assistance in general, the restraints imposed on counsel by ethical responsibilities, and the particular problems caused by multiple representation.

1. IN GENERAL

(13) Attorney Fitt, an experienced lawyer who had represented approximately 100 criminal defendants, was appointed to represent defendant Mulligan in a murder trial. When Mulligan said that he had been out of state with family, Fitt responded that a "family alibi" often results in conviction. When the prosecutor offered life imprisonment if Mulligan pleaded guilty, Fitt recommended taking the plea. Insisting on his innocence, Mulligan said he would plead not guilty.

Fitt then spoke to family members who corroborated, credibly Fitt believed, Mulligan's story. Fitt also spoke to the prosecutor about the state's eyewitnesses, told the prosecutor to put them in touch with him, but did not make any other efforts to speak with them before trial. Fitt said he knew he would have to show that these witnesses, which included three army officers, were mistaken or lying. Fitt did not talk to Mulligan's codefendant, who was planning to testify that Mulligan shot the victims. Fitt planned, however, to impeach the codefendant by revealing the grant of immunity he was receiving. Finally, believing he already knew the state's witnesses, Fitt turned down the prosecutor's offer to provide him a list of witnesses.

At trial, despite vigorous cross-examination, the eyewitnesses remained certain in their identification of Mulligan. After these witnesses testified, the prosecution called a fingerprint expert, who testified Mulligan's prints were found at the murder scene. Fitt objected because he did not know about this witness, but the judge rejected the objection upon learning that Fitt had declined the prosecutor's offer to provide him a witness list.

At this point, Mulligan whispered to Fitt that he had not told him the truth. Although Fitt had said in his opening statement that Mulligan and his family would testify that they were out of state, Fitt then decided not to call any witnesses for the defense. Instead, in closing argument, Fitt stressed the codefendant's motivation to lie.

What result on appeal after conviction?

(14) On September 23, Assistant Public Defender Cobb attended a lineup for defendant Griffin, who had been arrested for raping a thirteen-year-old girl. Between then and the preliminary hearing on November 11, at which Cobb represented Griffin, Cobb spoke to Griffin several

times, and Griffin gave Cobb the names of several witnesses, some of whom Cobb or his investigator interviewed. Cobb also examined the prosecutor's file, interviewed the arresting officers, and examined statements that Griffin had given the police.

After the preliminary hearing, Griffin indicated to Cobb his desire to retain counsel, and Cobb confirmed this in a letter to Griffin. Cobb presented a formal motion to withdraw on December 1, the day Griffin was indicted, but because Griffin had not succeeded in retaining counsel, the court denied the motion. Trial was scheduled for December 4. On December 3, Cobb asked for a continuance, stating that he was unprepared because he had been in court every day since December 1. The court denied the motion, but told Cobb that another Assistant Public Defender, one Bowling, who had no familiarity with Griffin's case, should help him prepare legal issues.

On December 3, Cobb was in court on another matter until 11:00 p.m. Thereafter, Cobb and Bowling worked on Griffin's case until 2:00 a.m. When trial began on the 4th, Cobb and Bowling unsuccessfully moved for a continuance. After a one-day trial at which no defense witnesses testified, the jury found Griffin guilty of rape.

What result on appeal?

(15) Carroll, Passarella, and Turner were charged with offenses growing out of the kidnapping of a man and his wife and the murder of the man. Pursuant to a plea bargain, Carroll agreed to cooperate and received a two-year sentence for simple kidnapping. Passarella was convicted by a jury of two counts of kidnapping and received a 70–year sentence.

Turner, who was represented by Bailey, his lead attorney, and Binkley, an out-of-state attorney, was charged with two counts of kidnapping and one count of murder. Before trial, the prosecutor made several plea offers, starting at four to ten years, which Turner rejected. Finally, the week before trial, the prosecutor offered two years, the same deal that Carroll had received. Binkley "recommended strongly" that Turner accept the two-year offer, but upon Bailey's advice, Turner countered with one year. When the prosecutor refused the counteroffer, Binkley again recommended accepting the offer of two years; indeed, he described the decision to go to trial as "ludicrous." Carroll's attorney told Binkley that Turner would "be crazy not to take the two-year offer." Relying on Bailey's advice, however, Turner let the deadline for settlement expire.

At trial, Turner was convicted on all three counts and sentenced to life imprisonment on the murder charge and two forty-year sentences on the kidnapping charges, the sentences to run concurrently. What result on appeal? If Turner is entitled to relief, what remedy is appropriate?

(16) Samuel and his codefendant Spencer were convicted of burglary after a two day trial. Their motion for a new trial was denied by the trial judge about six weeks after the trial, and they were sentenced to six years in prison. A year later, Samuel filed a petition for post-conviction relief, alleging that his experienced counsel was ineffective for failing to file a notice of appeal, thereby precluding his direct appeal. Samuel's counsel testified at a hearing on the petition that he had "off and on" conversations with Samuel about the possibility of an appeal, but that his client opted not to appeal if he received a sentence of six years or less. After sentencing, counsel stated that they talked about good time credits and where Samuel would serve his sentence, but he was emphatic that there was no further conversation about an appeal.

Samuel said that after sentencing he told counsel that he wanted to appeal and counsel at that time stood up to leave the room. Various family members and Samuel's girlfriend testified that his trial lawyer told them that he would handle the appeal, but counsel testified that he never told defendant or members of his family that he would file a notice of appeal on defendant's behalf. His only conversations with them related to the filing of a motion for new trial. After the hearing on the petition, Samuel contends that his counsel was not credible and, that even if he was credible, he performed in a professionally deficient manner because the failure to file an appeal fell below an objective standard of reasonableness. How should the court rule on the petition for post-conviction relief?

2. ETHICAL CONSIDERATIONS

(17) Henkel, charged with mail fraud, was represented by a lawyer who had previously represented him in two cases resulting in acquittals and one resulting in a hung jury. The present case was a retrial of the hung jury case. After both sides had rested and were about to begin closing arguments, counsel advised the court that, against his advice, Henkel wished to testify. When the court re-opened the case, counsel moved to withdraw, saying that he could not "professionally proceed." The court then commended counsel for not participating in his client's lies and said to Henkel, "I assume he just doesn't think the testimony will be honest." Henkel did not contradict these statements, but asked for a chance to confer with counsel. When Henkel indicated after conferring with his lawyer that he wanted to testify, the court denied counsel's motion to withdraw and permitted Henkel to testify without guidance.

What result on appeal following the jury's conviction of Henkel?

(18) Michael Hitch was indicted for murder. Diane Heaton, Hitch's girlfriend, told police investigators that the victim was in possession of a certain wristwatch before his death. Subsequently, Heaton told an investigator from the Public Defender's Office that she had found a watch in Hitch's suit pocket and that she did not want to turn it over to the police. The defendant's attorney then told the investigator to take possession of the watch and bring it to the attorney.

The attorney then requested an opinion from the Ethics Committee, which informed her that she was legally obligated to turn the watch over to the police and that she might also be compelled to testify as to its source. When the attorney informed the trial judge of the decision, the judge ordered her to give the watch to the police and to withdraw from the case.

What result on the attorney's appeal from the judge's order? What if the attorney received the watch from Hitch?

(19) While Fairbank was in jail waiting for trial on murder charges, the police obtained letters that Fairbank allegedly wrote to another inmate. The letters made reference to weapons that Fairbank had stashed away but that now were in his lawyers' hands. The prosecutor then moved the trial court for an order compelling the defense lawyers to produce the weapons. The court denied the order.

What result on the prosecutor's petition to a higher court for a writ of mandamus?

3. CONFLICTS OF INTEREST

(20) Hoffman was charged as an accessory to murder. Allegedly, at Hoffman's instigation, George Moose, Hoffman's brother-in-law, hired someone to kill the victim. When Moose was arrested, Hoffman paid to have Long represent him; when the police threatened to arrest Hoffman, he also retained Long. The day following Hoffman's arrest, Long negotiated a plea agreement for Moose.

When the case was called for trial, the judge ascertained that Hoffman knew that Long also represented Moose; that if he testified, his testimony might affect Moose; and that if Moose testified, Moose's testimony might affect him. Hoffman stated that he was satisfied with Long and that he had no problem with Long's representing Moose. The judge then repeated the inquiry with Moose. Long said that he saw no possibility of a conflict.

The next day, the court accepted a guilty plea from Moose. At Hoffman's trial, Moose, who received a sentence of twenty years when he could have been sentenced to death, testified that Hoffman had paid him to kill the person who had raped Hoffman's wife (who was also Moose's sister). Hoffman testified that he had told Moose the plan was off before the killing. The jury convicted Hoffman, and he subsequently received a life sentence.

At a habeas corpus hearing following unsuccessful state appeals, Moose testified that he had never informed Hoffman of his plea arrangement. Claiming that he had not known Moose was going to testify against him, Hoffman testified that he did not object to joint representation because he had thought that he and Moose would testify to the same facts. Long testified that he had told Hoffman that the police had asked Moose to cooperate, and that Hoffman had said to tell Moose to testify truthfully.

What result?

(21) Charged with robbery and murder, Horace Ford and his brother, Thomas, jointly retained one lawyer to represent both of them. Horace wanted to go to trial, but Thomas wanted to plead guilty and request mercy from the court. The prosecutor for the State of Georgia said that she would agree not to seek the death penalty, but only if both brothers pleaded guilty. Under pressure from his mother, Horace changed his mind and pleaded guilty. He received two consecutive life sentences.

What result on appeal?

(22) Defendants McCormick and Mahon, represented by the same retained counsel, were jointly charged with capital murder. In a pretrial hearing, the prosecutor moved for a severance. Each defendant had given a confession that strongly implicated the other, and the prosecutor viewed a severance as a way to avoid confrontation problems.

Aware that an actual conflict would arise if separate trials were ordered, which would force them to withdraw and refund a portion of their cash fees, defense counsel opposed the severance motion. (The conflict was that having learned of confidential information from a client who chose to testify in a separate trial, counsel would have been ethically precluded from using this information in cross-examination.) The judge denied the prosecutor's motion.

Because the court denied suppression motions for both confessions, counsel's strategy was to show that a promise of leniency had induced McCormick to confess and that the police used this confession, which implicated Mahon, to get Mahon to confess. When the case was tried, however, the prosecutor only introduced Mahon's confession, which contained references to McCormick that were not capable of being successfully excised. The court ruled, however, that McCormick had waived any confrontation problems by objecting to the severance. Both defendants were found guilty.

At sentencing, counsel called an equal number of reputation witnesses for both defendants. Counsel did not offer evidence that McCormick did not receive any significant remuneration for the killing, because this would imply that Mahon received the lion's share. Counsel also refrained from arguing theories of lesser culpability for McCormick. In nine pages of argument, counsel argued that the state had failed to prove beyond a reasonable doubt that "they" would be a continuing threat to society. Both men were sentenced to death.

What result when both defendants seek habeas corpus relief?

E.   THE EQUALITY PRINCIPLE

Indigent defendants sometimes need assistance other than counsel or at stages other than "the criminal prosecution." The Court has generally treated these issues under the heading of equal protection rather than due process or effective assistance of counsel. Given the Court's approach to equal protection, would it matter which label the Court used?

Supreme Court dicta once suggested that the kind of trial a person gets should not turn on the amount of money he has. Obviously, this dicta went too far. Can the state provide to every indigent the kind of defense O.J. Simpson was able to buy? (If not, the only way of making sure that money does not matter is to preclude the wealthy from spending their money on their own defenses.) Students should consider, however, whether the Court has drawn the necessary limiting line in the right place. If not the Court's line, what line?

(23) After defendant's one-day trial for armed robbery in Council Bluffs, Iowa, the court dismissed the deadlocked jury and scheduled a new trial six days later. Sixteen witnesses testified during the first trial, including three government eyewitnesses. Before the second trial, defense counsel petitioned the court for a free transcript of the first trial. The court denied the motion, stating that during the second trial defense counsel would be permitted to ask the court reporter to read back any testimony that might be helpful in cross-examination. Immediately after the mistrial, the government purchased a copy of the entire transcript.

On the morning of the second trial, the government furnished defense counsel the transcript of the three eyewitnesses' testimony, and counsel used this transcript to cross-examine these witnesses. Defense counsel never suggested to the trial court that any other witness had contradicted his earlier testimony and never asked the court reporter to read back any testimony from the first trial. After hearing testimony, the jury convicted the defendant.

What result on appeal?

(24) An information charged the defendant with murder. The victim died eight months after being shot. According to the county medical examiner, the victim died from a pulmonary embolism that resulted from a thrombosis in her leg, which in turn resulted from immobilization caused by paralysis from the shooting. Prior to trial, appointed counsel requested that the court provide $600 for an independent forensic pathologist to evaluate the medical evidence. Counsel argued that she could not personally evaluate the accuracy of the medical examiner's conclusions, that blood clots have many causes, and that the question of causation was pivotal in the case. Stating that she had no authority to provide such funds, the judge denied the motion.

At trial, the medical examiner conceded that it is unusual for a pulmonary embolism to occur as long as eight months after a trauma. The examiner also indicated that the victim had cirrhosis of the liver, an ailment that may cause an embolism. Questioned about his certainty concerning the causal connection between the shooting and the embolism, the examiner responded that he could not be 100% sure about anything in medicine but that he had the highest degree of medical certainty.

What result on appeal after conviction?

(25) An indictment charged the defendant and two co-defendants with raping a fourteen-year-old girl and her mother and with raping and beating to death her seventy-nine-year-old grandmother after breaking into their home early one morning in 1996. Prior to trial, defendant's appointed counsel requested the court to provide funds for a psychiatrist and a psychologist. Under state law, the trial court had discretion to make such expenditures in murder cases. The judge allocated funds for the psychiatrist, but denied funds for the psychologist.

Relying on psychological tests performed in 1982, 1985, 1989, and 1990, the defense psychiatrist at trial diagnosed the defendant as a psychopathic delinquent suffering from organic brain damage, unable either to deliberate prior to activity or to understand the nature and quality of his actions. The psychiatrist denied the need for more recent psychological tests, stating that test results do not significantly change after age six. A state psychiatrist described the defendant as having a psychopathic personality with no organic brain damage, capable of understanding his actions. He based his diagnosis on a pretrial test administered by a state-employed psychologist.

What result when the defendant seeks habeas corpus after conviction and appeal?

(26) The victim was raped early one morning by an assailant who had hidden in her closet. The assailant wore one of the victim's blouses over his head, but during the attack, it slipped off for about 60 seconds, allowing the victim to see a partial right profile of his face. Two days later, officer Lincecum hypnotized the victim, using the "T.V. screen" method of hypnosis. Under this technique, the subject views the events as though they are on a video; she can stop the action and zoom in for close-ups. In a session lasting several hours, the victim was unable to add to her description of the assailant. Lincecum, whose only training in hypnosis was a four-day course he attended at the Law Enforcement Hypnosis Institute, told the victim not to worry because her memory would improve in time.

On three subsequent occasions, the victim viewed photographs of men not including defendant Little. On the first occasion, she said a man in the display resembled the man who had raped her. Shown a fourth photo display one month later, the victim picked Little out as the man who had raped her. A month later, the victim picked Little out of a six-person lineup. Little claimed to have been 80 miles away when the crime occurred.

Prior to trial, the appointed lawyer representing Little requested funds for an expert in hypnosis. What result and why?

Chapter 17

TRIAL BY JURY

A. SCOPE AND MEANING OF THE RIGHT

The Sixth Amendment right to trial by jury does not apply to "petty" offenses. Although the Court has clarified the concept of a petty offense, there remains a gray area that can trouble the courts. In addition, the scope of the right to trial by jury is affected by issues concerning unanimity (at least in federal cases), jury nullification, and the anonymity of jurors.

(1) A federal information charged six defendants with violating the Freedom of Access to Clinic Entrances Act of 1994 for nonviolently blockading the entrances to an abortion clinic in Milwaukee. When the offense is nonviolent, it is punishable by imprisonment of not more than six months and/or a fine of not more than $10,000.

In 18 U.S.C. § 19, Congress in 1984 and 1988 defined an offense as "petty" if it is punishable by no more than six months in prison or by a fine not greater than $5,000 for an individual or $10,000 for an organization. While this provision does not create a statutory right to jury trial, its legislative history indicates Congressional awareness of the Supreme Court's practice in jury cases of looking to Congressional definitions of what is a petty offense.

What result when the defendants demand a jury trial? What if the Freedom of Access statute authorized a fine of one million dollars? How are courts to draw the line between petty and non-petty offenses?

(2) Under Nebraska law, conviction of a third offense for driving under the influence of alcohol is punishable by three to six months' imprisonment, revocation of the offender's driving license for 15 years, and a fine of up to $500. Before Nebraska amended its law, a third DUIL offense was punishable by up to five years' imprisonment, a $10,000 fine, and a one-year revocation of the offender's driving license. The penalty for failure to take a breathalyzer test is seven days' imprisonment, a $200 fine, and a six-month suspension of driving privileges. The penalties can be imposed to run consecutively.

Defendant Richter was charged with a third DUIL offense and with refusing to take a breathalyzer test. What result when Richter demands a jury trial? What if the Nebraska statute specifically precludes jury trial?

(3) An information charged the defendant with "molesting" for allegedly stroking the hair and neck of two eight-year-old girls. After plea bargaining, the prosecutor dismissed the molesting charge in return for the defendant's guilty plea to simple battery, a misdemeanor punishable by no more than six months' imprisonment and/or a $1,000 fine. A presentence report revealed that the defendant had a history of caressing, combing, and cutting the hair of young girls and that he had been committed several times to state mental hospitals.

The trial judge then adjourned sentencing and instituted the statutory procedure to determine whether the defendant was a "mentally disordered sex offender," defined by state law as "any person who by reason of mental defect, disease, or disorder is predisposed to the commission of sexual offenses to such a degree that he is dangerous to the health and safety of others." Under the law, mentally disordered sex offenders who can benefit from treatment are committed to a state hospital, while those who cannot benefit from treatment are committed to the custody of the Department of Health in a "state institution or institutional unit." Such "units" are typically on the grounds of regular prison facilities.

After the requisite diagnostic tests, the court held an evidentiary hearing to determine the defendant's status. Before beginning the hearing, the court denied the defendant's request for a jury trial, observing that state law did not require jury trials in civil commitment proceedings. Two doctors then testified that the defendant was a mentally disordered sex offender who posed potential dangers to the public, while a third doctor testified that the defendant had a mere personality defect and that he posed no risk of harm to society. The experts agreed that treatment would not cure his condition.

The court found the defendant to be a mentally disordered sex offender and a danger to the health and safety of others. Also finding that the defendant would not benefit from treatment in a mental hospital, the court committed him to the custody of the Department of Health "until such time as a finding is made that he is not a danger to others." What result on appeal?

(4) The defendant was tried in federal court for unlawfully accepting money to broadcast records on radio. After the jury twice reported itself deadlocked, a juror sent the court a note stating that he, as "the primary holdout," could not in good conscience change his opinion. Noting the possibility of other holdouts, the court asked whether defense counsel would accept a 10–2 verdict. After conferring with the defendant, counsel advised the court that they would only accept a unanimous verdict. The following colloquy then occurred.

Court: Take a verdict of ten jurors, agreement of ten?

Counsel: Eleven. If he says "I am holding out."

Court: He says, "I am the primary one."

Counsel: Let's see if we can get a jury of eleven.

Court: Is that agreeable?

Counsel (addressing the defendant): Would that be agreeable to you?
I suggest you do it. You are not going to get a better trial. I am
telling you right now.

Counsel: Yes, eleven, yes.

Court: All right, bring the jury back. I will dismiss this one juror and
tell the others.

A short while later, after further deliberation by the eleven remaining jurors, the court received another note that read, "I am under the
same opinion. May I be excused?" Before the court responded, the jury
sent word to disregard the note because it had agreed upon a verdict.
The jury found the defendant guilty.

What result on appeal?

(5) The defendant was tried before a federal jury for possession of
cocaine with intent to distribute. When the jury entered the courtroom
to return a verdict, the judge asked the foreperson whether they had
reached a unanimous verdict. The foreperson indicated that they had.
After the clerk read from a jury form indicating the verdict was guilty,
the judge immediately polled the jury as to whether this was each juror's
true and correct verdict. When the judge reached juror number seven,
the juror responded, "with reluctance, yes." When the judge had completed the jury poll, she announced that the verdict was unanimous and
entered it on the record.

What result on appeal?

(6) The defendant was charged with criminal sexual conduct. Under the
applicable statute, a person commits the offense by having sexual penetration with another if "(f) the actor causes personal injury to the
victim and force or coercion is used to accomplish the penetration."
Another statutory provision defines personal injury as "bodily injury,
disfigurement, mental anguish, chronic pain, pregnancy, disease.... "

The judge submitted the case to the jury under both the bodily
injury and mental anguish definitions of personal injury. Arguing that
these were alternate theories of guilt, the defendant alleges on appeal
that the trial judge erred in failing to instruct the jury to acquit if it did
not find one or the other unanimously. What result?

(7) A federal indictment charged defendant Veatch with bank fraud and
with making false statements to a federally insured financial institution.
At trial, Veatch elected to waive counsel and represent himself. During
closing arguments, the following occurred:

Veatch: There's little to add except to provide you that the U.S.
Constitution is the supreme law of the land. I love what's left of our
Constitution. You have the power to go ahead and give me to these

people; there's no doubt, they're my enemy. You also have the power as jurors to nullify any law.

Prosecutor: I object. That's not the law and it's contrary to the instruction of this court.

What is your ruling as trial judge?

(8) A federal indictment charged the defendant with being a felon in possession of ammunition in violation of 18 U.S.C. § 922(g)(1). Under the Armed Career Criminal Act, 18 U.S.C. § 924(e), the defendant faced a fifteen-year mandatory minimum sentence because he had three prior convictions for violent or drug crimes. Prior to jury deliberation, the defendant requested that the jury be informed of the fifteen-year mandatory minimum. The trial judge refused.

What result on appeal? What purpose would advice as to the mandatory minimum serve?

(9) An indictment charged Peter Vario, an official of Local 66 of the Laborers' International Union of North America, with conspiracy to violate the Racketeer Influenced and Corrupt Organizations Act (RICO). The indictment also charged that Vario had committed sixty-nine acts of racketeering in furtherance of the conspiracy, including the solicitation and receipt of payoffs from contractors in violation of the Taft–Hartley Act. More specifically, the indictment alleged that Vario had extorted payments from concrete contractors, who, in return for their payments, were permitted to violate collective bargaining agreements. Resistance to payment demands was met by economic reprisals from the union.

In a pretrial status conference, the government's attorney moved to empanel an anonymous jury—one in which the jurors' names, addresses, and places of work are not revealed to the defendant or defense counsel. In support of its motion, the government presented evidence that Vario was a member of the Lucchese organized crime family, that high-ranking members of the Lucchese family shared in the extortion payoffs, and that efforts to engage in jury tampering had recently occurred in the unrelated organized crime trial of John Gotti.

What result? What if the government also alleged that a coconspirator had contacted a known member of the grand jury before it returned the indictment? Why should the identities and addresses of jurors ever be disclosed?

B. JURY SELECTION: THE CROSS–SECTION REQUIREMENT

(10) An indictment charged the defendant with robbery. On the day of trial, 300 people were summoned for jury duty, 136 of whom were women. Twenty-five of the summoned women claimed an exemption under a statute excusing from jury service any woman with legal custody of a child or children under age 10. Once all statutory exemptions had been claimed, a court official, selecting at random from the remaining names, sent a group of 50 prospective jurors, 20 of whom were women, to the defendant's courtroom. The defendant's jury had eight men and four women.

What result on appeal after conviction?

(11) An indictment charged the defendant with smuggling marijuana. Before trial, the defendant moved to quash the entire jury venire on the ground that black males, young persons between 18–29, and the less advantaged were substantially underrepresented. The district in question selects names at random from voter registration lists and places them in a Master Jury Wheel. As jurors are needed, the clerk selects names from the wheel and mails each a Juror Qualification Questionnaire. Those people who are qualified to serve are determined from the returned questionnaires; those people not disqualified or excused are placed in a Qualified Jury Wheel.

A professor of mathematics and statistics testified for the defendant that black males comprise 8% of the district's population, 5.5% of the district's registered voters, and 4.9% of those who return the questionnaires. Fewer black males than white males were registered to vote, and fewer returned the questionnaires. In the professor's view, the data demonstrated, "in a statistical sense," that the juror selection system did not operate in a "purely random fashion." The clerk admitted that he did not follow up on persons who failed to file or who filed incomplete questionnaires.

With respect to the "less advantaged," unemployed persons comprised 13% of the population but only 3% of those in the Qualified Jury Wheel. For those not graduating from high school, the comparable figures were 8% and 2%. The defendant argued that these disparities resulted from the clerk's willingness to grant hardship exemptions to low-income people and from the clerk's authority to disqualify anyone "unable to read, write, and understand English with a degree of proficiency to fill out satisfactorily the Juror Questionnaire."

Assuming that the defendant presents comparable data on the 18–29 age group, what result on his various claims? Is statistical analysis necessary for each claim? If statistical analysis is used, what are the appropriate figures? For example, are black males underrepresented by 3.1%?

(12) Charged with attempted murder of a Des Plaines police officer, defendant Davis was tried in a branch of the Cook County Circuit Court located in Des Plaines, a northwest suburb of Chicago. Prior to trial, defense counsel observed that, although Cook County was 25.6% black, all of the forty prospective jurors in Davis's case were white. According to counsel, the array was composed of people who lived in predominantly white northwest suburbs of Chicago and the predominantly white northwest side of Chicago.

Counsel deposed Daniel Covelli, the county jury supervisor. Covelli, who did not remember the exact procedure used in Davis's case, outlined the steps he commonly took in selecting juries. Up to 1000 potential jurors reported to the Daly Center in Chicago every Monday. Members of Covelli's staff picked at random twice the number of jurors needed. Covelli then asked those persons living in or near the suburbs to volunteer for service at suburban courthouses. If not enough people volunteered for the suburban courthouses, Covelli would pick the rest randomly. Davis also deposed a statistician, who stated that the probability of selecting forty white jurors at random from Cook County was seven chances in a million.

What result on defendant's motion to quash the venire and why? Does it matter that an Illinois statute permits juries to be drawn from all of Cook County, its northern half, or its southern half? What if the statute specifically authorized jury selection from just the northern suburbs? Has the defendant done enough to prove systematic exclusion?

C. JURY SELECTION: THE VOIR DIRE

Constitutional issues play a minor role in the conduct of the *voir dire*. In examining the problems that follow, students should assess the importance of counsel's requested questions in developing challenges for cause and peremptory challenges. Students should also consider the issue of whether the judge or the lawyers should question the prospective jurors.

(13) A state indictment in Virginia charged Norwood and Linda Barber with the sale of marijuana. At the beginning of trial, defense counsel asked the judge to inquire whether any member of the panel would prejudge the defendants because they were an interracial couple: Norwood is black; Linda is white. The state's attorney objected that such a question would make race an issue in the case, but defense counsel argued the question would clear the air: "I'd like to clear the jurors' subconscious and agree that race is not an issue." The judge denied the request, explaining that it would inject race into the trial. The judge did ask whether the jurors knew of any reason why they could not "hear the facts of this case fairly and impartially and render a just verdict."

What result on federal habeas corpus after conviction and appeal? Does it matter that interracial marriage was a crime in Virginia until the Supreme Court invalidated the prohibition in 1967? Does it matter that a recent Gallup Poll found that 42% of Americans (54% of Southerners) disapproved of marriages between blacks and whites? What if the defendants were appealing a federal conviction?

(14) A federal indictment charged Basil and Geoffrey Kyles, both black, with armed bank robbery. Specifically, the indictment alleged that two men, armed with semi-automatic weapons, entered a bank in Connecticut, that one guarded the door, and that the other vaulted the counter and forced the tellers to stuff money into a plastic bag. None of the tellers was injured during the robbery.

Before jury selection, Basil's counsel, observing that all the bank tellers were white, requested the judge to ask the prospective jurors whether they had "any opinions or inclinations" about Basil because he was black. The judge declined, asking instead whether any of the prospective jurors ever had been crime victims or had relatives in law enforcement.

What result on appeal after conviction?

(15) An indictment charged Daniel Heller, a lawyer, with three counts of tax evasion and three counts of making false statements on income tax returns. After a complex 12–week trial, the case went to the jury. One day after deliberations began, the court received a note from the jury foreperson advising it that some jurors had made ethnic slurs and that a juror had discussed the case with an accountant outside the courtroom. When Heller moved for a mistrial, the judge decided to question each juror individually to "get rid of the taint we have seen here."

During the questioning, one of the jurors, Shatten, reported over-hearing another juror say the defendant was a Jew and "I say, let's hang him." Shatten said that when a rabbi testified for the defense, one juror provoked laughter by saying that the rabbi had come to bless Heller. Shatten also said that one of the jurors, in an apparent reference to the surnames of defense witnesses, asked with a smirk "how many Kaplans are we going to have." Shatten added that three or four people on the jury had "the appearance of a lynch mob."

Juror Nolan admitted making the comment about hanging the defendant, but said that he had been teasing. Other jurors verified that several jurors had made numerous racial and religious slurs and that one juror had told a story about a "rich Jew." In addition, the Court confirmed that one of the jurors, in violation of the court's instructions, had privately sought the opinion of an accountant.

The judge concluded his questioning of the jurors by asking whether they were prejudiced and whether, in light of what had occurred, they could decide the case strictly on the law and the evidence, free from bias. Following the individual assurances, the judge called the entire jury into the courtroom and got the same assurance from the group. Over defense objection, the judge then permitted the jury to resume deliberations. The jury returned a guilty verdict on all counts in 90 minutes.

What result on appeal? What were the judge's options?

(16) An indictment charged the defendant with sexually assaulting and murdering a seven-year-old girl. Prior to trial, the judge announced that she would not permit counsel to conduct the *voir dire,* but that they could submit questions for her consideration. The defense then informed the court that it would rely entirely on an insanity defense.

In conducting the *voir dire,* the trial judge rejected several of defense counsel's proposed questions concerning the insanity defense. One question sought to determine the prior experience of jurors in cases in which the insanity defense had been raised. Two other questions sought to determine the willingness of jurors to accept the insanity defense. In explaining her decision, the judge stated, "It isn't their attitudes. It is the law they have to comply with." Later she added, "We know the insanity defense is a very technical legal charge they have to get. It is like asking jurors if they agree with the presumption of innocence and burden of proof. I will instruct them in due course. I won't ask anything on insanity."

What result when the defendant appeals after conviction? To win relief, should the defendant have the burden of producing some evidence of the jurors' bias against the insanity defense? If so, how would he show this? Should the outcome turn on the care with which the judge conducted the rest of the *voir dire*?

(17) The defendant was charged with armed robbery. The prosecutor's evidence showed that a cab driver, who could not identify the defendant, informed the police that two men had stolen his cab. Shortly thereafter, an officer observed the cab and engaged it in a high speed chase, which ended when the cab crashed. The driver fled and was never apprehended. The officer testified, however, that a jammed door on the passenger side of the cab trapped the defendant. According to the officer, the defendant only had three cents and was trying to flee. The defendant testified that he could have emerged from the cab but chose not to do so. He also denied any knowledge of the robbery and claimed that he had five dollars on his person for cab fare.

Before jury selection, defendant requested that the judge ask whether any prospective jurors would believe the testimony of a police officer over that of a civilian. What result? Would an affirmative answer to the requested question subject a juror to removal for cause?

(18) An information charged the defendant with selling heroin and cocaine. The information was based on an arrest by Officer Bratcher, who claimed to have pursued the defendant after witnessing what appeared to be a narcotics sale on the street.

During *voir dire*, the judge asked the prospective jurors six questions: whether they had knowledge about this case; whether they knew any of the participants; whether they were related to anyone who had been a drug victim or a drug defendant; whether they would give more weight to the testimony of a police officer than that of a civilian; whether there was anything that would keep them from rendering a fair and impartial verdict; and whether there was any reason they should not sit on this case. The judge declined the defense's request to ask whether any of the jurors were or had been members of the law enforcement community or had a close relative who was or had been such a member. The defendant argued, among other things, that such a question would enhance his ability to exercise the ten peremptory challenges provided by law.

What result on appeal? Would an affirmative answer to the requested question subject a juror to removal for cause?

D. JURY SELECTION: CHALLENGES FOR CAUSE

(19) A state indictment charged the defendant with first-degree murder and negligent homicide in connection with the shooting to death of his father and sister. During *voir dire*, juror Stump admitted reading about the case and forming some "drastic opinions" about it, saying, "Well, I think it's pretty bad when you kill your family members." Nevertheless, Stump said that she could be fair and impartial and decide the case solely on the evidence produced in court. "A lot of things come out now that weren't in the paper, you know." Stump further said that "even if he did it, there might have been circumstances that it's just not as black and white as I thought at the beginning. But I still—it's hard. I'm really going through a wringer, because I still think, basically, you don't kill your family members." When Stump repeated that she could be fair and impartial, the judge rejected a defense request to remove her for cause.

Juror Earnshaw spoke up when the judge asked whether there was anyone who felt, for any reason, that he or she could not be impartial. She pointed to the fact the defendant was a teenager, and she said that her beliefs concerning capital punishment "caused her a problem." Without any further probing, the judge granted the prosecutor's motion to dismiss Earnshaw for cause.

What result on appeal from the defendant's conviction and sentence of death? (Assume the defendant used all his peremptories.)

(20) Defendant, who was sixteen years old, belonged to the "skinheads," a white supremacist organization. According to the indictment, defendant and two friends, also skinheads, engaged in a drive-by killing of an African–American male. The defendant entered a not guilty plea.

During *voir dire*, juror Booker said that he believed that defendant was a member of the skinheads and that he had murdered a black man. Booker, who is black, also said that he believed the defendant was his enemy. Booker also said that he would presume the defendant to be innocent and that he would require the state to prove its case. The judge refused to removed Booker for cause. At the end of the *voir dire*, counsel renewed the objection to Booker and requested one additional peremptory challenge. The judge denied both motions.

What result on appeal after conviction? Does it matter whether the defendant used all his peremptory challenges?

(21) A state indictment charged the defendant with murder in connection with the killing of a three-year-old child. Before jury selection, the judge informed the venire that the range of punishment was a minimum of five years' probation, when the defendant has no prior felony conviction, to a maximum of life imprisonment. During *voir dire*, defense counsel asked potential jurors whether they would be able to consider probation in a murder case in which a child had died. One of the panel answered the question negatively, but the judge, ruling the question improper as committing the jury to specific facts, refused to dismiss the juror for cause. The jury then convicted the defendant and imposed a thirty-year sentence.

What result on appeal?

(22) An indictment charged the defendants with burglary, armed robbery, and assault with a dangerous weapon. According to the government, the defendants entered the rectory of Saint Paul's Catholic Church, ostensibly to arrange a baptism. Instead, they robbed Fathers Kemp and Bouchard at gunpoint. At trial, the defendants requested that all Catholics be removed for cause from the jury panel. When the motion failed, the defendants requested that each juror be asked whether he or she could, if the evidence suggested it, find a priest's testimony untruthful. The court denied the request.

What result on appeal after conviction?

E. JURY SELECTION: PEREMPTORY CHALLENGES

(23) Defendant Branch, a black man, was tried for murder in Alabama. During *voir dire*, Branch moved to have the jury dismissed after the prosecution used six of its seven peremptory challenges to strike six of the seven blacks from the venire. When asked to explain the strikes, the prosecutor gave the following explanations:

"Regarding Mr. Harris, I was on a drug bust five months ago at a home close to Harris's. I saw him at the time, and I can't recall whether he was a relative of the person we busted. Besides, he appeared to be near in age and overall appearance to the defendant, not counting the fact that they're both black.

"Juror Maynor was undesirable because Gold Kist's employees, black and white, have not been attentive as jurors in other cases and because a number of them are being investigated for a variety of crimes.

"Juror Meadow's background as an unemployed, former student was unattractive, and she appeared to have a dumbfounded or bewildered look on her face.

"Juror Montgomery, as a scientist, would have put too great of a burden upon the prosecution, especially given the problems with one-hundred-percent mathematical aspects of a case like this.

"Juror Parmer was unkempt and gruff. He was also in credit management, and he might be at odds with other jury members.

"Juror Kelly as a single female the defendant's age might have felt like the defendant's sister. Moreover, she had a frown on her face and her mood seemed bad. She also seemed more friendly to the defense."

What do you do now as trial judge? Would it help you to know that the prosecutor did not strike two white jurors with jobs similar to

Montgomery's? What result if you find the prosecutor was being truthful in his responses? What if you do not believe the prosecutor was being truthful? What result on appeal if the trial judge does (does not) conclude that the prosecutor used the peremptories to exclude blacks?

(24) In selecting a jury in defendant's prosecution for selling drugs, the prosecutor struck the only black in the first panel of prospective jurors tendered to the defense, three of the six blacks in the second panel, and two of the four blacks in the third panel. The jury was composed of six blacks and six whites.

Does the prosecutor have to explain her use of peremptories? What result on appeal if the trial judge does (does not) conclude that the prosecutor used the peremptories to exclude blacks?

(25) An indictment charged the defendant, a black man, with armed robbery and attempted murder of a police officer. During *voir dire*, a total of ten blacks and thirty-seven whites were examined during nine rounds of questioning. The prosecutor used ten peremptory challenges, seven against blacks, three against whites. The seven blacks were from both sexes and had varied backgrounds, but two of the three blacks whom the prosecutor did not challenge had ties to law enforcement. Defense counsel used two peremptory challenges against these two jurors; the remaining black sat on the jury.

When the defense objected to the prosecutor's use of her peremptory challenges, the prosecutor pointed out the jury it had tendered the defense included 25% blacks (3/12), and that this closely approximated the 30% of the community represented by blacks.

Does the prosecutor have to explain her use of peremptories? What result on appeal if the trial judge does (does not) conclude that the prosecutor used the peremptories to exclude blacks?

(26) An indictment charged the defendant with murdering her husband by stabbing him in the back. In selecting the jury, the prosecutor exercised six peremptory challenges and one challenge for cause, with all but two of the peremptory challenges being against women. Trial began with a jury composed of nine men and three women. After a woman alternate replaced a man, the trial ended with a jury of eight men and four women.

Does the prosecutor have to explain her use of peremptories? What if the judge requires an explanation, and the prosecutor responds that the excluded women all had histories of being battered?

Chapter 18

SELECTED TRIAL ISSUES

Many issues that arise during a criminal trial, such as issues concerning the rights of cross-examination and compulsory process, are considered in Evidence, Criminal Law, or other courses. The problems that follow touch on just a few of the issues that may arise.

A. THE DEFENDANT'S RIGHT TO REMAIN SILENT

(1) An indictment charged the defendant with housebreaking having the intent to commit assault and steal property. At trial, the state's evidence disclosed that a fifteen-year-old girl, Courtney Whitten, came home with two friends, James Anderson and Charles Nowlin. Upon entering the apartment, they discovered the defendant attempting to hide behind a bedroom door. In explanation, the defendant claimed that he was waiting for the return of a friend, who had left him at the apartment. When the alleged friend did not appear, the girl called the police.

The defendant did not testify in his own behalf. During closing argument, the prosecutor said,

> Do you know what he said, "A friend brought me there." Now I will tell you something, I would like to know where is that friend today. That's what he told James Anderson and Charles Nowlin, and that is what he said in the presence of Courtney Whitten, "Oh, I am here. A friend told me to wait here." Where is the friend? Who is the friend? If you were on trial and wound up in somebody's house by mistake because a person that you trusted said, "Wait here, I'll be right back. I am going around the corner to run an errand," why, you would be screaming from the roof tops that the friend is John Brown or John Jones or whoever is was that asked you to stay there. He lives at such an address and you would have him down here. You would have him here to explain why you were in the house if you have an explanation, if you weren't a thief, if you weren't a burglar.

What result on appeal after conviction?

(2) A federal indictment charged the defendant with conspiracy to transfer machine guns. Before trial began, the trial judge read to potential jurors a list of witnesses, including the defendant, who would possibly testify at trial. The judge was seeking to ascertain whether any of the potential jurors were acquainted with any of the potential witnesses.

What result when the defendant argues that the judge's conduct called the jury's attention to whether he would remain silent?

(3) An indictment jointly charged the defendant and a codefendant with rape. At trial, the complainant testified that the codefendant held her hands while the defendant disrobed her and forced her to submit to sexual intercourse. Testifying in his own behalf, the defendant admitted intercourse with the complainant but claimed consent. The codefendant did not testify. During closing argument, the prosecutor improperly commented on the codefendant's failure to testify. After deliberating, the jury convicted both men as charged.

What result when the *defendant* appeals? Does this problem raise a Fifth Amendment issue? A standing issue? A confrontation issue?

B.   LIMITS ON CLOSING ARGUMENT

(4) At the defendant's trial for carrying a concealed deadly weapon, the prosecutor called only one witness, a police officer who testified that he discovered three pistols in an automobile after a traffic stop. The defendant, who had been a passenger, testified and denied knowing that guns were in the automobile. On cross-examination, the prosecutor probed extensively into the defendant's financial history, employment record, and means of supporting his family. In closing argument, the prosecutor, over objection, continued with this theme:

> Consider the fact too that the defendant had two cents in his pocket at the time he was arrested. Now, what are the proofs? Think about it. There's a man with two cents in his pocket and he hasn't worked for a long time; there's three guns, three fully loaded weapons in the vehicle. That is something that you can consider when you decide whether or not this defendant committed this particular violation.

What result on appeal after conviction? Should a *per se* rule exist about the argument made in this case? What if the defendant had been charged with attempted robbery? If the argument went too far, could a cautionary instruction from the judge have cured it? What result when the defendant seeks a federal writ of habeas corpus?

(5) An information charged the defendant with felonious assault of a police officer. At trial, a police officer testified that when he responded to a radio report of a shooting, he found the defendant holding a gun. The officer added that the defendant then pointed the gun at his chest. The defendant and his landlord testified that the defendant did not point the gun at the officer and that he dropped the gun when ordered to do so. During closing argument, the prosecutor said:

> Everyday policemen are called pigs, and people assault them with their fists and words. You know, they don't bring these things in. Those people are never charged with offenses. They don't bring these things into court unless they really happened. The point is the reason why they're here is this actually happened as the officers testified that it happened.

What result on appeal? What if the judge told the jury to disregard this argument? What result on federal habeas corpus?

(6) A paid informant testified as the state's principal witness at the defendant's trial for sale and delivery of heroin. In closing argument, defense counsel suggested that the only difference between the defendant and the informant was that the informant had decided to work for the police. In rebuttal, the prosecutor responded to the defendant's "equal justice theory" by rhetorically asking the jurors how the defendant had ever benefitted society except by selling heroin. The prosecutor warned the jurors that the defendant someday might sell heroin to the prosecutor's children or even to their children. He then added that an acquittal would mean that the jury was condoning drug usage and forbidding the police from using informants. The defendant, he predicted, would almost certainly tell his friends that they could continue selling drugs.

What result on appeal after conviction? Did the defendant invite this rebuttal argument? Was his argument proper?

(7) Defendant Foster was charged with possession of crack cocaine with intent to distribute. Prior to the defendant's arrest, a police officer observed him for about twenty minutes at 2:00 a.m. apparently selling drugs from a Washington, D.C., street corner. When arrested, Foster was standing near a bag that contained crack cocaine.

During closing argument, the prosecutor stated that Foster's drug activities perhaps started long before the day in question. The prosecutor also said that Foster had been selling drugs "all day long" on the day in question. No evidence supported either contention. Defense counsel objected and requested a curative instruction. The court upheld the objection but declined the curative instruction, saying that "the jury's recollection of the evidence will control." In charging the jury, however, the judge gave the standard instruction that arguments of counsel are not evidence.

What result on appeal after conviction?

C. DEADLOCKED JURIES

(8) The defendant was tried for breaking and entering. After deliberating about ninety minutes, the jury advised the court that it could not agree upon a verdict. The following then occurred:

Court: Well without saying for whom, how do you stand numerically?

Foreperson: Eleven to one.

Court: Well, that is not very far from a verdict. You have been at this an hour and a half. I have previously instructed you that it is your duty to determine that facts from the evidence received in open court and to apply the law to the facts and in this way decide the case. I am now asking you to return to your jury room for further deliberations. In your deliberations, you should examine the questions submitted with proper regard and consideration for the opinions of others. You should listen to each other's arguments with an open mind and make every reasonable effort to reach a verdict. You will now return to your jury room and resume your deliberations.

Shortly thereafter, the jury found the defendant guilty. What result on appeal? What if the judge made the same comments without asking the numerical division of the jury?

(9) After deliberating only seven minutes, a jury convicted the defendant of violating various sections of the Internal Revenue Code relating to the unlawful possession, transportation, and sale, of non-tax-paid distilled spirits. At defense counsel's request, the judge began polling the jury, and when she reached the fifth juror, the following occurred:

Court: Was it your verdict?

Juror: I didn't vote.

Court: Well, is it your verdict?

Juror: Yes, sir.

Court: Do you want to ask the juror any questions, Mr. Waller.

Mr. Waller (defense counsel): Judge, I think it is not a verdict.

Court: I am going to send the jury back to reconsider their verdict, and be sure that it is the verdict of each of you. It must be a unanimous verdict and you must vote on it.

Shortly thereafter, the jury returned to the courtroom and announced a unanimous guilty verdict, which a subsequent poll confirmed. The jury foreperson then indicated, in response to defense counsel's inquiry, that the jury reached its verdict through a secret ballot.

What result on appeal?

Chapter 19

DOUBLE JEOPARDY

Double jeopardy issues pertaining to joinder and severance were considered in Chapter 12. This chapter completes the double jeopardy picture by examining the issues of reprosecuting a defendant after a mistrial, both without and with his consent, reprosecuting the defendant after an acquittal or dismissal, and reprosecuting the defendant after a conviction from which he appeals.

A. REPROSECUTION AFTER A MISTRIAL

(1) An indictment charged the defendant with murder. Although the state planned to call fifteen witnesses, only two had substantial evidence connecting the defendant to the crime: fifteen year old David Luster, who had told the grand jury that he heard the defendant admit the killing, and Louis Banks, a codefendant who had agreed to testify in return for an oral promise to dismiss the indictment against him. On the morning of trial, both Banks and his lawyer reaffirmed that Banks would testify.

The trial proceeded as planned until Luster, the fourteenth witness, denied talking to the defendant about the crime. When Luster refused to recant after being reminded of his grand jury testimony, the prosecutor excused him (and at a later date charged him with perjury). After the prosecutor called Banks as the state's final witness, defense counsel asked for a moment to confer with Banks and his lawyer. Shortly thereafter, Banks invoked his Fifth Amendment privilege outside the jury's presence. At a subsequent hearing, Banks's lawyer said he felt uncertain about the prosecutor's commitment to drop the charges against Banks.

When Banks left the stand, the court, over defense counsel's objection, granted the prosecutor's motion for a mistrial. A few days later, the state tried Banks for murder, but the court directed an acquittal. Thereafter, the state reindicted the defendant, using Banks as a grand jury witness.

What result on the defendant's motion to quash the indictment?

(2) An indictment jointly charged Fincham and Odom with murder. After two days of trial, it became apparent that Odom's defense strategy was to portray Odom as a mere "underling" and Fincham as the "kingpin" in the killing. Despite admonitions from the court, Odom's lawyer during the two days was hostile in both tone and substance toward Fincham. The next day, over Odom's objection, the judge granted Fincham's renewed motion for a severance on the basis of antagonistic defenses. Although Fincham then asked to be severed and Odom asked to continue with the case against him, the judge granted the prosecutor's motion to proceed with Fincham's trial and to sever Odom. The prosecutor so moved because Fincham had already received a severance in a trial of the same charge with another codefendant: a second severance of Fincham would lead the public to think that Fincham was "beating the system."

What result when Odom moves to bar his retrial?

(3) An indictment charged the defendant with murder in the shooting death of the man with whom she lived. One of the officers who arrived on the scene took the defendant into the kitchen and, without giving her *Miranda* rights, took a statement. Shortly after obtaining this statement, the officer took the defendant to his cruiser and, again without giving her *Miranda* rights, took another statement. During the ride to the police station, but this time after giving *Miranda* warnings and obtaining a waiver, the officer took a third statement. In each of her statements, the defendant admitted shooting the victim, but she claimed that she had only intended to wound him.

Judge Gilmore denied a pretrial motion to suppress the statements. Subsequently, in a jury trial before Judge Thayer, the officer testified about the defendant's three statements. Thereafter, the judge called opposing counsel into chambers and expressed concern that the statements had been improperly admitted. The following morning, the judge indicated his belief that the statements were all the product of custodial interrogation. Noting that the defendant neither requested nor objected to a mistrial, the judge ordered a mistrial as the only means of being fair to the defendant: "it now would be a travesty to proceed to a conclusion in this case."

What result when the defendant seeks to bar her retrial?

(4) An indictment charged the defendant with sexual offenses against three children. Before trial, the defendant's lawyer obtained a discovery order from the court for transcripts of any taped interviews with the victims. When a dispute arose over the existence of such tapes, the court ordered the prosecutor to produce any tapes known to exist or to deny by sworn affidavit that there were any tapes. Thereafter, the prosecutor filed an affidavit claiming to have given the defense all known tapes and denying knowledge of any others.

After trial began, the defendant's lawyer went to a hospital and watched a videotaped interview with one of the victims. After being alerted to this by a nurse, the prosecutor informed the court that she had just learned of the videotape. The next day, the defendant, over the prosecutor's objection, obtained a mistrial.

Thereafter, the defendant moved to dismiss the indictment on double jeopardy grounds. After a hearing, the court concluded that the prosecutor had knowledge of the tape from the time it was made. The court also found the prosecutor's story "incredible" and "inconceivable," and it described the prosecutor's conduct as "reprehensible" and her affidavit as "fraudulent *ab initio.*" What result on the defendant's motion?

(5) Before her trial on murder charges, the defendant unsuccessfully moved to suppress her confession. Subsequently, after empaneling a jury, the trial judge entertained a second suppression motion and, disagreeing with the suppression hearing judge, suppressed the confession. In a conference held in the judge's chambers, the prosecutor said he had no choice but to cause a mistrial so that he could appeal both the merits of the court's ruling and the authority of the trial judge to overrule a suppression judge. (It turned out that state law did not permit such an interlocutory appeal.) Defense counsel then agreed that if the prosecutor would mention the suppressed confession in front of the jury, he would move for a mistrial. Defense counsel and the prosecutor disagreed over whether the defendant would be subject to reprosecution after the mistrial declaration.

What result when the defendant moves to dismiss the charge after the scene unfolds according to plan?

B. REPROSECUTION FOLLOWING ACQUITTALS AND DISMISSALS

One supposedly firm double jeopardy principle is that the government may not appeal an acquittal, at least when reversal of the acquittal would require another trial. Accordingly, courts must take care to distinguish true acquittals from dismissals that do not turn on factual guilt or innocence. Unfortunately, trial judges are not always so careful with the labels they use: just calling a dismissal an "acquittal" does not make it so. In addition, it is not always clear just what sort of further proceedings an acquittal bars. The problems in this section explore these issues.

(6) An information charged the defendant, a Native–American, with assaulting another Native–American in Native–American country, in violation of 18 U.S.C. § 1153, which provides that such an assault shall be defined and punished in accordance with state law. Prior to trial, the defendant moved to dismiss the information on equal protection grounds, alleging that had he not been a Native–American, federal assault law, rather than Utah law, would have been applicable. Federal assault law is more difficult to prove and carries a lighter penalty than Utah law. Refusing to decide the motion before trial, the judge directed the government to proceed with its proof. The government's evidence then showed that the defendant had stabbed his sister in the stomach with a file. At the close of the government's case, the defendant renewed his motion to dismiss and, after hearing argument, the judge granted the motion and entered a judgment of acquittal.

The defendant now challenges the government's appeal on double jeopardy grounds. What result?

(7) Before jury selection in the defendant's trial for first degree murder, the judge denied a motion to quash the information. The prosecutor then presented five witnesses, but before she completed presenting the state's case, the judge granted a defense motion for personal bond, commenting that "the proofs in this case are not strong." The defendant then indicated a willingness to plead guilty to manslaughter. Although state law prohibits a judge from accepting a plea to a reduced charge over the prosecutor's objection, the judge mistakenly concluded that the law did not apply when abuse of the prosecutor's charging discretion had occurred. The judge added that "the charge of murder should not have been made and that if the examination judge had heard this testimony, he would not have bound the defendant over for murder."

The judge then proceeded to establish a factual basis for the plea. The defendant stated that she took a shotgun to a hotel because a friend had phoned indicating that a man was trying to rape her. The defendant found her friend and the deceased in a car outside the hotel and, thinking that the deceased had attempted and still intended to rape her friend, shot him when he refused to leave the car.

When the prosecutor objected, the judge responded that she was only granting the defendant's pretrial motion to quash the information. The judge added that the state had not proved and could not prove that the defendant did not believe the killing was necessary to prevent a felony. The judge explained that he took a plea to manslaughter because the defendant did not limit herself to reasonable force to prevent what she perceived as a felony.

The defendant now raises a double jeopardy challenge to the state's appeal. What result?

(8) An indictment charged the defendants Kehoe and Bullock with embezzling land from a savings and loan association in violation of 18 U.S.C. § 657. When the government completed presenting its case after one day of trial, the defendants moved for a judgment of acquittal. They argued that the indictment failed to charge an offense because real property cannot be the subject of embezzlement under § 657. The trial judge, after hearing argument, granted a judgment of acquittal "on the grounds that the indictment failed to state an offense against the United States." In explaining his decision, the judge said, among other things,

> Had the evidence shown that the property was sold by and for the benefit of the savings and loan company but that the defendants in their fiduciary capacities diverted the proceeds for their own benefit, then an indictment alleging embezzlement under § 657 might have been proper. The circumstances of this case, however, accepted as true for purposes of this motion, show that the proceeds of sale were

never intended to flow to the company but only to the defendants. While the defendants ostensibly deprived the company of real estate holdings, they did not take any funds, credits, or securities belonging to the company.

If the government believes that the embezzlement statute does apply to real property, can it appeal the trial judge's decision?

(9) A federal indictment charged the defendant with three counts of perjury before a grand jury. After the jury returned a guilty verdict on all counts, defense counsel moved for a judgment of acquittal, alleging both insufficiency of the evidence and ambiguity in the questions asked by the grand jury. Alternatively, counsel moved for a new trial because of prejudicial newspaper publicity. After hearing argument, the trial judge granted the defendant's motion for a new trial because of prejudicial publicity. The judge then granted a judgment of acquittal with respect to two of the counts; on the one she allowed to survive, the judge concluded that the questioning by the grand jury was sufficiently precise and the falsity of the defendant's answers to these questions sufficiently established to sustain the conviction.

The defendant is challenging the government's appeal from the judgment of acquittal. What result?

(10) An information charged the defendant with one count of burglary and one count of misdemeanor theft. After both sides rested, the judge heard motions outside the jury's presence. Finding the evidence insufficient, the judge dismissed the theft charge. The following morning, however, and again outside the jury's presence, the judge reversed herself and reinstated the theft charge. The jury, which never learned of the judge's actions, then acquitted the defendant of burglary but convicted him of theft.

What result when the defendant appeals his theft conviction on double jeopardy grounds?

C. REPROSECUTION FOLLOWING CONVICTION

(11) A three-count Texas indictment charged the defendant with robbery by assault, robbery by firearms, and being a multiple offender, the substantive counts arising from the same transaction. Because robbery by firearms is a capital offense, the state elected to proceed with trial on that count alone. A jury found the defendant guilty, and he received a 99 year sentence. The conviction was reversed on appeal for failure to provide the defendant a pretrial competency hearing.

On retrial, the state elected to proceed on the other two counts. The defendant then moved to dismiss the indictment, claiming that trying him on the abandoned counts violates double jeopardy. What result? [What result if Texas follows the same transaction test?]

(12) A two-count state indictment charged the defendant with two robberies. After the state rested, the defendant announced that he wanted to plead guilty to the second count. When the court accepted the plea, the prosecutor dismissed the first count with the court's approval. Defense counsel then asked the court to make the sentence concurrent with one the defendant was already serving, but the defendant acknowledged the court's discretion to reject the request. When the court made the sentences consecutive, the defendant immediately moved to withdraw his plea, alleging that he had been told by his lawyer that the sentences would be concurrent. The court then vacated the plea.

Faced with a new trial on both charges, the defendant has moved to dismiss on double jeopardy grounds. What result?

(13) An indictment charged the defendants with bribery, receiving illegal gratuities, and extortion, the charges stemming from the defendants' congressional activities on behalf of the Wedtech corporation. The extortion was premised on two legal theories: (1) extortion by use of fear and (2) extortion under color of legal right. At the close of the evidence, the defendants unsuccessfully moved to dismiss the first theory for insufficient evidence. The jury then acquitted the defendants of the bribery and gratuity charges but convicted them of extortion. Though given an opportunity by the court, neither the defendants nor the government submitted special interrogatories for the jury.

On appeal, the court reversed, finding insufficient evidence for the first theory of extortion. The court held that "if there was insufficient evidence for one of the theories, the verdict is ambiguous and a new trial must be granted." What charge(s), if any, may the government retry?

(14) Defendant was tried under Tennessee law for being an habitual offender. Tennessee defines as habitual offenders those persons convicted of three felonies, either within Tennessee or any other government, two of which must be for felonies enumerated in the Tennessee statute.

The state offered proof that the defendant had been convicted of four felonies in Tennessee and two in federal court. Because only one of the defendant's state convictions was for a felony enumerated in the Tennessee statute, however, it was necessary for the state to prove that at least one of the federal convictions was for an enumerated offense. The state offered transcripts of defendant's guilty pleas in federal court to show that the acts on which the pleas were based would have constituted third degree burglary under Tennessee law, an enumerated offense for habitual offender purposes. The trial court erroneously excluded these transcripts on the ground that the state had failed to provide them in discovery. The jury nevertheless convicted the defendant, and he was sentenced to life imprisonment.

On appeal, the appellate court summarily reversed for insufficient evidence, the state having shown only one of defendant's convictions to be an enumerated felony. What result when the defendant seeks to bar the state from retrying him?

D.   INCREASED PUNISHMENT FOLLOWING A SUCCESSFUL APPEAL

Although, according to the Supreme Court, this topic raises a due process rather than a double jeopardy issue, it is considered here for lack of a more appropriate place. Students should examine the Court's conclusion that double jeopardy has no role to play in this area.

(15) A federal jury convicted the defendant of conspiracy and armed postal robbery. After receiving concurrent five and twenty-five year sentences, the defendant successfully appealed his conviction. The defendant then pleaded guilty to both offenses, and the court imposed consecutive five and twenty-five year sentences. At the defendant's request, however, the court suspended the latter sentence and imposed a five year term of probation. The court explained that consecutive terms were necessary because federal law did not permit a term of probation to exceed five years. The defendant expressed satisfaction with the sentence.

After serving the five year sentence, the defendant was released on probation. Sometime later, a court found the defendant to have violated his probation and sentenced him to the original twenty-five year term. What result when the defendant appeals?

(16) A jury convicted the defendant of two counts of possession of a controlled substance with the intent to distribute, and the judge sentenced him to two consecutive five year terms of imprisonment. On appeal, the court reversed count one for a jurisdictional defect and remanded to the trial judge for resentencing on count two. On remand the court sentenced the defendant to prison for ten years.

What result on the defendant's appeal?

CITATIONS TO CHAPTERS 1–19

Chapter 1

1. Thompson v. Anderson, 824 P.2d 712 (Alaska 1992).

2. Gundlach v. Janing, 401 F.Supp. 1089 (D.Neb.1975), *aff'd*, 536 F.2d 754 (8th Cir.1976).

3. Alston v. United States, 518 A.2d 439 (D.C.Ct.App.1986).

4. State v. Casconi, 94 Or.App. 457, 766 P.2d 397 (1988); State v. Owczarzak, 94 Or.App. 500, 766 P.2d 399 (1988).

5. Fixel v. Wainwright, 492 F.2d 480 (5th Cir.1974).

6. United States v. Cuevas–Sanchez, 821 F.2d 248 (5th Cir.1987).

7. State v. Gedko, 63 Wis.2d 644, 218 N.W.2d 249 (1974); United States v. Brown, 473 F.2d 952 (5th Cir.1973).

8. Commonwealth v. Oglialoro, 525 Pa. 250, 579 A.2d 1288 (1990).

9. United States v. Scherer, 673 F.2d 176 (7th Cir.), *cert. denied*, 457 U.S. 1120, 102 S.Ct. 2935, 73 L.Ed.2d 1334 (1982).

10. United States v. Giraldo, 743 F.Supp. 152 (E.D.N.Y.1990); People v. Jefferson, 43 A.D.2d 112, 350 N.Y.S.2d 3 (N.Y.App.Div.1973).

11. State v. Detroy, 102 Haw. 13, 72 P.3d 485 (2003).

12. Hause v. Commonwealth, 83 S.W.3d 1 (Ky. App. 2001).

13. State v. Lemmon, 318 Md. 365, 568 A.2d 48 (1990).

14. United States v. Wilson, 953 F.2d 116 (4th Cir.1991).

15. Llaguno v. Mingey, 763 F.2d 1560 (7th Cir.1985) (en banc), *cert. dismissed*, 478 U.S. 1044, 107 S.Ct. 16, 92 L.Ed.2d 783 (1986).

16. Campbell v. United States, 273 A.2d 252 (D.C.Ct.App.1971).

17. People v. Bower, 24 Cal.3d 638, 597 P.2d 115, 156 Cal.Rptr. 856 (1979).

18. United States v. Archuleta, 446 F.2d 518 (9th Cir.1971) (per curiam).

19. United States v. Reivich, 793 F.2d 957 (8th Cir.1986).

20. State v. Wasson, 615 N.W.2d 316 (Minn. 2000).

21. United States v. Basham, 268 F.3d 1199 (10th Cir. 2001); State v. Kelley, 265 Neb. 563, 658 N.W.2d 279 (2003).

22. United States v. Hendrixson, 234 F.3d 494 (11th Cir. 2000).

23. The facts are hypothetical.

24. United States v. Blalock, 578 F.2d 245 (9th Cir.1978).

25. United States v. Rengifo, 858 F.2d 800 (1st Cir.1988), *cert. denied*, 490 U.S. 1023, 109 S.Ct. 1752, 104 L.Ed.2d 189 (1989).

26. United States v. Cravero, 545 F.2d 406 (5th Cir.1976), *cert. denied sub nom.* Miller v. United States, 429 U.S. 1100, 97 S.Ct. 1123, 51 L.Ed.2d 549 (1977).

27. United States v. Goldenstein, 456 F.2d 1006 (8th Cir.1972), *cert. denied sub nom.* Ray v. United States, 416 U.S. 943, 94 S.Ct. 1951, 40 L.Ed.2d 295 (1974).

28. People v. Blasius, 435 Mich. 573, 459 N.W.2d 906 (1990).

29. United States v. Shye, 473 F.2d 1061 (6th Cir.1973), *appeal after remand*, 492 F.2d 886 (6th Cir.1974); *see also* State v. Murdock, 155 Wis.2d 217, 455 N.W.2d 618 (1990).

30. United States v. Hernandez, 941 F.2d 133 (2d Cir.1991).

31. United States v. Ibarra, 345 F.3d 711 (9th Cir. 2003).

32. State v. Tucker, 34 Or.App. 203, 578 P.2d 803 (1978), *aff'd*, 286 Or. 485, 595 P.2d 1364 (1979).

33. People v. Stoffle, 1 Cal.App.4th 1671, 3 Cal.Rptr.2d 257 (1991).

34. United States v. Arango, 879 F.2d 1501 (7th Cir.1989), *cert. denied*, 493 U.S. 1069, 110 S.Ct. 1111, 107 L.Ed.2d 1019 (1990).

35. State v. Pallone, 236 Wis.2d 162, 613 N.W.2d 568 (2000).

36. United States v. Brookins, 228 F.Supp.2d 732 (E.D.Va.2002), *reversed on other grounds*, 345 F.3d 231 (4th Cir. 2003).

37. See problems 33 and 34.

38. Osban v. State, 726 S.W.2d 107 (Tex.Crim.App.1986) (en banc), *reversed on other grounds by* Heitman v. State, 815 S.W.2d 681 (Tex.Crim.App. 1991).

39. People v. White, 68 Mich.App. 348, 242 N.W.2d 579 (1976).

40. State v. Boyd, 275 Kan. 271, 64 P.3d 419 (2003).

41. United States v. Johnson, 862 F.2d 1135 (5th Cir.), *cert. denied*, 492 U.S. 909, 109 S.Ct. 3223, 106 L.Ed.2d 572 (1989).

42. People v. Galak, 80 N.Y.2d 715, 610 N.E.2d 362, 594 N.Y.S.2d 689 (1993).

43. Cabbler v. Superintendent, 528 F.2d 1142 (4th Cir.1975), *cert. denied*, 429 U.S. 817, 97 S.Ct. 60, 50 L.Ed.2d 77 (1976).

44. People v. Brow, 67 Mich.App. 407, 241 N.W.2d 227 (1976).

45. Riddick v. State, 319 Md. 180, 571 A.2d 1239 (1990), *overruled in part by* Wengert v. State, 364 Md. 76, 771 A.2d 389 (2001).

46. State v. Riedinger, 374 N.W.2d 866 (N.D.1985).

47. People v. Clark, 68 Mich.App. 674, 243 N.W.2d 914 (1976).

48. United States v. Vasey, 834 F.2d 782 (9th Cir.1987).

49. United States v. Maragh, 756 F.Supp. 18 (D.D.C.1991).

50. People v. Crenshaw, 9 Cal.App.4th 1403, 12 Cal.Rptr.2d 172 (1992).

51. Silva v. State, 344 So.2d 559 (Fla.1977).

52. United States v. Burrell, 286 A.2d 845 (D.C.Ct.App.1972).

53. Commonwealth v. Pegram, 450 Pa. 590, 301 A.2d 695 (1973).

54. Sanders v. State, 385 So.2d 735 (Fla.App.1980).

55. United States v. Nelson, 284 F.3d 472 (3d Cir. 2002); Jackson v. Commonwealth, 39 Va.App. 624, 576 S.E.2d 206 (2003).

56. State v. Brown, 256 Wis.2d 695, 647 N.W.2d 469 (2002).

57. State v. Moffatt, 450 N.W.2d 116 (Minn.1990).

58. United States v. Tapia, 309 F.3d 1283 (10th Cir. 2002).

59. People v. McGaughran, 22 Cal.3d 469, 585 P.2d 206, 149 Cal.Rptr. 584 (1978), *reversed on reh'g*, 25 Cal.3d 577, 601 P.2d 207, 159 Cal.Rptr. 191 (1979).

60. United States v. Brown, 913 F.2d 570 (8th Cir.), *cert. denied*, 498 U.S. 1016, 111 S.Ct. 590, 112 L.Ed.2d 594 (1990).

61. United States v. Riggs, 474 F.2d 699 (2d Cir.), *cert. denied*, 414 U.S. 820, 94 S.Ct. 115, 38 L.Ed.2d 53 (1973).

62. Williams v. State, 261 Ind. 547, 307 N.E.2d 457 (1974).

63. Wrigley v. State, 248 Ga.App. 387, 546 S.E.2d 794 (2001).

64. United States v. Davis, 143 F.Supp.2d 1302 (M.D.Ala. 2001).

65. Petersen v. City of Mesa, 204 Ariz. 278, 63 P.3d 309 (2003).

66. United States v. Ward, 131 F.3d 335 (3d Cir. 1997).

67. Commonwealth v. Rodriquez, 532 Pa. 62, 614 A.2d 1378 (1992).

68. People v. Marshall, 69 Mich.App. 288, 244 N.W.2d 451, *leave to appeal denied*, 397 Mich. 851 (1976).

Chapter 2

1. United States v. Christopher, 956 F.2d 536 (6th Cir.1991), *cert. denied*, 505 U.S. 1207, 112 S.Ct. 2999, 120 L.Ed.2d 875 (1992).

2. Duncan v. State, 291 Ark. 521, 726 S.W.2d 653 (1987).

3. United States v. Murphy, 763 F.2d 202 (6th Cir.1985), *cert. denied sub nom.* Stauffer v. United States, 474 U.S. 1063, 106 S.Ct. 812, 88 L.Ed.2d 786 (1986).

4. State v. Carl, 310 Minn. 365, 246 N.W.2d 192 (1976).

5. F. INBAU, J. REID & J. BUCKLEY, CRIMINAL INTERROGATION AND CONFESSIONS 133–34 (3d ed. 1986).

6. Welch v. Butler, 835 F.2d 92 (5th Cir.), *cert. denied*, 487 U.S. 1221, 108 S.Ct. 2877, 101 L.Ed.2d 912 (1988). *But see* State v. Nelson, 69 Haw. 461, 748 P.2d 365 (1987).

7. State v. Amaya–Ruiz, 166 Ariz. 152, 800 P.2d 1260 (1990), *cert. denied*, 500 U.S. 929, 111 S.Ct. 2044, 114 L.Ed.2d 129 (1991).

8. State v. Lale, 141 Wis.2d 480, 415 N.W.2d 847 (Wis.Ct.App.1987), *review denied*, 143 Wis.2d 911, 422 N.W.2d 860 (1988).

9. In re Pack, 420 Pa.Super. 347, 616 A.2d 1006 (1992), *leave to appeal denied*, 535 Pa. 669, 634 A.2d 1117 (1993), *abrogated by* Texas v. Cobb, 532 U.S. 162, 121 S.Ct. 1335, 149 L.Ed.2d 321 (2001).

10. People v. Patterson, 39 Mich.App. 467, 198 N.W.2d 175 (1971); State v. Smith, 107 Ariz. 100, 482 P.2d 863 (1971).

11. United States v. York, 933 F.2d 1343 (7th Cir.), *cert. denied*, 502 U.S. 916, 112 S.Ct. 321, 116 L.Ed.2d 262, *reh'g denied*, 502 U.S. 1010, 112 S.Ct. 651, 116 L.Ed.2d 668 (1991), *overruled by* Wilson v. Williams, 182 F.3d 562 (7th Cir. 1999).

12. Alston v. Commonwealth, 264 Va. 433, 570 S.E.2d 801 (2002).

13. United States v. Martinez, 972 F.2d 1100 (9th Cir.1992).

14. United States v. Conley, 779 F.2d 970 (4th Cir.1985), *cert. denied*, 479 U.S. 830, 107 S.Ct. 114, 93 L.Ed.2d 61 (1986).

15. Commonwealth v. Mitchell, 445 Pa. 461, 285 A.2d 93 (1971).

16. United States v. Griffin, 922 F.2d 1343 (8th Cir.1990).

17. State v. Rosse, 478 N.W.2d 482 (Minn.1991).

18. United States v. McCain, 556 F.2d 253 (5th Cir.1977).

19. State v. Jones, 386 So.2d 1363 (La.1980).

20. Shedelbower v. Estelle, 885 F.2d 570 (9th Cir.1989), *cert. denied*, 498 U.S. 1092, 111 S.Ct. 975, 112 L.Ed.2d 1060 (1991).

21. State v. Weedon, 342 So.2d 642 (La.1977).

22. Grooms v. Keeney, 826 F.2d 883 (9th Cir.1987).

23. State v. Fuller, 118 N.J. 75, 570 A.2d 429 (1990).

24. State v. Harvey, 121 N.J. 407, 581 A.2d 483 (1990), *cert. denied*, 499 U.S. 931, 111 S.Ct. 1336, 113 L.Ed.2d 268 (1991).

25. United States v. Porter, 764 F.2d 1 (1st Cir.1985).

26. United States v. Wright, 962 F.2d 953 (9th Cir.1992).

27. State v. Ikaika, 67 Haw. 563, 698 P.2d 281 (1985).

28. Commonwealth v. Franklin, 438 Pa. 411, 265 A.2d 361 (1970).

29. Fleming v. Collins, 954 F.2d 1109 (5th Cir.1992).

30. State v. Provost, 490 N.W.2d 93 (Minn.1992), *cert. denied*, 507 U.S. 929, 113 S.Ct. 1306, 122 L.Ed.2d 694 (1993).

31. State v. Dailey, 53 Ohio St.3d 88, 559 N.E.2d 459 (1990).

32. United States v. Cruz, 910 F.2d 1072 (3d Cir.1990), *cert. denied*, 498 U.S. 1039, 111 S.Ct. 709, 112 L.Ed.2d 698 (1991).

Chapter 3

1. Moore v. Oliver, 347 F.Supp. 1313 (W.D.Va.1972).

2. Boyd v. Henderson, 555 F.2d 56 (2d Cir.), *cert. denied*, 434 U.S. 927, 98 S.Ct. 410, 54 L.Ed.2d 286 (1977).

3. United States v. Luck, 447 F.2d 1333 (6th Cir.1971).

4. United States v. Bierey, 588 F.2d 620 (8th Cir.1978), *cert. denied*, 440 U.S. 927, 99 S.Ct. 1260, 59 L.Ed.2d 482 (1979); United States v. Cunningham, 423 F.2d 1269 (4th Cir.1970); People v. Williams, 3 Cal.3d 853, 478 P.2d 942, 92 Cal.Rptr. 6 (1971).

5. People v. Settles, 46 N.Y.2d 154, 385 N.E.2d 612, 412 N.Y.S.2d 874 (1978), *overruled as stated in* People v. Claudio, 85 A.D.2d 245, 447 N.Y.S.2d 972 (1982).

6. People v. Hutton, 21 Mich.App. 312, 175 N.W.2d 860 (1970).

7. United States v. Field, 625 F.2d 862 (9th Cir.1980).

8. Smith v. Coiner, 473 F.2d 877 (4th Cir.), *cert. denied sub nom.* Wallace v. Smith, 414 U.S. 1115, 94 S.Ct. 848, 38 L.Ed.2d 743 (1973).

9. *See* Doob & Kirshenbaum, *Bias in Police Lineups—Partial Remembering*, 1 J. Pol. Sci. & Admin. 287 (1973).

10. United States v. Williams, 436 F.2d 1166 (9th Cir.1970), *cert. denied*, 402 U.S. 912, 91 S.Ct. 1392, 28 L.Ed.2d 654 (1971).

11. United States v. Telfaire, 469 F.2d 552 (D.C.Cir.1972); Regina v. Peterkin, 125 C.S. 228 (Quebec Ct. Sessions 1959).

12. Regina v. Sutton, (1970) 2 O.R. 358 (Ont. Ct. App. 1969).

13. State v. Willis, 240 Kan. 580, 731 P.2d 287 (1987).

14. United States v. Fosher, 590 F.2d 381 (1st Cir.1979).

Chapter 4

1. United States v. Harrelson, 754 F.2d 1153 (5th Cir.), *cert. denied*, 474 U.S. 908, 1034, 106 S.Ct. 277, 599, 88 L.Ed.2d 241, 578 (1985).

2. United States v. Passarella, 788 F.2d 377 (6th Cir.1986).

3. United States v. San Martin, 469 F.2d 5 (2d Cir.1972).

4. United States v. Koyomejian, 946 F.2d 1450 (9th Cir.1991), *vacated*, 970 F.2d 536 (9th Cir.) (en banc), *cert. denied*, 506 U.S. 1005, 113 S.Ct. 617, 121 L.Ed.2d 550 (1992).

5. People v. Shapiro, 50 N.Y.2d 747, 409 N.E.2d 897, 431 N.Y.S.2d 422 (1980).

6. United States v. Silberman, 732 F.Supp. 1057 (S.D.Cal.1990), *aff'd in part sub nom.* United States v. Petti, 973 F.2d 1441 (9th Cir.1992), *cert. denied*, 507 U.S. 1035, 113 S.Ct. 1859, 123 L.Ed.2d 480 (1993).

7. United States v. King, 335 F.Supp. 523 (S.D.Cal.1971), *aff'd in part*, 478 F.2d 494 (9th Cir.1973), *cert. denied*, 417 U.S. 920, 94 S.Ct. 2628, 41 L.Ed.2d 226 (1974).

8. United States v. David, 940 F.2d 722 (1st Cir.1991), *cert. denied*, 504 U.S. 955, 112 S.Ct. 2301, 119 L.Ed.2d 224 (1992).

9. United States v. Homick, 964 F.2d 899 (9th Cir. 1992).

10. United States v. Feiste, 961 F.2d 1349 (8th Cir.1992).

11. United States v. Suarez, 906 F.2d 977 (4th Cir.1990), *cert. denied sub nom.* Lucero–Romero v. United States, 498 U.S. 1070, 111 S.Ct. 790, 112 L.Ed.2d 852 (1991).

Chapter 5

1. Henderson v. United States, 261 F.2d 909 (5th Cir.1958).

2. State v. DeAngelo, 113 Or.App. 192, 830 P.2d 630, *review denied*, 314 Or. 391, 840 P.2d 709 (1992).

3. Bowser v. State, 555 So.2d 879 (Fla.Ct.App.1989), *disapproved of in* Munoz v. State, 629 So.2d 90 (Fla. 1993).

4. People v. Perry, 75 Mich.App. 121, 254 N.W.2d 810 (1977), *leave to appeal denied*, 402 Mich. 857, 261 N.W.2d 533 (1978).

5. State v. Glosson, 462 So.2d 1082 (Fla.1985). *See also* United States v. Gonzales, 927 F.2d 139 (3d Cir.1991).

6. United States v. Johnston, 426 F.2d 112 (7th Cir.1970).

Chapter 6

1. In re Grand Jury Subpoena (Battle), 748 F.2d 327 (6th Cir.1984).

2. In re Grand Jury Proceedings: Subpoenas Duces Tecum, 827 F.2d 301 (8th Cir.1987).

3. In re Nwamu, 421 F.Supp. 1361 (S.D.N.Y.1976).

4. In re Grand Jury Subpoenas, 906 F.2d 1485 (10th Cir.1990).

5. In re Grand Jury Subpoena Served upon John Doe, 781 F.2d 238 (2d Cir.) (en banc), *cert. denied sub nom.* Roe v. United States, 475 U.S. 1108, 106 S.Ct. 1515, 89 L.Ed.2d 914 (1986).

6. In re Grand Jury Subpoena Duces Tecum Dated January 2, 1985 (Simels), 767 F.2d 26 (2d Cir. 1985).

7. In re Grand Jury Subpoena Duces Tecum, 782 F.Supp. 1518 (N.D.Ala.1992).

8. In re Grand Jury Subpoena Duces Tecum Dated October 29, 1992, 1 F.3d 87 (2d Cir.1993), *cert. denied sub nom.* Doe v. United States, 510 U.S. 1091, 114 S.Ct. 920, 127 L.Ed.2d 214 (1994).

9. In re January 1976 Grand Jury, 534 F.2d 719 (7th Cir.1976).

10. In re Zuniga, 714 F.2d 632 (6th Cir.), *cert. denied*, 464 U.S. 983, 104 S.Ct. 426, 78 L.Ed.2d 361 (1983).

11. In re Grand Jury Matter, Gronowicz, 764 F.2d 983 (3d Cir.1985) (en banc), *cert. denied*, 474 U.S. 1055, 106 S.Ct. 793, 88 L.Ed.2d 770 (1986).

12. In re Grand Jury Proceedings, 831 F.2d 228 (11th Cir.1987).

13. Commonwealth v. Columbia Inv. Corp., 222 Pa.Super. 30, 292 A.2d 533 (1972).

14. Flanders v. Schoville, 350 F.Supp. 371 (N.D.Iowa 1972).

Chapter 7

1. People v. Mack, 100 Mich.App. 45, 298 N.W.2d 657 (1980).

2. People v. Moreno, 2 Cal.App.4th 577, 3 Cal.Rptr.2d 66 (1992).

3. Welfare of B.R.K., 658 N.W.2d 565 (Minn. 2003).

4. United States v. Jefferson, 925 F.2d 1242 (10th Cir.), *cert. denied*, 502 U.S. 884, 112 S.Ct. 238, 116 L.Ed.2d 194 (1991).

5. State v. Sanders, 5 Kan.App.2d 189, 614 P.2d 998 (1980).

6. State v. Cude, 14 Utah 2d 287, 383 P.2d 399 (1963).

7. United States v. Cassell, 542 F.2d 279 (5th Cir.1976), *cert. denied*, 430 U.S. 985, 97 S.Ct. 1684, 52 L.Ed.2d 380 (1977).

8. People v. Bisogni, 4 Cal.3d 582, 483 P.2d 780, 94 Cal.Rptr. 164 (1971).

9. People v. Walker, 27 Mich.App. 609, 183 N.W.2d 871 (1970).

10. Commonwealth v. Whitaker, 461 Pa. 407, 336 A.2d 603 (1975).

11. Sossamon v. State, 816 S.W.2d 340 (Tex.Crim.App.1991).

12. United States v. Morales, 788 F.2d 883 (2d Cir.1986).

13. State v. Madruga–Jiminez, 485 So.2d 462 (Fla.Dist.Ct.App.), *review denied*, 492 So.2d 1335 (Fla.1986).

14. United States v. Eaton, 890 F.2d 511 (1st Cir.1989), *cert. denied*, 495 U.S. 906, 110 S.Ct. 1927, 109 L.Ed.2d 291 (1990).

15. United States v. Andrade, 784 F.2d 1431 (9th Cir.1986).

16. United States v. Drosten, 819 F.2d 1067 (11th Cir.1987).

17. People v. Taylor, 8 Cal.3d 174, 501 P.2d 918, 104 Cal.Rptr. 350 (1972), *cert. denied*, 414 U.S. 863, 94 S.Ct. 35, 38 L.Ed.2d 83 (1973).

18. United States v. Cichon, 48 F.3d 269 (7th Cir.1995), *cert. denied*, 516 U.S. 1111, 116 S.Ct. 908, 133 L.Ed.2d 840 (1996), *overruled on other grounds*, United States v. Baldwin, 60 F.3d 363 (7th Cir. 1995).

19. Phelps v. Duckworth, 772 F.2d 1410 (7th Cir.) (en banc), *cert. denied*, 474 U.S. 1011, 106 S.Ct. 541, 88 L.Ed.2d 471 (1985).

20. Stephens v. State, 290 Ark. 440, 720 S.W.2d 301 (1986).

21. United States v. Spencer, 955 F.2d 814 (2d Cir.1992).

22. United States v. Leake, 998 F.2d 1359 (6th Cir.1993).

23. United States v. Ferra, 948 F.2d 352 (7th Cir.1991), *cert. denied*, 504 U.S. 910, 112 S.Ct. 1939, 118 L.Ed.2d 545 (1992).

Chapter 8

1. United States v. Cramer, 451 F.2d 1198 (5th Cir.1971).

2. United States v. McConnell, 842 F.2d 105 (5th Cir.1988).

3. Allen v. United States, 386 F.2d 634 (D.C.Cir.1967).

4. Quinn v. Crowder, 625 So.2d 1247 (Fla.Dist.Ct.App.1993).

5. Mott v. Indiana, 490 N.E.2d 1125 (Ind.Ct.App.1986).

6. State v. O'Neal, 108 N.C.App. 661, 424 S.E.2d 680 (1993).

7. The facts are hypothetical. They were suggested by the "Son of Sam" killings in New York.

8. United States v. Contreras, 776 F.2d 51 (2d Cir.1985).

9. United States v. Millan, 4 F.3d 1038 (2d Cir.1993), *cert. denied sub nom.*, Rivera v. United States, 511 U.S. 1011, 114 S.Ct. 1386, 128 L.Ed.2d 60 (1994).

10. United States v. Baker, 890 F.Supp. 1375 (E.D.Mich.1995).

11. United States v. Stanley, 469 F.2d 576 (D.C.Cir.1972).

Chapter 9

1. United States v. Librach, 536 F.2d 1228 (8th Cir.), *cert. denied*, 429 U.S. 939, 97 S.Ct. 354, 50 L.Ed.2d 308 (1976).

2. Redmond v. United States, 384 U.S. 264, 86 S.Ct. 1415, 16 L.Ed.2d 521 (1966).

3. The facts are hypothetical. They are based on an incident that occurred in Detroit.

4. The facts are a variation on a problem in F. MILLER, THE DECISION TO PROSECUTE 35 (1969).

5. The facts are hypothetical, but not atypical.

6. The facts are a variation on a problem in W. LaFAVE, ARREST: THE DECISION TO TAKE A SUSPECT INTO CUSTODY 149 (1965).

7. Peek v. Mitchell, 419 F.2d 575 (6th Cir.1970).

8. State v. Unnamed Defendant, 150 Wis.2d 352, 441 N.W.2d 696 (1989).

9. United States v. Steele, 461 F.2d 1148 (9th Cir.1972).

10. United States v. Cammisano, 413 F.Supp. 886 (W.D.Mo.), *vacated and remanded*, 546 F.2d 238 (8th Cir.1976), *on remand* 433 F.Supp. 964 (W.D.Mo.1977).

11. State v. Kennedy, 247 N.J.Super. 21, 588 A.2d 834 (1991).

12. United States v. Meyer, 810 F.2d 1242, *vacated on reh'g en banc*, 816 F.2d 695 (D.C.Cir.), *reinstated on reconsideration en banc sub nom.* Bartlett ex rel. Neuman v. Bowen, 824 F.2d 1240 (D.C.Cir. 1987), *cert. denied*, 485 U.S. 940, 108 S.Ct. 1121, 99 L.Ed.2d 281 (1988).

13. United States v. Litton Systems, Inc., 573 F.2d 195 (4th Cir.), *cert. denied*, 439 U.S. 828, 99 S.Ct. 101, 58 L.Ed.2d 121 (1978).

14. State ex rel. Ronan v. Stevens, 93 Ariz. 375, 381 P.2d 100 (1963).

Chapter 10

1. Commonwealth v. Lynch, 270 Pa. Super. Ct. 554, 411 A.2d 1224 (1979), *aff'd in part and rev'd in part sub nom.* Commonwealth v. Wojdak, 502 Pa. 359, 466 A.2d 991 (1983).

2. People v. Hall, 435 Mich. 599, 460 N.W.2d 520 (1990).

3. Hooker v. Sheriff, 89 Nev. 89, 506 P.2d 1262 (1973).

4. Ysaguirre v. Superior Court, 204 Cal.Rptr. 66 (1984), ordered by the Supreme Court not to be published in the official reports.

5. United States v. King, 482 F.2d 768 (D.C.Cir.1973).

6. People v. Paille, 383 Mich. 621, 178 N.W.2d 465 (1970).

7. McKeldin v. Rose, 482 F.Supp. 1093 (E.D.Tenn.), *rev'd*, 631 F.2d 458 (6th Cir.1980), *cert. denied*, 450 U.S. 969, 101 S.Ct. 1488, 67 L.Ed.2d 619 (1981); Commonwealth v. Taylor, 219 Pa. Super. Ct. 334, 280 A.2d 405 (1971).

Chapter 11

1. United States v. Armored Transport, Inc., 629 F.2d 1313 (9th Cir.1980), *cert. denied*, 450 U.S. 965, 101 S.Ct. 1481, 67 L.Ed.2d 614 (1981).

2. United States v. Yellow Freight Sys., Inc., 637 F.2d 1248 (9th Cir.1980), *cert. denied*, 454 U.S. 815, 102 S.Ct. 91, 70 L.Ed.2d 84 (1981).

3. United States v. James, 290 F.2d 866 (5th Cir.), *cert. denied*, 368 U.S. 834, 82 S.Ct. 60, 7 L.Ed.2d 36 (1961).

4. United States v. Yost, 24 F.3d 99 (10th Cir.1994).

5. United States v. Harris, 973 F.2d 333 (4th Cir.1992).

6. State v. Foster, 845 So.2d 393 (La.App. 2003).

7. United States v. Lopez, 854 F.Supp. 41, *motion denied*, 854 F.Supp. 50 (D.P.R.1994).

Chapter 12

1. People v. Tobey, 401 Mich. 141, 257 N.W.2d 537 (1977).

2. People v. Thompson, 410 Mich. 66, 299 N.W.2d 343 (1980).

3. People v. Bracey, 52 Ill.App.3d 266, 9 Ill.Dec. 917, 367 N.E.2d 351 (1977).

4. State v. Washington, 386 So.2d 1368 (La.1980).

5. United States v. Colon–Osorio, 10 F.3d 41 (1st Cir.1993), *cert. denied*, 512 U.S. 1239, 114 S.Ct. 2749, 129 L.Ed.2d 867 (1994).

6. United States v. Seda, 978 F.2d 779 (2d Cir.1992), *overruled by* United States v. Chacko, 169 F.3d 140 (2d Cir. 1999).

7. Wayne County Prosecutor v. Recorder's Court Judge, 406 Mich. 374, 280 N.W.2d 793 (1979), *overruled in part by* People v. Robideau, 419 Mich. 458, 355 N.W.2d 592 (1984).

8. United States v. Rodgers, 18 F.3d 1425 (8th Cir.1994).

9. United States v. Smith, 470 F.2d 1299 (5th Cir.), *cert. denied*, 411 U.S. 952, 93 S.Ct. 1929, 36 L.Ed.2d 415 (1973).

10. Simon v. Commonwealth, 220 Va. 412, 258 S.E.2d 567 (1979).

11. People v. Johnson, 62 Mich.App. 240, 233 N.W.2d 246 (1975).

12. Cupo v. United States, 359 F.2d 990 (D.C.Cir.1966), *cert. denied*, 385 U.S. 1013, 87 S.Ct. 723, 17 L.Ed.2d 549 (1967).

13. People v. Slate, 73 Mich.App. 126, 250 N.W.2d 572 (1977), *overruled in part by* People v. Cochran, 84 Mich.App. 710, 270 N.W.2d 502 (1978).

14. United States v. Shuford, 454 F.2d 772 (4th Cir.1971).

15. State v. White, 50 Wash. App. 858, 751 P.2d 1202 (1988).

16. People v. Hurst, 396 Mich. 1, 238 N.W.2d 6 (1976). *See also* People v. Hana, 447 Mich. 325, 524 N.W.2d 682 (1994).

17. United States v. Logan, 210 F.3d 820 (8th Cir. 2000).

Chapter 13

1. Arrant v. Wainwright, 468 F.2d 677 (5th Cir.1972), *cert. denied*, 410 U.S. 947, 93 S.Ct. 1369, 35 L.Ed.2d 613 (1973).

2. United States v. Hanna, 347 F.Supp. 1010 (D.Del.1972).

3. Dodge v. People, 178 Colo. 71, 495 P.2d 213 (1972).

4. People v. Laskowski, 72 Misc.2d 580, 340 N.Y.S.2d 787 (Nassau County Ct. 1973).

5. United States v. Sairafi, 801 F.2d 691 (4th Cir.1986).

6. United States v. Garcia, 995 F.2d 556 (5th Cir.1993).

7. United States v. Thompson, 866 F.2d 268 (8th Cir.), *cert. denied*, 493 U.S. 828, 110 S.Ct. 94, 107 L.Ed.2d 59 (1989).

8. Pittman v. State, 301 A.2d 509 (Del.1973).

9. Penney v. Superior Court, 28 Cal.App.3d 941, 105 Cal.Rptr. 162 (1972).

10. Woody v. United States, 370 F.2d 214 (D.C.Cir.1966).

Chapter 14

1. United States v. Ahmad, 53 F.R.D. 194 (M.D.Pa.1971).

2. United States v. Walk, 533 F.2d 417 (9th Cir.1975).

3. United States v. Roberts, 811 F.2d 257 (4th Cir.1987) (en banc) (per curiam).

4. In re United States, 918 F.2d 138 (11th Cir.1990).

5. State v. Cloutier, 302 A.2d 84 (Me.1973); State v. McArdle, 156 W.Va. 409, 194 S.E.2d 174 (1973).

6. United States v. Peters, 937 F.2d 1422 (9th Cir.1991).

7. Moore v. United States, 353 A.2d 16 (D.C.Ct.App.1976).

8. People v. Bellanca, 386 Mich. 708, 194 N.W.2d 863 (1972).

9. People v. Chard, 808 P.2d 351 (Colo.), *cert. denied*, 502 U.S. 863, 112 S.Ct. 186, 116 L.Ed.2d 147 (1991).

10. State v. Grove, 65 Wash. 2d 525, 398 P.2d 170 (1965); State v. Olwell, 64 Wash. 2d 828, 394 P.2d 681 (1964); State v. Perkerewicz, 4 Wash. App. 937, 486 P.2d 97, *review denied*, 79 Wash. 2d 1006 (1971).

11. State v. Pawlyk, 115 Wash. 2d 457, 800 P.2d 338 (1990).

12. United States v. Wright, 489 F.2d 1181 (D.C.Cir.1973).

13. United States v. Johnson, 752 F.2d 206 (6th Cir.1985).

14. Chappee v. Vose, 843 F.2d 25 (1st Cir.1988).

15. United States v. Griley, 814 F.2d 967 (4th Cir.1987).

16. Commonwealth v. Powell, 449 Pa. 126, 295 A.2d 295 (1972).

17. United States v. Phillip, 948 F.2d 241 (6th Cir.1991), *cert. denied*, 504 U.S. 930, 112 S.Ct. 1994, 118 L.Ed.2d 590 (1992).

18. People v. McSherry, 14 Cal.Rptr.2d 630 (1992), ordered by the Supreme Court not to be published in the official reports.

19. Commonwealth v. Brison, 421 Pa.Super. 442, 618 A.2d 420 (1992).

Chapter 15

1. Little v. Smith, 347 F.Supp. 427 (N.D.Ga.1971); Burks v. State, 490 S.W.2d 34 (Mo.1973). (Most of the problem is hypothetical.)

2a–2c. People v. Callahan, 80 N.Y.2d 273, 604 N.E.2d 108, 590 N.Y.S.2d 46 (1992).

2d. People v. Butler, 43 Mich.App. 270, 204 N.W.2d 325 (1972).

3. Smith v. State, 717 P.2d 402 (Alaska.Ct.App.1986).

4. State v. Horning, 158 Ariz. 106, 761 P.2d 728 (Ariz.Ct.App.1988).

5. United States v. Bruce, 976 F.2d 552 (9th Cir.1992).

6. In re Lewallen, 23 Cal.3d 274, 590 P.2d 383, 152 Cal.Rptr. 528 (1979).

7. United States v. Swinehart, 614 F.2d 853 (3d Cir.), *cert. denied*, 449 U.S. 827, 101 S.Ct. 90, 66 L.Ed.2d 30 (1980).

8. United States v. Kurkculer, 918 F.2d 295 (1st Cir.1990).

9. People v. Clark, 43 Mich.App. 476, 204 N.W.2d 332 (1972).

10. People v. Stevens, 45 Mich.App. 689, 206 N.W.2d 757 (1973).

11. Mosher v. LaVallee, 351 F.Supp. 1101 (S.D.N.Y.1972), *aff'd*, 491 F.2d 1346 (2d Cir.), *cert. denied*, 416 U.S. 906, 94 S.Ct. 1611, 40 L.Ed.2d 111 (1974).

12. Cancino v. Craven, 467 F.2d 1243 (9th Cir.1972).

13. United States v. Riles, 928 F.2d 339 (10th Cir.1991).

14. United States v. Broadus, 450 F.2d 639 (D.C.Cir.1971); United States v. Myers, 451 F.2d 402 (9th Cir.1972).

15. United States v. Leming, 532 F.2d 647 (9th Cir.1975), *cert. denied*, 424 U.S. 978, 96 S.Ct. 1485, 47 L.Ed.2d 749 (1976).

16. Moore v. Balkcom, 716 F.2d 1511 (11th Cir.1983), *cert. denied*, 465 U.S. 1084, 104 S.Ct. 1456, 79 L.Ed.2d 773 (1984).

17. United States v. Stead, 746 F.2d 355 (6th Cir.1984), *cert. denied*, 470 U.S. 1030, 105 S.Ct. 1403, 84 L.Ed.2d 790 (1985).

18. United States v. DeCicco, 899 F.2d 1531 (7th Cir.1990).

19. United States v. DeFusco, 949 F.2d 114 (4th Cir.1991), *cert. denied*, 503 U.S. 997, 112 S.Ct. 1703, 118 L.Ed.2d 412 (1992).

20. State v. Johnston, 17 Wash. App. 486, 564 P.2d 1159, *review denied*, 89 Wash. 2d 1007 (1977).

21. State v. Harris, 266 Wis.2d 200, 667 N.W.2d 813 (2003).

Chapter 16

1. United States v. Mendoza–Cecelia, 963 F.2d 1467 (11th Cir.), *cert. denied sub nom.* Marin–Hernandez v. United States, 506 U.S. 964, 113 S.Ct. 436, 121 L.Ed.2d 356 (1992).

2. United States v. Hicks, 948 F.2d 877 (4th Cir.1991).

3. Smith v. Lockhart, 923 F.2d 1314 (8th Cir.1991).

4. United States v. Perez–Macias, 335 F.3d 421 (5th Cir. 2003).

5. Cottle v. Wainwright, 477 F.2d 269 (5th Cir.), *vacated*, 414 U.S. 895, 94 S.Ct. 221, 38 L.Ed.2d 138 (1973); Clay v. Wainwright, 470 F.2d 478 (5th Cir.1972).

6. Savage v. Estelle, 924 F.2d 1459 (9th Cir.1990), *cert. denied*, 501 U.S. 1255, 111 S.Ct. 2900, 115 L.Ed.2d 1064 (1991).

7. McMahon v. Fulcomer, 821 F.2d 934 (3d Cir.1987).

8. Menefield v. Borg, 881 F.2d 696 (9th Cir.1989).

9. McKee v. Harris, 649 F.2d 927 (2d Cir.1981), *cert. denied*, 456 U.S. 917, 102 S.Ct. 1773, 72 L.Ed.2d 177 (1982).

10. People v. Durfee, 215 Mich.App. 677, 547 N.W.2d 344, *leave to appeal held in abeyance*, 554 N.W.2d 321 (Mich.1996).

11. Linton v. Perini, 656 F.2d 207 (6th Cir.1981), *cert. denied*, 454 U.S. 1162, 102 S.Ct. 1036, 71 L.Ed.2d 318 (1982).

12. Giacalone v. Lucas, 445 F.2d 1238 (6th Cir.1971), *cert. denied*, 405 U.S. 922, 92 S.Ct. 960, 30 L.Ed.2d 793 (1972).

13. Mulligan v. Kemp, 771 F.2d 1436 (11th Cir.1985), *cert. denied*, 480 U.S. 911, 107 S.Ct. 1358, 94 L.Ed.2d 529 (1987).

14. Griffin v. Aiken, 775 F.2d 1226 (4th Cir.1985), *cert. denied*, 478 U.S. 1007, 106 S.Ct. 3301, 92 L.Ed.2d 715 (1986).

15. Turner v. Tennessee, 664 F.Supp. 1113 (M.D.Tenn.1987), *aff'd*, 858 F.2d 1201 (6th Cir.1988), *vacated on other grounds*, 492 U.S. 902, 109 S.Ct. 3208, 106 L.Ed.2d 559 (1989).

16. People v. Rovito, 327 Ill.App.3d 164, 261 Ill.Dec. 72, 762 N.E.2d 641 (2001).

17. United States v. Henkel, 799 F.2d 369 (7th Cir.1986), *cert. denied*, 479 U.S. 1101, 107 S.Ct. 1327, 94 L.Ed.2d 178 (1987).

18. Hitch v. Pima County Superior Ct., 146 Ariz. 588, 708 P.2d 72 (1985).

19. People v. Superior Ct., 192 Cal.App.3d 32, 237 Cal.Rptr. 158 (1987).

20. Hoffman v. Leeke, 903 F.2d 280 (4th Cir.1990).

21. Ford v. Ford, 749 F.2d 681 (11th Cir.), *cert. denied*, 474 U.S. 909, 106 S.Ct. 278, 88 L.Ed.2d 243 (1985).

22. Ex parte McCormick, 645 S.W.2d 801 (Tex.Crim.App.1983) (en banc).

23. United States v. Talbott, 454 F.2d 1111 (8th Cir.), *cert. denied*, 407 U.S. 922, 92 S.Ct. 2467, 32 L.Ed.2d 808 (1972).

24. Williams v. Martin, 618 F.2d 1021 (4th Cir.1980).

25. United States ex rel. Dessus v. Commonwealth of Pennsylvania, 452 F.2d 557 (3d Cir.1971), *cert. denied*, 409 U.S. 853, 93 S.Ct. 184, 34 L.Ed.2d 96 (1972).

26. Little v. Armontrout, 835 F.2d 1240 (8th Cir.1987) (en banc), *cert. denied*, 487 U.S. 1210, 108 S.Ct. 2857, 101 L.Ed.2d 894 (1988).

Chapter 17

1. United States v. Soderna, 82 F.3d 1370 (7th Cir.), *petition for cert. filed*, 65 U.S.L.W. 3086, 1996 WL 442631 (1996).

2. Richter v. Fairbanks, 903 F.2d 1202 (8th Cir.1990).

3. People v. Feagley, 14 Cal. 3d 338, 535 P.2d 373, 121 Cal. Rptr. 509 (1975).

4. United States v. Vega, 447 F.2d 698 (2d Cir.1971), *cert. denied*, 404 U.S. 1038, 92 S.Ct. 712, 30 L.Ed.2d 730 (1972).

5. United States v. Netter, 62 F.3d 232 (8th Cir.1995), *vacated*, 517 U.S. 1130, 116 S.Ct. 1411, 134 L.Ed.2d 538 (1996), *reh'g granted* (8th Cir., 1996), *reh'g en banc denied* (8th Cir. 1996).

6. People v. Asevedo, 217 Mich.App. 393, 551 N.W.2d 478 (1996) (per curiam).

7. United States v. Sealander, 91 F.3d 160 (10th Cir. 1996).

8. United States v. Johnson, 62 F.3d 849 (6th Cir.1995).

9. United States v. Vario, 943 F.2d 236 (2d Cir.1991), *cert. denied*, 502 U.S. 1036, 112 S.Ct. 882, 116 L.Ed.2d 786 (1992).

10. Johnson v. State, 548 S.W.2d 700 (Tex.Crim.App.1977).

11. United States v. Blair, 493 F.Supp. 398 (D.Md.1980), *aff'd*, 665 F.2d 500 (4th Cir.1981).

12. Davis v. Warden, 867 F.2d 1003 (7th Cir.), *cert. denied*, 493 U.S. 920, 110 S.Ct. 285, 107 L.Ed.2d 264 (1989).

13. United States v. Barber, 80 F.3d 964 (4th Cir.), *cert. denied*, 519 U.S. 876, 117 S.Ct. 198, 136 L.Ed.2d 134 (1996).

14. United States v. Kyles, 40 F.3d 519 (2d Cir.1994), *cert. denied*, 514 U.S. 1044, 115 S. Ct. 1419, 131 L.Ed.2d 302 (1995).

15. United States v. Heller, 785 F.2d 1524 (11th Cir.1986).

16. United States v. Cockerham, 476 F.2d 542 (D.C.Cir.1973) (per curiam).

17. Langley v. State, 281 Md. 337, 378 A.2d 1338 (1977).

18. Davis v. State, 333 Md. 27, 633 A.2d 867 (1993).

19. State v. Sparks, 147 Ariz. 51, 708 P.2d 732 (1985).

20. Brosky v. State, 915 S.W.2d 120 (Tex.App.1996), *review refused* (July 31, 1996).

21. Maddux v. State, 862 S.W.2d 590 (Tex.Crim.App.1993) (en banc), *overruled by* Standefer v. State, 59 S.W.3d 177 (Tex.Crim.App. 2001).

22. Coleman v. United States, 379 A.2d 951 (D.C.Ct.App.1977).

23. Ex parte Branch, 526 So.2d 609 (Ala.1987).

24. People v. Jenkins, 84 N.Y.2d 1001, 646 N.E.2d 811, 622 N.Y.S.2d 509 (1994) (mem).

25. People v. Jenkins, 75 N.Y.2d 550, 554 N.E.2d 47, 555 N.Y.S.2d 10 (1990).

26. People v. Macioce, 197 Cal.App.3d 262, 242 Cal.Rptr. 771 (1987), *cert. denied*, 488 U.S. 908, 109 S.Ct. 258, 102 L.Ed.2d 247 (1988).

Chapter 18

1. Bradley v. United States, 433 F.2d 1113 (D.C.Cir.1969).

2. United States v. Goodapple, 958 F.2d 1402 (7th Cir.1992).

3. Kinser v. Cooper, 24 Ohio Misc. 141, 413 F.2d 730 (6th Cir.1969).

4. People v. Johnson, 393 Mich. 488, 227 N.W.2d 523 (1975).

5. People v. Farrar, 36 Mich.App. 294, 193 N.W.2d 363 (1971).

6. People v. Meir, 67 Mich.App. 534, 241 N.W.2d 280 (1976).

7. United States v. Foster, 982 F.2d 551 (D.C.Cir.1993).

8. People v. Wilson, 44 Mich.App. 137, 205 N.W.2d 75 (1972), *aff'd*, 390 Mich. 689, 213 N.W.2d 193 (1973).

9. United States v. Sexton, 456 F.2d 961 (5th Cir. 1972).

Chapter 19

1. McNeal v. Collier, 353 F.Supp. 485 (N.D.Miss.1972), *rev'd*, 481 F.2d 1145 (5th Cir.1973).

2. United States v. Odom, 888 F.2d 1014 (4th Cir. 1989).

3. State v. Crutchfield, 318 Md. 200, 567 A.2d 449 (1989), *cert. denied*, 495 U.S. 905, 110 S.Ct. 1926, 109 L.Ed.2d 289 (1990).

4. Morrison v. State, 946 F.2d 1340 (8th Cir.1991), *cert. denied*, 504 U.S. 959, 112 S.Ct. 2312, 119 L.Ed.2d 232 (1992).

5. Commonwealth v. Warfield, 424 Pa. 555, 227 A.2d 177 (1967).

6. United States v. Appawoo, 553 F.2d 1242 (10th Cir.1977).

7. People v. Anderson, 409 Mich. 474, 295 N.W.2d 482 (1980), *cert. denied*, 449 U.S. 1101, 101 S.Ct. 896, 66 L.Ed.2d 827 (1981).

8. United States v. Kehoe, 516 F.2d 78 (5th Cir.1975), *cert. denied*, 424 U.S. 909, 96 S.Ct. 1103, 47 L.Ed.2d 313 (1976).

9. United States v. Alberti, 568 F.2d 617 (2d Cir.1977).

10. Lowe v. State, 242 Kan. 64, 744 P.2d 856 (1987).

11. Vardas v. Estelle, 715 F.2d 206 (5th Cir.1983), *cert. denied*, 465 U.S. 1104, 104 S.Ct. 1603, 80 L.Ed.2d 133 (1984).

12. State v. Calvert, 211 Kan. 174, 505 P.2d 1110 (1973).

13. United States v. Garcia, 938 F.2d 12 (2d Cir.1991), *cert. denied*, 502 U.S. 1030, 112 S.Ct. 868, 116 L.Ed.2d 774 (1992).

14. Duffel v. Dutton, 785 F.2d 131 (6th Cir.1986).

15. Thurman v. United States, 423 F.2d 988 (9th Cir.), *cert. denied*, 400 U.S. 911, 91 S.Ct. 148, 27 L.Ed.2d 151 (1970).

16. United States v. Pimienta–Redondo, 874 F.2d 9 (1st Cir.), *cert. denied*, 493 U.S. 890, 110 S.Ct. 233, 107 L.Ed.2d 185 (1989).

†